ROUTLEDGE LIBRARY EDITIONS:
SMALL BUSINESS

Volume 6

SMALL AND MEDIUM SIZE ENTERPRISES AND REGIONAL DEVELOPMENT

SMALL AND MEDIUM SIZE ENTERPRISES AND REGIONAL DEVELOPMENT

Edited by
MARIA GIAOUTZI, PETER NIJKAMP AND
DAVID J. STOREY

LONDON AND NEW YORK

First published in 1988 by Routledge

This edition first published in 2016
by Routledge
2 Park Square, Milton Park, Abingdon, Oxon OX14 4RN

and by Routledge
711 Third Avenue, New York, NY 10017

Routledge is an imprint of the Taylor & Francis Group, an informa business

© 1988 Maria Giaoutzi, Peter Nijkamp and David J. Storey

British Library Cataloguing in Publication Data
A catalogue record for this book is available from the British Library

ISBN: 978-1-138-67308-3 (Set)
ISBN: 978-1-315-54266-9 (Set) (ebk)
ISBN: 978-1-138-68273-3 (Volume 6) (hbk)
ISBN: 978-1-315-54491-5 (Volume 6) (ebk)

Publisher's Note
The publisher has gone to great lengths to ensure the quality of this reprint but points out that some imperfections in the original copies may be apparent.

Disclaimer
The publisher has made every effort to trace copyright holders and would welcome correspondence from those they have been unable to trace.

SMALL AND MEDIUM SIZE ENTERPRISES AND REGIONAL DEVELOPMENT

Edited by
MARIA GIAOUTZI, PETER NIJKAMP
AND DAVID J. STOREY

ROUTLEDGE

First published in 1988 by
Routledge
11 New Fetter Lane, London EC4P 4EE

Printed and bound in Great Britain by
Mackays of Chatham PLC, Chatham, Kent

British Library Cataloguing in Publication Data

Small and medium size enterprises and
   regional development.
   1. Regional economic development. Role
of small firms & medium-sized firms
I. Giaoutiz, Maria II. Nijkamp, Peter,
1946-   III. Storey, D.J. (David John),
1947-
330.9
ISBN 0–415–00415–2

Contents

Part Two: Case Studies

List of Figures

List of Tables

Abbreviations

CAD	Computer-aided design
CEC	Commission of the European Communities
CGTC	Component Generation Technology Cycle
CNC	Computerised numerically controlled
CURDS	Centre for Urban and Regional Development Studies
DGV	Directorate General for Employment and Social Affairs of the CEC
NC	Numerically controlled
R&D	Research and development
RPE	Regional production environment
RPI	Regional performance indicator
RPS	Regional production structure
RSE	Regional sector evaluation
SBA	Small Business Administration
SMEs	Small and medium-sized enterprises

List of Contributors

Neil Alderman
CURDS
University of Newcastle
Newcastle Upon Tyne, NEI 7RU
England

Theo Alsters
Coreo
P.O. Box 1010
Venlo
The Netherlands

Philippe Aydalot (*deceased*)
Formerly Université de Paris I
Panthéon Sorbonne
90, Rue de Tolbiac
F–75634 Paris Cedex 13
France

Juan R. Cuadrado Roura
Dept of Political Economics
University de Alcala de Henares
Rafael Calvo, 17
28010 Madrid
Spain

Han Dieperink
Nederhorst den Berg
The Netherlands

Manfred M. Fischer
Dept of Geography
University of Vienna
Universitatsstrasse 7/v
A – 1010 Vienna
Austria

Maria Giaoutzi
Dept of Geography and Regional
Planning
National Technical University
Zographou Campus
Athens 157 10
Greece

Charlie Karlsson
Institute for Economics
University of Karlstad
Box 9501
65009 Karlstad
Sweden

Alfred Kleinknecht
Dept of Economics
Limburg University
Maastricht
The Netherlands

Gabriel Lipshitz
Dept of Geography
Hebrew University
Mount Scopus
Jerusalem
Israel

Denis Maillat
Institute for Regional Economic Research
Université de Neuchatel
Pierre-à-Mazel
CH–2000 Neuchatel
Switzerland

Ronald van der Mark
Institute for Policy Research
Stationsweg 25
2312 AS Leiden
The Netherlands

Peter Nijkamp
Dept of Economics
Free University
P.O. Box 7161
1007 MC Amsterdam
The Netherlands

Piet H. Pellenbarg
Dept of Geography
State University of Groningen
P.O. Box 800
9700 AV Groningen
The Netherlands

Piet Rietveld
Dept of Economics
Free University
P.O. Box 7161
1007 MC Amsterdam
The Netherlands

David J. Storey
School of Industrial and Business Studies
University of Warwick
Coventry
England

Luis Suarez-Villa
Program in Social Ecology
University of California
Irvine, Cal. 92717
USA

Morgan D. Thomas
Dept of Geography
University of Washington
Seattle, Wash. 98195
USA

Alfred T. Thwaites
CURDS
University of Newcastle
Newcastle Upon Tyne NEI 7RU
England

Pooran Wynarczyk
CURDS
University of Newcastle
Newcastle Upon Tyne NEI 7RU
England

Preface

In recent years the small and medium-sized enterprise sector has become a focal point of scientific and policy interest. It is — sometimes uncritically — widely believed that this sector contains the rejuvenation potential that is necessary for revitalising the industrial and service sector in our stagnating economies. Small and medium-sized firms are consequently also often regarded as the vehicles for regional development planning. In this context, many myths have come into being and there is a clear need for a critical look at both the spatial economic theoretical basis and the empirical evidence concerning the regional development potential of small and medium-sized enterprises. A broad cross-national view is here a prerequisite for judging whether we have not set our expectations regarding this sector too high.

The present volume aims at covering the above-mentioned issues. It is the result of an expert meeting on the theme of 'small and medium-sized enterprises and regional development', which was held in the autumn of 1986 on the beautiful island of Samos, Greece. This volume is dedicated to the memory of Professor Philippe Aydalot (Paris), who unexpectedly passed away a few months after the Samos meeting. His active participation at this meeting and more generally his scientific contribution to the area of regional dynamism were a rich source of inspiration for many colleagues.

We would like to acknowledge the generous support for this meeting given by EOMMEX (the Hellenic Organisation for Small and Medium-sized Firms), OAEΔ (the Hellenic Employment Organisation), the Industrial Bank of Greece, the Commercial Bank of Greece, the Greek Office of the European Community in Athens, and the city of Karlovasi (Samos).

Maria Giaoutzi (Athens)
Peter Nijkamp (Amsterdam)
David J. Storey (Newcastle)

1

Small is Beautiful — The Regional Importance of Small-scale Activities

Maria Giaoutzi, Peter Nijkamp and David J. Storey

PROLOGUE

In recent years the economies of most countries have gone through a phase of structural change. In this context, Bluestone and Harrison (1982), amongst others, refer to the deindustrialisation trend in America, by which they mean a widespread, systematic disinvestment in the nation's basic productive capacity. Clearly, in other countries different definitions of deindustrialisation are used, reflecting the differences in the perceived nature of the problem. In the UK, for example, a variety of different definitions have been used. Some cite 1966 as the beginning of deindustrialisation since it was in this year that manufacturing employment peaked. Others may regard deindustrialisation as occurring when a country's share of world trade in manufactured goods declines, whilst others may regard it as the time when imports of manufactured goods exceed exports (cf. Blackaby, 1979). In addition, the primary sector (agriculture, resource extraction) also shows signs of dramatic qualitative changes, while finally the tertiary sector is increasingly influenced by the products of technological progress (telecommunication, computerisation etc.). Altogether our era exhibits drastic change patterns in its production base.

This observation is certainly not a new one, as it is in perfect agreement with Schumpeter's view that capitalist economies can only evolve to higher levels of prosperity through a process of creative destruction. In order to survive, a healthy economy requires a permanent transformation, a reincarnation leading to a higher qualitative level. Without such a morphogenetic transformation, the economy will stagnate and eventually crumble.

In the light of the above-mentioned qualitative evolutionary patterns of our economies, it is no surprise that in many countries industrial revitalisation is regarded as a source of new progress, reflected in the current emphasis on industrial innovation and technological change (cf. Planque, 1983, Piore and Sabel, 1984, and Nijkamp, 1986).

As certain regions and cities encompass - either in a spontaneous or in a planned way — the seedbeds for specific new technologies (cf. Silicon Valley, Greater Boston, Sophia-Antipolis), it is evident that new structural developments will have serious implications for the distribution of welfare over the regions of a national economic system. It turns out that in many cases the first fruits of technological changes (which sometimes take the form of technological 'revolutions') are mainly beneficial to the major agglomerations, thus creating a widening gap between central and peripheral world regions.

Many of these peripheral areas are often characterised by small and medium-sized activities (tourism, traditional services, handicrafts, etc.), and the question is often raised as to whether such activities provide a satisfactory platform for a solid and stable economic progress. On the other hand, it is increasingly realised that the small and medium-sized industrial and service sector encompasses an enormous employment potential, which is — unfortunately — not fully recognised nor exploited in most countries. Consequently, it is an important research task to assess the regional employment perspectives provided by the small and medium-sized industrial and service sector.

In recent years, when the economies of most industrialised countries have shown various signs of stagnation and structural decline, a variety of studies have been undertaken which demonstrate clearly that small and medium-sized firms may be regarded as generators of new growth, as primary sources of technological change and, via job creation, as one of the major factors in maintaining socio-economic stability (see Rothwell and Zegveld, 1982).

Small and medium-sized enterprises (SMEs) have increasingly become the focus of attention by public policy-makers in a variety of countries with very different political traditions. It is our purpose to investigate the reasons which underlie these changes. Several explanations can be provided, notably technological changes, increased levels of unemployment, the growth of the service sector, changes in cultural attitudes and value systems, and political pressures exerted by changes in governments in Europe and North America.

The key question for policy is the extent to which these developments are a reflection of the world recession of the 1970s and 1980s, therefore being expected to disappear in the event of improved world economic conditions; and how much they reflect fundamental changes in the sectoral, technical and value systems in developed economies. If we believe the former to be the prime explanation, then policies to promote the small-firms sector should be primarily short-term palliatives designed to mitigate the ravages of unemployment. On the other hand, if we believe that there are major structural changes taking place, then policies to promote the small-firms sector need to be of a long-term and fundamental nature.

It is also increasingly realised that new economic growth does not uniformly take place on a nation-wide scale. Specific places provide a specific incubator function for specific new activities. Research on this so-called incubator hypothesis already has a long history since the early attempts of Hoover and Vernon (1959). A review of discussions and arguments on this hypothesis can be found in Davelaar and Nijkamp (1988). Incubator hypotheses have not always turned out in the ways expected: for example, it was argued that inner cities would be good incubators for the establishment of new firms since there was a close market and abundant cheap premises, both of which were very important for the new firm. It was also argued that once these firms began to grow, they were likely to move outside the cramped environs of the inner city. Empirical testing of this hypothesis, however, has demonstrated that firms do not always develop in the manner suggested. Sometimes, both rates of new firms in the inner cities were no higher than in the outer areas, while the growth rates of firms in the outer areas were actually greater than those in the inner city areas (primarily because they were initiated by middle-class founders who lived in the suburbs). In fact, very few firms which began in the inner city moved to larger premises in the outer areas. This was because the firms founded in the inner city were located there because of the specific locational advantages which the site or sites provided. The main question here is the identification of favourable locational conditions that act as attractors of new activities. While conventional regional policy has primarily addressed itself to providing various incentives to firms to locate branch plants in development regions and to subsidising establishments already located in such regions, local authorities are nowadays increasingly focusing attention on the revitalisation of indigenous regional resources which may trigger off the creation of new, often knowledge-based, activities, particularly in the small and medium-sized firm sector (see also Storey, 1982, Keeble and Wever, 1986). Thus, the regional development potential offered by SMEs deserves closer attention.

SMALL AND MEDIUM-SIZED ENTERPRISES IN PERSPECTIVE

The role which SMEs play in the economy varies from nation to nation and reflects the cultural background of the different countries. In the US economy, for example, SMEs are considered to be the cornerstone of a free market economy where free entry into business is a central element. SMEs are seen here as major forces for economic dynamism. Thus, socio-political support for (both existing and new) small businesses in the US has been — and still is — normal practice (see Bannock, 1981).

In Japan the situation is rather different. SMEs in Japan play a more indirect role as suppliers of low-cost, high-quality and often innovative product components to larger firms (see Anthony, 1983). Larger Japanese corporations seem to demonstrate — in contrast to large American and European firms — a remarkable degree of internal flexibility and technical progressiveness (especially with respect to new technological areas such as bio-technology, video systems, etc.).

In Europe, even though there are large differences between different countries, the focus has been primarily on the socio-economic position of the existing SMEs in the traditional and medium-technology sectors of the economy (for more details on this issue see Rothwell and Zegveld, 1982).

SMEs do not only play a different role in different countries, but also in different time periods in different industries in a national economy. In this respect it is useful to consider Rothwell's (1981) simplified scheme for the patterns of post-war industrial development in which the role of SMEs in an industry varies as the industry develops from newness to maturity. In this model of industrial evolution three major stages are distinguished.

4

(a) *Dynamic growth stage* (1945 to about 1964): emergence of new industries such as electronics, synthetic materials, pharmaceuticals, petro-chemicals, agro-chemicals based on new technological capabilities that emerged during the pre-Second World War period; production initially in small units; introduction of many new products; rapidly growing new markets; new employment generation (output growth greater than productivity growth).

(b) *Consolidation stage* (mid to late 1960s): increasing industrial concentration; growing static scale economies; increasing emphasis on process and organisational innovations; rapid productivity growth; markets still growing rapidly; output growth and productivity growth in rough balance (manufacturing employment).

(c) *Maturity and market saturation stage* (early 1970s to date): highly concentrated industry; very large production units; increasing production process and organisational rationalisation; growing automatisation; stagnating and replacement markets; productivity growth higher than output growth; rapidly growing manufacturing unemployment.

In the early stage of the Rothwell typology, SMEs are seen as seed-corn of the new industry. Their role over time as a major force of industrial development diminishes, partly through the entry of already-established larger corporations from other areas, partly through take-overs and mergers, but also through successful growth. In the later stages such firms can play another, nevertheless important role as subcontractors to large firms, as suppliers of specialised services and for narrow market niches.

It is worth mentioning that, whilst the Rothwell taxonomy may apply to certain sectors, most small firms are not in those sectors. Firstly, most firms are in the primary and service sectors (and always have been), so that the taxonomy does not apply to them. Secondly, even within the manufacturing sector, most small firms are in very traditional sectors such as textiles, furniture, mechanical engineering, food, etc. Thirdly, when one talks about the small-firms sector one must be absolutely clear that whilst the sector may change relatively modestly over a period of time, the individual firms that comprise the sector change very rapidly. In the UK, for example, the annual failure rate of all businesses registered for VAT is 10.8 per cent. More importantly, the failure rate of firms with a turnover of less than £13,000 in 1980 was 25 per cent annually. It is the high failure rate of small firms which is an important feature distinguishing small from large firms. Hence, whilst in principle small firms are the seed-corn of tomorrow's large firms and new industries, the probability of any individual firm experiencing substantial growth is very modest. Perhaps 50 per cent of firms which began in year t will not be in business in year $t+5$, while the chances of a firm established in year t growing to 100 employees by year $t+10$ is smaller than 0.5 per cent.

Even so, one of the ways to reverse the evolution of industry from a state of saturation may be the generation of new industries based on new technologies such as, for example, energy-related technologies (solar and wind energy systems, heat pumps, etc.), bio-technology (bio-engineering, biomass), robotics technology, electronic office equipment and advanced information and communication technologies. In the area of these new technologies, existing and new technology-based small firms may enjoy many innovative opportunities (see Rothwell and Zegveld, 1982, and Bollard 1983).

The important role of SMEs as triggers of development is often explained in terms of the specific entrepreneurial spirit in this sector, characterised *inter alia* by independence, responsibility, simple organisational structures, rapid decision-making, tailor-made production organisation, and so on (see also Fischer and Nijkamp, 1988).

During the past decade the interest in SMEs has increased in most European countries. Much of this interest is based upon the belief in the ability of these enterprises to generate employment and innovations in a period of economic stagnation. A very interesting contribution to the discussion on employment generation of small firms can be found in Birch (1979). Birch studied employment change in 5.6 million business establishments (82 per cent of all manufacturing and private sector service establishments) in the United States between 1969 and 1976. His major conclusions from this study, based on a component of change (or job accounting) framework, were (see Storey, 1982):

(a) gross job loss through closure and contraction was about 8 per cent per year;

(b) about 50 per cent of the gross job gains were created

through expansions of existing companies and about 50 per cent through new openings;

(c) about 50 per cent of gross jobs created by openings were produced by independent, free-standing entrepreneurs and 50 per cent by multi-plant corporations (in-moves);

(d) firms with less than 20 employees generated 66 per cent of net new jobs in the United States.

When the Birch results for the 1969–76 period were published, they caused great controversy. For this reason the US Small Business Administration (SBA) issued a research contract to the Brookings Institution to look at the 1978–80 period using the same Dun and Bradstreet data base that has been used by Birch. They found that, for this period, firms with 100 employees or less created about 38 per cent of all jobs in the US economy. The Brookings results therefore suggested that small firms were growing no faster in terms, of employment than other sizes of firm in the economy (Armington and Odle, 1982).

Since the original Birch study covered the period 1969–76 and the Armington and Odle study covered 1978–80, there was the possibility of conflicting results. For this reason the SBA then provided a copy of the Dun and Bradstreet data tapes for the 1978–80 period to Birch and asked him to compute his estimate of the contribution to job creation made by firms with less than 100 workers. Using the identical input data to Armington and Odle, he obtained a figure of 70 per cent.

In Storey and Johnson (1987), the authors examined the causes of the results and broadly concluded that they reflect a different treatment of firms which are not included in the data base. They also suggest that Birch significantly overestimated the role of small firms, but that if anything, the Brookings procedure led to an underestimate. In their view the data support a result that about 50 per cent of new jobs in the US were created by firms with less than 100 workers, at a time when this sector employed 38 per cent of the labour force. This suggests that small firms are creating jobs faster than other sizes of firms, but at a lower growth rate than suggested by the Birch report.

In many European countries, there is also some empirical evidence that particularly small firms (up to 100 employees) contribute considerably more than proportionately to the net growth of jobs and that employment expectations decrease with increasing firm size. The shift of employment growth to small

7

firms can be observed in nearly all sectors. There are several explanations for this phenomenon. Firstly, because of their strong engagement in standard mass production, larger firms had — and still have — more opportunities to substitute capital for labour. Secondly, small firms are much more engaged in producing specialities and supplying products for market niches and spatially limited markets which are not so strongly affected by international competition. Thirdly, the new international divisions of labour affects especially the mass production of mature goods and, thus, the activities of larger firms. Fourthly, larger firms tend to be more strongly affected by labour market regulations which have been strengthened in the 1970s in most European countries (see Ewers, 1986).

In general, SMEs may exhibit relative growth for a variety of different reasons and these reasons may vary over space. In areas such as Birmingham, UK, for example, the relative growth in small firms may be attributable to the decline and rationalisation of the large firms in the area. These firms are shedding labour, which, having no alternative employment opportunities, means that the only option to unemployment is to start a small firm. The large firm also sheds functions so that activities which were formerly undertaken within the firm are now either undertaken by subcontractors, or in the hived-off 'independent' firms.

In contrast, a region such as Boston, USA has a highly developed small-firms sector, primarily in services, due to the demand created by the high-tech sector. In Boston the wealth is created by what is now the large-firm dominated high-tech sector, but the jobs are created in the small-firm dominated service sector. The final contrast is with Bologna in Italy where there has also been a massive growth in the small-firms sector in industries such as textiles, clothing, footwear, musical instruments, toys, etc. Here production takes place in small firms, generally in a rural environment, but the marketing and organisation of this system of production takes place in towns such as Bologna. It is worth noting that the developments are not in the high-tech sectors, but emphasis is placed upon high-quality market goods (Storey and Johnson, 1987).

The purpose of the previous distinction is to show that small firms can become relatively more important for a variety of very different reasons, and that the policy implications of each scenario are very different. Certainly, each of the major European countries has areas which correspond to the Birmingham and Boston models and therefore what is needed is a small-firms policy that is sensitive to these regional and structural differences.

Besides the growth of existing firms, new openings also contribute to employment growth in the small-firms sector. Although there is a negative correlation between age of the firm and growth rates, the question as to whether new or existing businesses contribute most to employment growth is not clear, since not only the birth rates, but also the death rates of young firms are generally high. Even though detailed empirical research is missing, there are plausible reasons to assume that new small (especially technology-based) businesses are generating a considerable number of jobs in producer-related and market consumer services, even in the short run, at least in the United States. Even when a new firm employs only relatively few workers and, thus, has only small direct employment effects, the indirect multiplier effects may be substantial. Many small businesses induce — via subcontracting arrangements — indirect employment effects. In an assessment of the role of business start-ups for regional development, such effects have to be taken into account.

FIRM SIZE AND INNOVATION

In the framework of a Schumpeterian analysis much attention has been given to the role of SMEs in innovations. The analysis of the effect of firm size upon technical innovations and on the transformation of research input into output has not yielded entirely conclusive answers, but many studies have indicated that new investment projects would tend to be more efficiently under-taken in a relatively small firm than it would in a large one (for a review, see Kamien and Schwartz, 1975, 1982). However, whether the intensity of innovational effort increases with firm size is still an unresolved question.

Kamien and Schwartz, in their overview of market structure and innovation, make a helpful distinction between firm size and inventive effort on the one hand, and firm size and inventive output on the other. As for the former relationship, they come to the conclusion that there is no direct and simple proportional rela-tionship between R&D expenditures (or the intensity of innova-tional effort) and firm size. In general, there is even some evidence that for large firms innovational intensity appears to be

9

constant or decreasing with size. Kleinknecht (1986) even argues that current surveys on R&D in most OECD countries are biased towards considerably underestimating R&D in small firms. In any case, there are remarkable inter-industry differences in the relation between size and innovational effort. Furthermore, it has to be realised that there is also a big difference between large and small firms in terms of sustained R&D programmes.

For the second relation — that is, between firm size and inventive output — the authors conclude that there is some evidence on the positive effect of small firm size on innovational effort, but here too the results differ by industry.

Recent results for significant innovations in the UK have been published by Pavitt *et al.* (1987). They examine 4,378 significant innovations introduced into British industry since 1945. More than 80 per cent of the innovations are in the manufacturing sector, and within the sectors there are some major differences. Thus, for example, when the sectors are normalised by employment size, innovations per employee are almost fifteen times higher in the instruments sector than they are in either printing or food. In the present context, Pavitt *et al.* also show that there has been a change in the innovativeness of different sizes of firms since 1945. Broadly they show that innovativeness per employee has increased for both small and large firms, with the medium-sized firms experiencing a relative decline. Innovativeness therefore appears to be becoming *U*-shaped when related to size. It must, however, be pointed out that when the analysis is conducted at a sectoral level, there is very little evidence that the *U*-shape is occurring in each sector. In fact, what appears to be happening is that in certain sectors there is a movement towards large firms becoming a more significant source of innovations (e.g., mechanical engineering and electrical engineering), and in some sectors it is the small firms that are becoming relatively more important (e.g., machinery, shipbuilding and vehicles). Indeed, the clear *U*-shaped pattern is restricted to instruments, electronics and electricals. For all the remaining 17 sectors analysed, there is no clear pattern.

It is also suggested that in order to stimulate indigenous regional development by means of an SME policy, access to higher education and scientific and technological research institutions should be improved, venture capital and other innovative structure-improving infrastructure should be provided, and the establishment of regional technology networks should be promoted. In general, independent SMEs may be thought to have a greater impact on regional development than branch plants because of their more even balance between direct and indirect labour, their more stable employment development over time, and their close commitment to regional interests (see Rothwell and Zegveld, 1982).

However, one word of warning is in order here. SMEs are not a homogeneous sector, so the benefits ascribed to this sector do not equally apply to all firms. For instance, one may distinguish SMEs in old-line industries, SMEs in modern industries, and high-tech oriented SMEs: all have different impacts on regional development. Despite the diversity in this sector, however, SMEs may act as important vehicles for a technology-based indigenous regional innovation and development strategy, not only in central locations but also in intermediate and peripheral regions (cf. Meyer-Krahmer, 1985). In all cases, however, density of information, accessibility to customers, availability of highly qualified manpower, and access to finance and business services are *sine qua non* for SMEs as incubators of technological innovation. This also has direct implications for regional SME policies, as will be outlined in the next section.

REGIONAL POLICY AND THE SME SECTOR

Most SMEs are firmly rooted in the economic structure of a region and constitute part of its indigenous development resources. Given the innovation potential of SMEs (see previous section), it is important for regional policies to focus on those technological conditions which support innovative SME firms.

Policy approaches to deal with the problems of SMEs require both a sectoral and a spatial perspective. A *within-sector* approach is needed to address the question of which firms require attention and which of them are more or less biased toward small and medium-size entrepreneurship. At such a level it should be possible (necessary) to identify which entrepreneurial roles are crucial and which are (or can be) potential sources of bottlenecks for economic development. At a *spatial* level, the question of interregional disparities needs to be dealt with, considering which regions have greater or lesser shares of industries where SMEs are significant, and how well these perform with respect to average national and interregional performance. Both the sectoral

11

and spatial perspectives need to consider (explicitly) the *temporal* dimensions of each industry's product and process development trajectory.

In this respect it has to be realised that some firms in the SME sector have many favourable characteristics such as flexibility, resilience, efficient management and organisation, and tailor-made production systems. Given these features, an effective regional policy should attempt to reinforce these elements and to remedy the negative features.

A bottleneck for many SMEs is the lack of interaction with knowledge centres (the source of technological innovation) and promising but distant markets (the source of significant revenues). Such disadvantages are usually shared by larger firms. In this context, the design of efficient information, marketing and sales networks (sometimes of an informal nature) is an extremely important issue. In addition, regional policy should aim at providing many stimuli for developing such internal and external communication (including knowledge transfer networks and trade networks), for instance via the banking system, the system of regional development corporations, a close co-operation with university research institutes, a joint promotion and marketing system, and so on.

At the level of the European Community, it is proposed to establish a Community Information Centre for small firms, and currently a number of pilot schemes for SMEs are in operation (see CEC, 1986, 7 August, Resolution to the Council).

Special attention should be given to the creation of an information system for SMEs on export opportunities, advising where their products can be potentially competitive, and placing these in contact, and serving as their liaison with, import–export agencies and customers abroad.

Access to such networks also reduces the distance perception, especially for those SMEs which are located in peripheral areas. Geographical distance is essentially a cost factor, which has a negative impact on both the production efficiency and the sales market. Sufficient venture capital (or alternative regional financing systems to provide 'seed' capital, e.g. tax incentives) is therefore also a necessary condition for an effective regional development strategy for SMEs, not only for expansion but also for enterprise start-up. In particular, a regional development fund in backward areas might be useful, which is specifically targeted to the SME sector. This fund might be financed by setting aside a fraction of tax revenues collected from the area or by utilising part of the pension funds collected from both small and large enterprises. In addition to appropriate financing schemes, it is also evident that infrastructure provisions (including information technology) directly geared to the interest of SMEs are of the utmost importance.

Labour market conditions, of course, also play an important role in the development of the SME sector. In the case of a regional mismatch of labour *vis-à-vis* the requirements of the SME sector, it may be useful to establish an apprenticeship system to train unskilled labour in SMEs, (possibly) along with the establishment of a management–labour relations board that can mediate labour problems in the SME sector.

In general, policy programmes and incentives should be targeted to specific entrepreneurial activities (or roles) that are major bottlenecks to enterprise growth, profitability or cost reduction, instead of providing blanket subsidies or incentives (which are often wasteful). Thus, for example, if better knowledge of productive organisation and co-ordination in the SME sector is targeted from, say, household industries that attempt to grow larger, then an assistance programme may be structured to address this issue in a systematic way. In this context, the mode of outreach or diffusion is important here (including dissemination techniques). In all cases, regional SME policies should aim at fully exploiting the 'entrepreneurial spirit' (à la Schumpeter) which is incorporated in the SME sector.

THE PAPERS

Given these technical and macroeconomic developments the chapters in this volume address the central question of the impact of these changes for regional economies. To focus upon these issues the volume makes a clear distinction between those chapters which discuss developments in the context of more than a single country or region, and those which focus upon developments in a single country or region. The former group are found in Part 1 and the latter group in Part 2.

The single unifying question which is addressed in all the chapters is whether the changing size distribution of enterprises is likely to lead to economic development, particularly in the currently less prosperous areas. In order to obtain insights into this question it is necessary to recognise that some countries or regions are relatively poor because they have never experienced industrialisation, whilst others may be suffering from industrialisation which has taken place in the past. In the latter regions the legacy of prior industrialisation can shape attitudes to enterprise, whereas in formerly agricultural areas there are more obvious problems of a shortage of wealth to finance investment. The majority of the text is devoted to the performance of the old industrialised areas, but in order to introduce a balance the final four chapters examine the smaller firm in an essentially rural or less developed setting.

The chapters in the volume are therefore designed to offer an insight into how the map of regional prosperity is likely to change over the next 20 or so years if the current trends in firm size continue. As is perhaps inevitable in such a collection of essays there is no single clear answer either on the impact of developments or on the choice of appropriate policies to be pursued to reach chosen objectives. Since the editors have contributed to this discussion it would be inappropriate for us to be both player and referee in this debate — we leave matters of judgement to the reader.

To set out the issues, however, we have arranged the chapters to begin with two contributions, by Suarez-Villa and Thomas, which set the discussion in context, particularly that of technical change. We find that the Suarez-Villa chapter presents a persuasive case that the role of the entrepreneur in stages of economic development varies considerably in importance and emphasis from one time period to another and from one economy to another. If enterprise and entrepreneurship are two of the key themes of the volume, then the essay by Thomas emphasises a third — that of innovation and technical development.

The remaining chapters in Part 1 develop these twin Schumpeterian themes of entrepreneurship and innovation but, the perspectives taken by each differ very markedly, and their regional prescriptions are therefore equally disparate. Maillat's review focuses upon innovative small firms and finds that whilst small innovative firms are well-equipped to withstand the currently turbulent technical and economic changes, such firms are dependent, to a possibly surprising degree, on their locality for inputs of know-how or inputs of complementary manufacturing or services. Maillat proposes that the new focus of regional policy should be to promote the development of small innovative firms through a series of measures such as the reduction of business burdens and the provision of 'market-lead' services.

The contributions by Fischer, Alderman *et al.* and Storey, however, are rather less sanguine in their views either of the role which small firms play in economic development or in the efficacy of the measures advocated by Maillat. Fischer, in his careful review of the evidence, is at pains to point to the diversity of criteria upon which the impact of small firms on regional economic development is judged. He distinguishes between studies which look only at manufacturing firms compared with those looking at all sectors. He also emphasises the importance of assessing the total impact, taking into account multiplier and displacement effects, rather than some of the narrower criteria which are sometimes used.

Alderman *et al.* also emphasise the need for balance in assessing the role of high-tech firms in promoting economic development. They show that in the less prosperous regions of Britain the majority of new jobs being created in the small-firms sector are in firms in the traditional industries. It is inferred that such regions would be better advised to concentrate upon policies to strengthen such industries by making them more competitive, rather than turning over exclusively to policies to promote innovative small firms in the new technology sectors. It is this approach which Alderman *et al.* refer to as 'balanced'.

The chapters by Fischer, Alderman *et al.* and Storey all touch upon the question of whether current changes in the size distribution of firms will lead to greater regional equity or to an increase in divisiveness. This question is addressed directly in the chapter by Nijkamp *et al.* who present the results of a strength–weaknesses analysis of European regions for small and medium-sized enterprises. Their results suggest that in the peripheral regions of Europe small and medium-sized firms' performance was superior to that of similar firms in the traditional industrial, but declining, regions. In our view there is a case for more disaggregated and detailed studies of the traditional regions to investigate further the nature of this differential performance.

Part 2 of the volume begins with Philippe Aydalot's analysis of developments in France. His richly illustrated contribution emphasises the interaction between growth in the small-firms sector and the performance of the large firm. Illustrating many of the points made in the earlier essays by Suarez-Villa and Thomas,

Aydalot shows that the large firm is often a key actor in taking initiatives to promote small firms. In some cases these initiatives are purely altruistic, being designed to mitigate the effects of the closure of a plant, but in others the promotion of small firms can be seen to provide a clear commercial return since the large firms then obtain access to new research ideas. The large firm, for example, may be an important source of venture capital or a source of major orders, yet it may act in this way so as to provide itself with an 'inside track' for potential acquisitions.

As was noted earlier, much of the interest in the role of small firms in promoting economic development in the 1980s stems from the work of Birch in the United States, which attempted to quantify the contribution which small firms made to job creation. It is only possible to undertake this type of work where data on employment are available on individual enterprises or establishments. The chapter by Karlsson presents an analysis of such data for the Värmland province in Sweden, and its importance is twofold. Firstly, it shows that in both Värmland, and in Sweden as a whole, it is small firms that are shedding labour fastest — a result which stands in contrast with the developments chronicled elsewhere in this volume. Secondly, however, Karlsson shows that, even though the small-firms sector is in relative and absolute decline in Värmland, the probability of a small firm growing in terms of employment is almost identical to those estimated from small-firm cohort studies in northern England and in Ireland where the small-firms sector is performing much better than the large-firms sector.

The essay by Pellenbarg sees a return to the question of whether there are changes in the relative position of regions as a result of the changing size distribution of firms and the growth, in particular, of small firms in the high-technology sectors. Using an analysis of the Netherlands he finds that whilst the older 'core' areas continue to dominate, the intermediate areas, particularly in the south of the country, appear to be leading a modest realignment of economic power amongst the Dutch regions. Similar issues are raised in the chapter by Dieperink et al.

The final four chapters examine economies which are significantly less developed than those discussed elsewhere in the volume, but even here the developments discussed are far from homogeneous. In both the chapter on Spain by Cuadrado Roura and on Greece by Giaoutzi, it is observed that the drive for economic development has led to a conflict with the objectives of regional policy. The need to promote economic growth, and particularly the growth of new technology-based firms, has meant that developments have become increasingly centralised or clustered in a few areas, thereby leading to a widening of regional disparities.

The impact of changes in average firm size upon migration patterns in Israel is examined in the chapter by Lipshitz, who presents an optimistic picture of the impact of public policies. He shows that the government of Israel has been effective in creating the type of 'human infrastructure' necessary to facilitate the growth of new small industries in the peripheral regions of the country. On the other hand, the chapter by Rietveld, which draws upon the Indonesian experience, indicates that focused and targeted policies to promote small-scale industry are likely to be less effective than more general policies designed to supplement rural incomes.

Perhaps it is inevitable that amongst such a wide-ranging set of essays covering many countries, there would be no uniform policy prescription. What does remain clear is that economic policy-makers in all countries have to recognise that the new techno-logies and the new momentum for economic growth amongst formerly less developed countries will lead to significant changes. In most cases small firms are seen to be an important vehicle for promoting these changes, but the conditions under which their contribution is maximised varies widely. What does remain clear is that such changes will lead to significant redistributions of regional prosperity which, in turn, may lead to conflicts between output-orientated economic policy and regional policies which have a strong redistributive element.

REFERENCES

Anthony, D. (1983) Japan. In D. J. Storey (ed.), *The small firm: an international survey*. Croom Helm, London, 46–83.

Armington, C. and M. Odle (1982) Small business: how many jobs?. *Brookings Review*, Winter, 14–17.

Bannock, G. (1981) *The economics of small firms*. Basil Blackwell, Oxford.

Birch, D. L. (1979) *The job generation process*. MIT Program on Neighbourhood and Regional Change, Cambridge, Mass.

Blackaby, F. (1979) *De-industrialization*. National Institute of Social and

Economic Research, Cambridge University Press, Cambridge.

Bluestone, B. and B. Harrison (1982) *Deindustrialization of America*. Basic Books, New York.

Bollard, A. (1983) Technology, economic change and small firms. *Lloyds Bank Review*, *147*, 42–56.

Commission of the European Communities (CEC) (1986) *Draft resolution of the Council concerning the action programme for SMEs*. COM(86)445 final, Brussels, 7 August.

Davelaar, E. J. and P. Nijkamp (1988) The incubator hypothesis: revitalisation of metropolitan areas? *Annals of the Regional Science*, forthcoming.

Ewers, H. J. (1986) Spatial dimensions of technological developments and employment effects. In P. Nijkamp (ed.), *Technological change, employment and spatial dynamics*. Springer, Berlin, 157–76.

Fischer, M. M. and P. Nijkamp (1988) The role of small firms for regional revitalisation. *The Annals of Regional Science*, 22, SPED, 28–42.

Hoover, E. M. and R. Vernon (1959) *Anatomy of a metropolis*. Harvard University Press, Cambridge, Mass.

Kamien, M. I. and N. L. Schwartz (1975) Market structure and innovation: a survey. *Journal of Economic Literature*, *13*(1), 1–77.

—— (1982) *Market structure and innovation*. Cambridge University Press, Cambridge.

Keeble, D. and E. Wever (eds) (1986) *New firms and regional development in Europe*. Croom Helm, London.

Kleinknecht, A. (1986) Measuring R&D in small firms: how much are we missing? *Research Memorandum, State University Limburg, Maastricht*, RM 86-017.

Meyer-Krahmer, F. (1985) Innovative behaviour and regional indigenous potential. *Regional Studies*, *19*(6), 523–34.

Nijkamp, P. (ed.) (1986) *Technological change, employment and spatial dynamics*. Springer, Berlin.

Pavitt, K., M. Robson and J. Townsend (1987) The size distribution of innovating firms in the UK: 1945–1983. *Journal of Industrial Economics*, *35*(3), 297–316.

Piore, M. J. and C. F. Sabel (1984) *The second industrial divide*. Basic Books, New York.

Planque, B. (1983) *Innovation et développement régional*. Economica, Paris.

Rothwell, R. (1981) Aspects of government policy towards technological innovation policy. *Futures*, June.

—— and W. Zegveld (1982) *Innovation and the small and medium size firm*. Frances Pinter, London.

Storey, D. J. (1982) *Entrepreneurship and the new firm*. Croom Helm, London.

—— and S. Johnson (1987) *Job generation and labour market change*. Macmillan, London.

Part One

The Regional Importance of Small and Medium-sized Enterprises

Part One

The Regional Importance of Small and
Medium-sized Enterprises

2

Innovation, Entrepreneurship, and the Role of Small and Medium-sized Industries: A Long-term View

Luis Suarez-Villa

INTRODUCTION

The rapid international diffusion of manufacturing activities and innovations has become one of the major economic characteristics of our time. Nations that had scarcely industrialised over three decades ago have now become major exporters of industrial goods where manufacturing makes a substantial contribution to national development.

Enterprise size has been one of the most significant variables influencing industrialisation and the international diffusion of innovations. Small and medium-sized industrial enterprises have, in particular, been major vehicles for both employment creation and the diffusion of innovations at local and regional levels, especially in less developed economies. In advanced nations, small and medium-sized enterprises have also played significant roles in the diffusion of innovations, especially in the earlier phases of product and process development.

The relationship between entrepreneurship and firm size in promoting these developments has been neither adequately acknowledged nor researched. Usually, both entrepreneurship and firm size have been treated in highly fragmented ways to focus on such aspects as investment, R&D, and internal organisational questions. While such studies have yielded very significant insights on the issues they have researched, the broader aspects related to the various entrepreneurial roles and their relationship to form size and evolution have been conspicuously missing.

This chapter will attempt to relate the broader and most significant aspects of entrepreneurial innovation and its diffusion by considering the role of small and medium-sized industrial enterprises in product and process development. A concise survey of the historical literature will first define the major innovative entrepreneurial roles, to be followed by a brief discussion of the role of small and medium-sized industries in the long-term process of industrialisation and economic development. The relationship between the entrepreneurial roles, innovation diffusion, product and process development, and firm size will then be explored in the final section. Emphasis will be placed on examining the general relevance of these relationships rather than on analysing their microanalytic details or assembling empirical evidence.

ENTREPRENEURSHIP AND INNOVATION — A BROAD PERSPECTIVE

While technological innovation has attracted much attention in recent times, its relation to the broader and very significant question of entrepreneurship has remained considerably neglected in the economic literature. Such neglect has been one of the most pervasive features of the orthodox economic paradigm. An emphasis on unrealistic behavioural principles, compounded by Walrasian static analysis, and by equilibrium and optimisation assumptions, have tended to view entrepreneurial activities as automatic, if not downright trivial.[1] This bias has also been significant in the economic development literature, where its 'macro' approach, based on national income accounting, has all but completely ignored the role of entrepreneurship as the most important factor in development. To a great extent, this neglect has been part of the Keynesian legacy and its emphasis on economic aggregates.[2] At the same time, the study of economic development, whether macro or micro, has depended greatly on the study of flows, whereas entrepreneurship can only be considered, from this perspective, as a stock variable.

It is interesting to note that a recent survey of 25 general works on economic development, many of them textbooks, found that while several of them contained a section or chapter on entrepreneurship, the ideas developed in those sections were, for the most part, not applied in other chapters.[3] At the same time, their treatment of export promotion and industrialisation policies has not considered the impact of shortfalls of entrepreneurial skills in the implementation of those strategies. This neglect has, for example, also become obvious in our prevailing ignorance of the obstacles and frictions that interfere with entrepreneurial opportunities. Institutional obstacles that arise both from divergent economic interests and established inertia have thus been important obstructions to economic growth and innovation. Obstacles related to a lack of skills and knowledge, along with the effort required to overcome the little-noticed but important friction of space and distance, especially in international and interregional trade, have also been greatly ignored.

Clearly, a definition of entrepreneurship that focuses on technological innovation alone is insufficient to consider the myriad other innovative activities and roles that are part of the entrepreneurial function, and their relationship to firm size dynamics. Only when entrepreneurship is differentiated with respect to its various economic and innovative roles can it be expected to provide adequate insights on its effects on the processes of industrialisation and economic change. At the same time, it is obvious that enterprise size has different impacts on, and is variously affected by, each entrepreneurial role. Larger firms may thus be able to afford entrepreneurial capabilities that are virtually unknown to smaller firms, while the latter can enjoy greater flexibility in making decisions that take better advantage of rapidly changing conditions.

Although a precise definition of entrepreneurial roles has not emerged, the historical literature on this topic has revealed diverse facets that can be used to develop a comprehensive typology.[4] Capital investment and accumulation, and the inherent risk involved, have constituted the oldest and most common role ascribed to entrepreneurship. This definition can be traced historically to Cantillon's eighteenth-century conceptualisation of the entrepreneur as the bearer of non-insurable risk. It became enshrined in economic thinking after Adam Smith's mercantile interpretation of entrepreneurship as the provision and accumula tion of capital, to the exclusion of other possible roles, a legacy that was later adopted and expanded upon by Marx and, in our own time, by the neoclassical paradigm. Almost half a century after Smith, J. B. Say provided a distinction between investment and organisational decision-making that was largely ignored for over a century, but would be made more explicit by Schumpeter's well-known differentiation between innovative and routine decision-making.

A second but less common role assigned to entrepreneurship is that of managerial or productive co-ordination. After Say's contribution, noted above, Marshall equated entrepreneurship with the co-ordinative role by regarding it as the fourth factor of production. Contrary to the opinion of some scholars, however, Schumpeter did not exclude the potential for innovation from this role, inasmuch as he regarded the development of new organisational forms to be a major component of the innovative process. This role was also related to the process of economic development when, in the 1950s, Harbison (1956) observed that managerial and organisational capability were the most scarce skills in less developed economies. Then, since the 1960s, the co-ordinative role has attracted significant attention through Leibenstein's (1968, 1978) X-efficiency conceptualisation that focuses on organisational motivation as a major factor in economic change.[5] The co-ordinative role becomes most obvious in the X-efficiency paradigm through the definition of 'input completing' activities, where the ability to obtain and use factors of production that are not well marketed is most seriously tested. For such factors, markets may not even exist, and prices will not usually yield the necessary signals required to anticipate quality or performance levels. It is also in this role where small and medium-sized industrial enterprises have been most effective in fulfilling economic needs. Such commonplace activities as the adaptation of production processes to allow the employment of less skilled labour, or the restructuring of production tasks to implement a new productive process, are familiar examples of this element.

The Schumpeterian focus on innovation attracted increasing attention to a third major component of the entrepreneurial function: invention. Schumpeter's (1934) implicit, yet well-known distinction between process and product innovation basically equated the latter to the type of experimentation and discovery that is now commonly associated with corporate R&D and individual inventiveness. Nelson and Winter (1982) have been the most recent and best-known exponents of this approach, focusing on one major and very significant aspect of invention: corporate R&D and its effects on economic change. Their extension and conceptualisation of this aspect of innovation as an evolutionary process, rooted in natural selection mechanisms, have extended and enriched the Schumpeterian paradigm and its dynamic underpinnings.[6]

A fourth major component of entrepreneurship that is much related to organisational form, structure and size is that of strategic planning and decision-making. This role can also be related to Schumpeter's broad perspective on innovation through the very direct effect it exercises on such activities as the creation and opening of new markets and sources of inputs. The evolution of this role can be traced to the historical development of industrial organisations as they changed from being primarily single-product, single-function enterprises to single-product, multi-function and finally multi-product, multi-function organisations. Its context is therefore much related to questions of enterprise size and to changes in managerial knowledge. Chandler and Redlich (1961) and Chandler and Daems (1980) have related this typology to the geographical expansion of markets of industrial enterprises as these evolved from serving primarily local or regional markets to multi-region and to national and international markets. In this sense, this role also has a substantial and explicit linkage to the international diffusion of entrepreneurial innovations through the decision processes it activates.

At a microbehavioural level, the strategic planning role can also be related to McClelland's (1961) elaboration of the 'n-Achievement' (need for achievement) concept in its implications for risk-taking and decision-making. Because strategic decisions often affect all of the other entrepreneurial roles substantially, at least in so far as corporate organisations are concerned, its significance for entrepreneurial innovation and diffusion cannot be underestimated. More recently, Leibenstein's definition of 'gap filling' activities in the X-efficiency paradigm is also central to this role, through the identification and coverage of market deficiencies and opportunities it exercises.[7]

Finally, the connection of distinct markets is yet another role that has received substantial attention in modern times. Hirschman's (1958) contribution, viewing entrepreneurship as central to the creation of forward and backward linkages in manufacturing industries, was very significant in this respect. This view was also quite compatible with Schumpeter's perspective on the opening up of new markets or sources of inputs as major elements of innovation. Leibenstein (1978) has also expanded significantly on this role, considering it a major outcome of entrepreneurial motivation in the X-efficiency paradigm.

Differences between the stategic planning and inter-market connection roles are mainly due to the scope of their activities. Strategic planning is assumed to be more concerned with the enterprise's internal operations and their relationship to demand influences and strategies. Inter-market connection is, on the other hand, more related to broader market restructuring efforts that may have little to do with an enterprise's internal questions. Horizontal integration with activities that have little relationship to an enterprise's main function, or the formation of conglomerates, would be examples of activities included in this role.

The supply characteristics of these entrepreneurial roles in various enterprise sizes constitute one of the most important questions facing the study of firm size dynamics. Some roles, such as strategic planning, may very likely be more scarce in smaller firms than in medium-sized or larger enterprises. The impact of varying supply characteristics on firm size may therefore pose significant obstacles to long-term economic development and industry evolution. In the next section, the significance of enterprise size in the long-term process of industrialisation and economic development will be explored, as a prerequisite to the general analysis of industry evolution. The relationship between the latter and enterprise size, and the supply of any of the entrepreneurial roles defined in this section, will then be the focus of the fourth section.

LONG-TERM PERSPECTIVES ON INDUSTRIALISATION AND THE ROLE OF SMALL AND MEDIUM-SIZED FIRMS

A study of the significance of the entrepreneurial roles and innovation in the process of economic development cannot ignore the historical importance of firm size in any of the various stages of development. Previous work on industrial studies and economic development has shown that small and medium-sized industries (and particularly the former) have accounted for the larger share of manufacturing employment in most nations.[8] Only in some of those countries that are now in the most advanced stages of industrialisation have large industries accounted for a significant share of industrial employment.

Small and medium-sized industries are, furthermore, more spatially dispersed and can make a better contribution to local and regional development, especially in hinterland regions, than large industries, which are usually concentrated in primate or major metropolitan areas.[9] Small and medium-sized industries are also generally more labour-intensive than large ones and can make a more significant contribution to both local and national employment, especially since they account for the lion's share of the manufacturing labour force. Most of the time, these industries have also served as significant incubators of large enterprises. In this respect, Anderson (1982), for example, found that the share in employment expansion of large industrial firms attributable to the growth of small industries ranged between 40 and 53 per cent for Korea, the Philippines, Turkey and Taiwan, and was 67 and 70 per cent for India and Colombia, respectively.[10]

The relationship between firm size and the process of economic development has previously been explored by some authors through the analysis of historical stages of development. Thus, for example, Parker (1979) and Anderson (1982) developed general growth phase typologies based on the experience of the industrialised nations.[11] In these schemes, the contribution of industries becomes most obvious in the early phases of industrial development, where household (cottage) manufacturing can account for as much as 50 to 75 per cent of total industrial employment (first phase, see Figure 2.1). Garment-makers, smiths, shoemakers, handicrafts, and crop processing are typical examples of these industries. The predominance of these rudimentary industries in this stage is therefore best explained by their relationship to agricultural production, as providers of inputs and processing capacity, and of the non-food needs of rural areas and small towns.

Figure 2.1: Manufacturing enterprise size and development stages

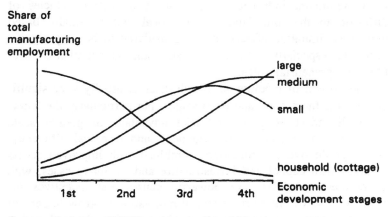

Source: Anderson (1982) and author's modifications and addenda

Small workshops and factories have been found to grow rapidly and displace household manufacturing in many industries during the second stage of development. Over the long term, these firms have generally been considered to be a significant source of income.[12] While many have thought small industrial firms to be engaged primarily in traditional activities, Norcliffe and Freeman (1980) have found that only a small range of such activities is actually practised in many rural industries. A wider range of activities than has so far been thought possible in both rural (particularly resource-based and agro-processing) and urban 'informal' small industries therefore attests to, and complements, the very significant employment share of these industries. In so far as the entrepreneurial roles are concerned, it can be expected that productive co-ordination and inter-market connection may be most important for small household firms in these early stages. Investment capital is usually obtained from family or partners, and the role of institutionalised capital markets (except for some government-sponsored lending programmes) is generally insignificant for these industries.[13] Similarly, invention and strategic planning are usually present only at a very rudimentary level, if at all. Some elementary technological experimentation can occur, however, through some equipment modernisation and production readjustments. International innovation diffusion and adoption during the first two stages of development have traditionally been considered to follow a simple pattern, originating in the advanced nations acting as global locomotives of economic growth and being diffused, with significant and varying time-lag, to the less developed economies. In this process, primate cities and their most significant industries usually serve as major vehicles of diffusion to the hinterland and its local and regionally based industries. Imitation effects can be considered to be very significant here, especially in the co-ordinative and inter-market connective entrepreneurial roles.

The growth of medium-sized industries is usually very significant during the second and third stages, but particularly the latter, as small industries grow and take advantage of greater scale economies in production, management, and technical efficiency. Better productive co-ordination, combined with improved access to investment capital and infrastructure and, in many cases, with government subsidies, are powerful causes and incentives for firms with sufficient entrepreneurial motivation to grow larger. At the same time, taking advantage of increasing demand and a larger market niche also requires some strategic planning to guide firm expansion and marketing efforts.

The transition from household and small firms to medium-sized industries varies greatly between sectors. Anderson (1982), for example, has found that small industries in light-engineering activities can grow very rapidly during this stage. Similarly, small and medium-sized clothing and footwear manufacturers can grow rapidly through 'putting out', undertaken by many as a secondary source of income, and subcontracting. Small, and some medium-sized producers in food processing can, on the other hand, decline significantly, as a result of the mechanisation of processing operations for some agricultural products. Spatially, some urban 'informal' small industries may grow while their rural counterparts decline. This is usually the case for small urban industries that increase their work-force by providing employment to recent rural–urban migrants, or that act as low income, near-subsistence activities in the informal sector. At the same time, small and medium-sized metropolitan industries serving high-income segments can also grow very rapidly, providing incomes that exceed the levels of skilled labour in the formal sector. Many of these small industries that grow to medium or even large size serve as convenient starting points for new entrepreneurs that want to reduce risks and overhead costs.

While the growth of large manufacturers is very conspicuous during both the third and fourth stages of development, it must be noted that these industries seldom account for a significant share of total manufacturing employment, except in the most advanced nations (fourth stage). At the same time, even the smaller industries of some sectors, such as electronics in the advanced nations, can be very significant in the latter stages as sources of invention.[14] Household and small industries have also served a very significant role in many economies during these later stages, as substantial 'putting out' and subcontracting can help isolate larger firms from the effects of major economic downturns and labour strife.

Industrial innovation can become most significant in the advanced nations in the third and fourth phases, and especially the latter, as substantial R&D investments and organisations are developed. In the less developed nations, innovation absorption and imitation can attain unprecedented levels, through the establishment of capital-goods industries and foreign-owned subsidiaries. For small and medium-sized firms, the development of infrastructure and communications can result in substantial advantages, including the opportunity to serve larger markets and attain larger threshold size. At the same time, these industries can also serve as significant vehicles of innovation diffusion in hinterland areas by increasing productivity and aggregate income.

The rapid growth of small and medium-sized industries over long periods in the second and third phases can best be explained by their spatial market dispersion, due to the lack of adequate infrastructure and the resulting high transport and marketing costs. Anderson (1982) notes that small industries benefiting from this condition are those processing a spatially dispersed raw material where transport costs can be lowered through weight reduction, those producing heavy, bulky, or perishable products, and the service or repair industries. In most cases, large industries located in the primate or major cities are unable to compete with these firms because, in addition to inadequate infrastructure, the establishment of branch operations in the hinterland requires substantial capital investment, knowledge of local markets, and the training of local labour.

The rapid growth of small and medium-sized industries in these stages can also be attributed to an increase in the amount of subcontracting and local assembly in such activities as forging, foundry work, machine-shop processing, and agricultural equipment manufacturing. Subcontracting has, in particular, been found to improve capacity utilisation while it helps larger firms avoid labour problems during economic recessions, and the payment of uniformly high union wages in all or most stages of the production process. Low scale-economies found in the production of differentiated products, sometimes also serving limited local markets, have in many cases contributed to the rapid growth of small and medium-sized firms. The tailoring and garment industries, specialty foods manufacturers, and handicrafts are examples of industries benefiting from this situation.

Not all small and medium-sized industries are equally affected by this growth process, however. Firm size dynamics will be very much determined by the character of industry evolution. More specifically, the trajectories of product and process development in any given industry will influence how quickly small or medium-sized enterprises grow to larger sizes. Average firm size between industries can therefore be expected to vary significantly, depending on the species of product demand and production process characteristics. This is, furthermore, affected by national comparative advantages and resource availability for any given industrial activity.

INDUSTRY EVOLUTION, INNOVATION, AND FIRM SIZE

A better understanding of the process of change in enterprise size and its potential economic development impact can best be obtained by focusing on the patterns of product and process evolution that condition the firm's existence and its utilisation of the entrepreneurial roles. It should be obvious from the preceding discussion that, while certain industrial firm sizes are predominant in each stage of development, individual changes in firm size are better related to the dynamics of product and process evolution that are, in turn, conditioned by innovating entrepreneurship and external demand conditions.

Product and process innovation and development have become the means through which firm sizes change and make their impact on local and regional economies.[15] Quantum improvements in communications infrastructure and information technology have helped to diffuse many advances to even the smallest producers, thereby accelerating the pace of diffusion and innovation adoption in many nations. At the same time, advances in organisational practices and the fragmentation of production processes have helped the growth of small and medium-sized firms by making them more capable of being integrated in the international division of labour in manufacturing.

Product innovation and development have been conceptualised as life cycle-type phenomena with distinct phases of invention, growth, maturity, and decline.[16] While demand-side preferences have been found to be crucial in determining the life cycle span of a product, the degree of patent protection afforded by institutional mechanisms and the amount of investment devoted to invention and research have also been found to be very significant. In contrast, in process innovation, Nelson (1984) found secrecy rather than patent protection to be more important in preserving appropriability and limiting adoption and imitation. At the same time, the complex nature of process innovations makes them harder to decipher than product innovations, where advances are usually embodied and can be more easily analysed and imitated. Product innovation may therefore more easily benefit smaller and medium-sized industries than process innovations,

Table 2.1: Entrepreneurship and product innovation and development

| | Phases | | | |
	I	II	III	IV
R&D	Invention (individual/ corporate)			
Finance		Investment		
Marketing		Strategic Planning		(Strategic Planning)
Production			Co-ordination	Co-ordination
Enterprise Size[a]	Small	Medium	Medium–Large	Large–Medium[b]

Notes: a. Relative to average of industry firm size.
      b. Small complementary firms (subcontractors) likely in many industries.

where substantial resources may be required for innovation or imitation.

In a life cycle model of product innovation and development, some entrepreneurial roles can be more significant than others in the various phases of change (see Table 2.1). A look at entrepreneurial performance through the various functions of an enterprise would, for example, reveal individual or corporate inventiveness to be a crucial role during the first phase of product development. Risk-taking is an essential element of this phase, and its degree of success will determine whether a new product will be marketed at all. An invention that results in a patent may not necessarily translate into a new product, however, as investment and marketing capabilities do not always follow automatically. More often than not, inventions that are patented are never developed because the follow-up entrepreneurial roles required are not available, or because substantial investment in products that accomplish a similar function has already been made. This is especially applicable to smaller firms lacking the necessary resources for subsequent investment. In addition, although corporate R&D does account for the majority of product innovations, the role of small businesses has been important in some industries, such as electronic computing.[17]

The investment and strategic planning roles are then essential during the subsequent phase of initial production, where meeting the rapid growth in demand and productive capacity is crucial to maintain appropriability and the benefits of a head start. It is also in this phase where smaller firms have a significant opportunity to grow to a medium or large size, through rapid market expansion. Stategic planning capabilities will therefore be especially important to the smaller and medium-sized firms in developing marketing strategies. Well-developed capital markets can be essential to these firms in channelling investment in this phase, and can help some of the smaller firms to grow substantially. In addition, as competition begins to develop, smaller and medium-sized firms located in relatively lower-wage regions may derive significant advantages over their metropolitan competitors, especially in the advanced nations.

Productive co-ordination is a significant entrepreneurial role in the mature and declining phases (III–IV) of the product cycle (see Table 2.1). The adaptation of productive processes to accommodate less skilled labour or greater automation, often combined with significant difficulties in labour–management relations, is a major challenge. Competitive pressures usually act as major catalysts of this role, as firms strive to adjust to and survive relative product obsolescence. A tendency in the literature to think of this role as being merely 'routine' is quite unjustified, however. At a microbehavioural level, the possibilities for innovative behaviour, on the part of both labour and management, are usually not as limited as some would think, if the proper incentives and motivation exist. It is also during the mature phase that significant subcontracting to smaller and medium-sized firms can occur, reducing uncertainty and the negative effects of economic downturns. Significant diffusion of production towards less developed regions usually occurs in this phase, through branch plant creation and the growth of small and medium-sized enterprises in those regions.[18]

Significant differences in patterns of product decline during the last phase of product development have been documented in the management literature. The demise of a product may, in this sense, be as much due to innovations that render it less effective as to changing exogenous conditions that require a different application. Increasing competition may actually cause many industrial firms to shrink in size, as efforts to reduce costs occur and some operations are subcontracted out or transferred to lower-wage regions or nations. At the same time, opportunities for product differentiation also exist, especially in oligopolised industries where resources for innovation are likely to be available only to the existing corporate groups. Whenever product differentiation occurs, the strategic planning role again becomes essential, though not as crucially as in the second phase, since possibilities for significant market expansion are usually more limited. Even in oligopolised industries, however, product differentiation can be expected to help small and medium-sized firms through vertical disintegration and the resulting trend towards subcontracting.

These patterns of product change are underlain by a concurrent though different temporal dynamic in the processes that are applied to manufacture any given product. A process life cycle may therefore be assumed to span over several phases of process innovation and development and encompass one or more product cycles (see Table 2.2 and Figure 2.2).[19] Process innovations have traditionally been considered under the general rubric of 'technology', but a review of the various entrepreneurial roles involved in process life cycles should reveal many other opportunities for innovation. The design of organisational structures to accommodate a new productive process or to make it work more effectively is one such example. This, and the fact that process development often requires new ways of making decisions, planning corporate activities, facilitating investment or new access to capital markets, requires a much broader definition of innovation than is afforded by the usually narrow visions of technological invention. Furthermore, technological invention itself often requires new modes of self-organisation on the part of individuals and units searching for ideas and new combinations. Similarly, such 'micro' yet significant innovations as developing new negotiating strategies to acquire or merge with other firms so as to achieve greater vertical or horizontal integration, devising new forms of work organisation, supervision, and work-force participation in quality control, are usually ignored by the orthodox focus on 'technology' as the only source of process innovation.

Process innovations must therefore be thought of in broader terms than product innovations, since they often represent whole 'new ways of doing things' that are complex and cannot be embodied in any given product or commodity.[20] Such new approaches can often be better structured in newer and smaller firms where set ways and complex bureaucracies do not become obstacles to creative exploration. In addition, the revolutionary

Table 2.2: Process Innovation and the Entrepreneurial Roles

	Phases					
	A	B	C	D	E	F
R&D	Invention					
Finance		Investment	Investment			
Marketing		Strategic Planning				
Production					Co-ordination	Co-ordination
Inter-firm/ Inter-industry			Inter-market Connector	Inter-market Connector	Inter-market Connector	
Enterprise Size[a]	Small	Medium	Medium–Large	Large[b]	Large[b]	Large–Medium[b]

Notes: a. Relative to average of industry firm size.
b. Reduction of average firm and plant size possible in some industries, through segmentation of productive process.

Figure 2.2: Process and product cycles

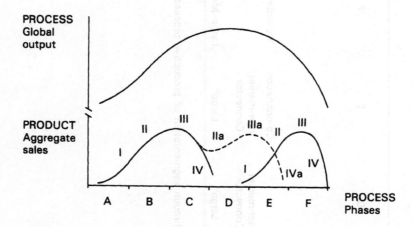

implications that such innovations have for the structure of any economy as well as for many 'micro' aspects related to the workplace, managing, and investing, among others, cannot be ignored. Many process inventions today occur through medium-sized corporate actors, and this role can therefore be most closely associated with the modern corporate R&D function.

As with the product cycle, and for very similar reasons, the strategic planning and investment roles are crucial during the second phase of the process cycle. Innovative strategic planning can, however, be expected to include a broader range of activities, with deeper implications for medium- and long-term firm survival, than with product innovation and development. This can include all the logistics of planning the various product lines to be generated and the markets to be targeted, deciding on the geographical distribution of branch operations or subsidiaries and the division of labour of each within the firm's scope of activities, and promoting the firm's abilities to marshal and manage financial resources. This phase is therefore especially crucial for small and medium-sized firms hoping to grow and acquire a larger product market share.

A third phase of process innovation and development then involves investment as a crucial role in increasing the capacity and outreach of process activities and output (see Table 2.2). A need for greater vertical integration and co-ordination with suppliers and customers may also require inter-market connection to play a major innovative role during this and the fourth phase of process development. At the same time, during the third phase, significant diffusion of process know-how can be expected to occur, firstly, to less developed export-oriented regional and national economies, especially in industries manufacturing consumer durables or involved in significant assembly of these products. This can only be expected to help small and medium-sized manufacturers in those areas, as they apply their comparative advantages in labour costs to vie for additional productive capacity. The rapid diffusion to, and development of, electronics manufacturing in several Asian nations, particularly South Korea, is a significant example of this phenomenon. It is significant to note that some of the larger firms in these nations actually started out as relatively small concerns that grew rapidly with government support and significant investment and strategic planning. Such diffusion can become more significant during the fourth phase for economies involved in significant import substitution, whether in capital goods or consumer durables manufacturing and, to some extent, in those natural resource-related industries in which preliminary processing capabilities are being expanded. The industrialisation and adoption of innovations in nations such as Brazil, Argentina and Mexico are major examples of this development.

The international diffusion of process know-how during the fourth and fifth phases (D, E) of the process cycle has been a subject of much attention in recent years. Grunwald and Flamm (1985), for example, assign a very important role to labour costs in attracting assembly-type processes to less developed nations. Industries applying such processes are usually relatively small by international standards. Cost advantages in this area must, however, be offset by any additional transport costs incurred in shipping products to markets in the advanced nations. Nations with potentially large markets for any of these products, where substantially lower labour costs can offset any additional transport and transaction costs, can therefore enjoy a much more significant advantage than nations with smaller potential markets.

Inter-market connection can be expected to become a significant entrepreneurial role in the fifth phase of the process cycle, by promoting greater horizontal integration between a firm with an increasingly obsolescent productive process and other, usually smaller, service enterprises with certain medium-term stability.

This would most likely apply to industries facing significant competition, but may also affect oligopolised industries facing uncertain or highly competitive international markets. The most obvious manifestation of this development is the emergence of conglomerates and increasing rates of acquisitions and mergers involving various sectors. Increasing horizontal integration is also combined in many cases with substantial vertical integration, especially as the limits of the latter are reached, through either institutional or functional constraints, and disintegration and subcontracting to smaller and medium-sized firms begin to develop.

Organisational problems in dealing with labour issues and endogenous–exogenous environmental pressures during the last two phases of the process cycle then ensure a significant role for co-ordinative entrepreneurship. As with the product cycle, innovation in this role may be found in experimentation with organisational and work-force arrangements that attempt greater participation of the work-force in the productive process, or substitute more machinery for labour. In the case of relocations to lower wage nations or regions, a significant aspect of this role may therefore involve the substitution of less skilled for more skilled labour for machinery, and the fragmentation of a production process into smaller units and firms.

The temporal dimensions of the product and process cycles also reflect differences that are inherent in the scale and complexity of their innovations (see Figure 2.2). Product differentiation and its added lease on the life of a commodity is a very common strategy in product development, especially in situations where no distinct or competitive substitute has emerged. In contrast, significant process differentiations have historically been very limited, since whenever they are feasible, the investment required is generally substantial and their longevity is usually quite uncertain. At the same time, it is obvious that a single but perhaps slightly differentiated process can accommodate more than one product's life cycle and, in some cases, several parallel product lines and their differentiations. Differentiated processes can as a whole be expected to establish greater articulation with smaller and medium-sized industries, as large firms discover the disadvantages of introducing substantial in-house modifications and capital investment.

CONCLUSIONS

This chapter has related entrepreneurial innovation and its various roles to firm size dynamics in the process of economic development and industry evolution. Special emphasis has been placed on the role of small and medium-sized industries in the analysis of these processes and their economic impacts. The approach has been general in scope, and has stressed the interrelations that exist at each stage of the long-term processes of economic and industrial change.

Some of the entrepreneurial roles defined in this essay are more important in some stages of economic and industrial development than in others. Thus, whenever any of the crucial roles are less available to smaller and medium-sized firms, it may be expected that major obstacles to firm growth and development may occur. The lack of institutionalised capital markets that can serve the needs of small and household firms can, for example, prevent the development of these enterprises whenever the entrepreneurial investment role becomes an essential component of any product or process development phase. Similarly, the lack of sufficient societal educational resources can hamper the advancement of small entrepreneurs whenever invention becomes a crucial element for advancement, as in the first phases of product and process innovation.

Such disparities in the supply of innovative entrepreneurial roles available to small and medium-sized firms, and the temporal requirements of industrial and general economic progress, can be expected to introduce significant bottlenecks in the process of regional and local economic development. The fact that these considerations have been so conspicuously missing from the development literature only reinforces our ignorance about the general processes of economic and social change.

It is hoped that the general analytical framework presented in this chapter can provide a better understanding of the role of firm size and of small and medium-sized industries, in particular, in the long-term processes of industrial and economic change. Hopefully, this effort may stimulate others to seek empirical evidence and to provide further analytical and conceptual insights on the processes outlined in this discussion.

NOTES

1. A significant discussion of these shortcomings, based on the neoclassical approach, is in Baumol (1968, 1983).

2. See, for example, Giersch's (1984) provocative account of the Schumpeterian paradigm and its relation to current and previous trends.

3. See Leibenstein (1985). The same pattern was found in discussions with economists who teach courses on economic development. Similarly, a recent survey of the regional science and regional development literature by Nijkamp (1987) revealed that the question of entrepreneurship was never explicitly addressed, although most areas of research were implicitly related to its function.

4. Some discussion on the need to approach entrepreneurship from a broad, multidisciplinary perspective has emerged in the literature from time to time: see, for example, Redlich (1966), Kilby (1971), Giersch (1984) and Suarez-Villa (1987a, b).

5. A major argument for this approach is based on Solow's (1957) finding of a substantial residual (87.5 per cent) left unaccounted for by labour and capital in the production function specification.

6. See also Greenfield and Strickon (1981).

7. Examples of 'gap filling' provided by Leibenstein (1968) are the search, discovery and evaluation of economic opportunities and information, marshalling financial resources for the enterprise and translating these into new markets.

8. See, for example, Staley and Morse (1965), Banerji (1978), Anderson (1982), Rothwell and Zegveld (1982) and Chuta and Sethuraman (1984).

9. For the purposes of this discussion, small industry will be considered to include both household (or cottage) industries and small factories or workshops. In so far as size thresholds are concerned, industries employing less than 30 employees are usually considered small; those employing between 30 and 100 are normally considered to be of medium size, while large industries are generally thought to employ over 100.

10. The time periods covered were 1920–40 (Taiwan), 1953–73 (Colombia), 1961–71 (India: Uttar Pradesh), 1963–75 (Korea), 1967–75 (Philippines) and 1970–7 (Turkey).

11. See also Hoselitz (1959) and Livingstone (1980).

12. See, for example, Beesley and Hamilton (1984).

13. Over the years, many have argued for policy-induced shifts of investment opportunities toward these industries in less developed economies. Anderson (1982), for example, believes that this would improve earning opportunities for a large share of the labour force, while encouraging regional industrial development.

14. See Storey (1982).

15. In this section, enterprise size will be considered analogous to the firm's total productive capacity.

16. See Vernon (1966, 1970) and Hirsch (1967).

17. See Jewkes et al. (1969) and Nelson (1981).

18. See, for example, Thomas (1975), Hansen (1979) and Oakey *et al.* (1982).

19. See, for example, Abernathy and Townsend (1975), Hayes and Wheelwright (1979) and Suarez-Villa (1983, 1985, 1987a).

20. The advantage of a head start, especially in semiconductors, computers and aerospace manufacturing, and advancing down the learning curve, have been found by Nelson (1984) to be most important in preserving appropriability for both process and product innovations. In semiconductors and computers, at least initially, the contribution of small firms has been very significant.

REFERENCES

Abernathy, William J. and Peter L. Townsend (1975) Technology, productivity and process change. *Technological Forecasting and Social Change*, 7, 379–96.

Anderson, Dennis (1982) Small industry in developing countries: a discussion of issues. *World Development*, 10, 913–48.

Banerji, Ranadev (1978) 'Small scale' production units in manufacturing: an international cross-section overview. *Weltwirtschaftliches Archiv*, 114, 62–82.

Baumol, William J. (1968) Entrepreneurship in Economic Theory. *American Economic Review, Papers and Proceedings*, 58, 64–71.

—— (1983) Toward operational models of entrepreneurship. In Joshua Ronen (ed.), *Entrepreneurship*, Lexington Books, Lexington, Mass, pp. 29–48.

Beesley, M. E. and R. T. Hamilton (1984) Small firms' seedbed role and the concept of turbulence. *Journal of Industrial Economics*, 33, 217–31.

Chandler, Alfred D. and Herman Daems (eds.) (1980) *Managerial hierarchies: comparative perspectives on the rise of the modern industrial enterprise.* Harvard University Press, Cambridge, Mass.

Chandler, Alfred D. and Fritz Redlich (1961) Recent developments in American business administration and their conceptualization. *Business History Review*, 35, 1–27.

Chuta, E. and S. V. Sethuraman (eds) (1984) *Rural small-scale industries and employment in Africa and Asia.* International Labor Organization, Geneva.

Giersch, Herbert (1984) The age of Schumpeter. *American Economic Review, Papers and Proceedings*, 74, 103–9.

Greenfield, Sidney M. and Arnold Strickon (1981) A new paradigm for the study of entrepreneurship and social change. *Economic Development and Cultural Change*, 29, 467–99.

Grunwald, Joseph and Kenneth Flamm (1985) *The global factory: foreign assembly in international trade.* Brookings Institution, Washington DC.

Hansen, Niles M. (1979) The new international division of labor and manufacturing decentralization in the United States. *Review of Regional Studies*, 9, 1–11.

Harbison, Frederick H. (1956) Entrepreneurial organization as a factor in economic development. *Quarterly Journal of Economics*, *70*, 364–79.

Hayes, Robert and Steven Wheelwright (1979) The dynamics of process–product life cycles. *Harvard Business Review*, *57*, 127–36.

Hirsch, Seev (1967) *Location of industry and international competitiveness*. Oxford University Press, Oxford.

Hirschman, Albert O. (1958) *The strategy of economic development*. Yale University Press, New Haven.

Hoselitz, Bert F. (1959) Small industry in underdeveloped countries. *Journal of Economic History*, *19*.

Jewkes, John, David Sawers and Richard Stillerman (1969) *The sources of invention*, 2nd ed. Norton, New York.

Kilby, Peter (1971) Hunting the Heffalump. In Peter Kilby (ed.), *Entrepreneurship and economic development*. The Free Press, New York, pp. 1–40.

Leibenstein, Harvey (1968) Entrepreneurship and development. *American Economic Review*, *58*, 72–83.

—— (1978) *General X-efficiency theory and economic development*. Oxford University Press, New York.

—— (1985) Entrepreneurship, entrepreneurship training, and economics: the case of the missing inputs. Mimeo.

Livingstone, Ian (ed.) (1980) *Development economics and policy: readings*. Allen and Unwin, London.

McClelland, David C. (1961) *The achieving society*. Van Nostrand, Princeton.

Nelson, Richard R. (1981) Competition, innovation, productivity growth, and public policy. In Herbert Giersch (ed.), *Towards an explanation of economic growth*, 1980 Symposium, Belknap, Tübingen, pp. 151–79.

—— (1984) Incentives for entrepreneurship and supporting institutions. *Weltwirtschaftliches Archiv*, *120*, 646–61.

—— and Sidney G. Winter (1982) *An evolutionary theory of economic change*. Belknap, Cambridge, Mass.

Nijkamp, Peter (1987) Twenty-five years of regional science. *Sistemi Urbani*.

Norcliffe, G. B. and D. B. Freeman (1980) Non-farm activities in market centers of central province, Kenya. *Canadian Journal of African Studies*, *14*, 503–17.

Oakey, R. P., P. A. Nash and A. T. Thwaites (1982) Technological change and regional development: some evidence on regional variations in product and process innovation. *Environment and Planning A*, *14*, 1073–86.

Parker, W. N. (1979) Industry. In Peter Burke (ed.) *The new Cambridge modern history*. Cambridge University Press, London.

Redlich, Fritz (1966) Toward the understanding of an unfortunate legacy. *Kyklos*, *19*, 709–16.

Rothwell, R. and W. Zegveld (1982) *Innovation and the small and medium sized firm: their role in employment and in economic change*. Frances Pinter, London.

Schumpeter, Joseph A. (1934/1912) *The theory of economic development:*

an inquiry into profits, capital, credit, interest, and the business cycle. Harvard University Press, Cambridge, Mass. (Originally published as *Theorie der Wirtschaftlichen Entwicklung*, Leipzig.)

Solow, Robert M. (1957) Technological change and the aggregate production function. *Review of Economics and Statistics, 39,* 312–30.

Staley, E. and R. Morse (1965) *Modern small-scale industry for developing countries.* McGraw-Hill, New York.

Storey, David (1982) *Entrepreneurship and the new firm.* Croom Helm, London.

Suarez-Villa, Luis (1983) El Ciclo del Proceso de Manufactura y la Industrialización de las Zonas Fronterizas de México y Estados Unidos. *Comercio Exterior, 33,* 950–60.

——— (1985) Los Enclaves Industriales para las Exportación y el Cambio en las Manufacturas. *Comercio Exterior, 35,* 466–80.

——— (1987a) Entrepreneurship and the international diffusion of innovations in manufacturing: a general approach. *Rivista Internazionale di Scienze Economiche e Commerciali, 34,* 369–91.

——— (1987b) Entrepreneurship in the space-economy. *Revue d'Economie Régionale et Urbaine, 28,* 59–76.

Thomas, Morgan D. (1975) Growth pole theory, technological change and regional economic growth. *Papers of the Regional Science Association, 34,* 3–25.

Vernon, Raymond (1966) International investment and international trade in the product cycle. *Quarterly Journal of Economics, 80,* 190–207.

——— (1970) The location of economic activity. In John Dunning (ed.), *Economic analysis and multinational enterprise.* Allen and Unwin, London, pp. 89–114.

3

Innovation and Technology Strategy: Competitive New-technology Firms and Industries

Morgan D. Thomas*

INTRODUCTION

During the last decade and a half there has been a significant increase in interest in the role played by technical innovation in the growth of economies, industries and firms. Theorising with respect to this role has been greatly stimulated by the rediscovery of innovation as the key explanatory element in Schumpeter's seminal theory of economic development in a capitalist economy (Schumpeter, 1934, 1939, 1950).

The critical economic development implications of the relationship between innovation and behavioural competition at firm and industry levels are enunciated in Schumpeter's theory. Contemporary studies are providing major contributions to the clarification and further development of some important aspects of this relationship (Abernathy, 1978; Porter, 1980; Rosenbloom, 1981; Nelson and Winter, 1982; Rosenberg, 1982; Abernathy *et al*. 1983; Clark, 1983; Abernathy and Clark, 1985). In these studies, among other things, questions are asked about the role of innovations in shaping the competitive environments of not only firms and industries but also sub-national and national economies. Concomitantly, key decision-makers in innovative firms are increasingly grappling with the problem of incorporating innovation into the development of long-term firm strategy.

* I wish to thank Patrick Aldwell, Ed Delaney, Gunter Krumme and Scott MacCready for their helpful comments. This material is based partly upon work supported by the National Science Foundation under Grant No. SES 8411692.

This essay represents a response to the growing recognition that there are very important reasons why we need a better understanding of the way in which the process of technical innovation shapes the competitive environment of firms and industries. This response, largely conceptual in form, primarily focuses attention on selected relationships between innovation and technology strategy development within competitive 'new technology' firms and industries. In the sections of the chapter which follow, several heuristic frameworks are articulated: the first presents a way of viewing the competitive behaviour of 'new technology' firms and industries; the second, provides a perspective on key elements in the development process of a new technological paradigm; the third focuses attention on the process of innovation and selected technical and economic relationships; and the fourth concentrates on technology-based strategy issues in competitive new-technology firms and industries. The concluding section provides a brief assessment of the frameworks.

BEHAVIOURAL COMPETITION: SELECTED CONCEPTUALISATIONS

A great deal of theorising concerning the role of innovations and technical change in the process of economic development has been based on the seminal contributions on the subject by Schumpeter (1934, 1939, 1950). One of his key ideas was the notion of behavioural competition. He argued that it was not price competition, but the competition founded on the entrepreneurial behaviour of the entrepreneur who carried out the innovation, that was responsible for the process of 'creative destruction'. Firms which continued to innovate successfully grew and drove non-innovating firms out of their industry. Major, radical and commercially successful innovations eventually destroyed even well-established monopolies, but in so doing, Schumpeter believed that the vigorous new industries created offered the promise of a more prosperous future.

In essence, Schumpeter argued that innovations, manifested in the development of new technical possibilities by innovator firms, were a most potent source of competitive advantage, at both the firm and industry level. Consequently, innovations may be viewed as a vital means of generating various kinds of scalar, structural and locational changes in firms and industries. How do we now utilise Schumpeter's conceptualisation of the process of 'creative destruction' to achieve a better understanding of the competitive behaviour of innovative firms? In other words, how do these firms use technical innovations to create new industries and/or to enhance their competitive position within their respective industries?

Conceptually, we may assume that firms in the same industry produce products that are close substitutes for each other. We may also assume that competition between firms in an industry continually works to drive down the rate of return on invested capital towards the competitive floor rate of return where 'normal' profits are earned. A firm whose long-run rate of return is customarily less than the competitive floor rate of return would be expected to go out of business. High, long-run, rates of return in an industry would be expected to stimulate an inflow of investments by new entrants and existing firms (Porter, 1980, 1983). Technical innovation as a competitive variable may then be viewed as a powerful force which has the potential of increasing significantly the competitive position of the innovator firm within its industry. The firm may be able to do this by altering the industry's competitive structure.

Industry competitive structure

In any industry, if we view competition broadly, there are five fundamental competitive forces at work. The collective strength of these forces determines the ability of firms to earn rates of return on investment in excess of the opportunity cost of capital. The five forces are:

(1) the threat of entry;
(2) substitution;
(3) bargaining power of suppliers;
(4) bargaining power of customers; and
(5) rivalry among incumbent competitors.

Underlying each of these five forces are sets of economic, technical and situational determinants which define the rules of competition in the industry (Porter, 1983).

Firm competitive strategy

One may view the objective of a firm's competitive strategy, over its planning period, to be the creation for itself of a defensible position against the competitive forces it believes it will encounter. These underlying competitive forces are both generated within its industry as well as by potential new entrant firms currently associated with other industries. One approach a firm may adopt to accomplish its strategy objective is to find the least vulnerable industry position with respect to the competitive forces: for example, a particular market segment may provide a safe niche against the threat of substitute products.

The other approach to strategy formulation is to develop a strategy that is meant to change industry competitive structure in ways that would enhance the firm's competitive advantage (Nelson and Winter, 1982; Porter, 1983). Clearly, technical innovation can and does play a powerful role in the use of this approach in the formulation of competitive strategies by innovative science- and technology-based firms.

Recently, Porter (ibid., pp. 3–4) drawing on his own extensive studies and those carried out by other researchers, concluded that:

> What makes technology unique as a strategic variable is its considerable power to change the competitive rules of the game . . . Where a firm's technological innovations are appropriable, these impacts of technological change on structure are the fundamental motivations underlying the firm's choice of technological strategies.

These technological strategy choices may be made on the basis of evaluations and assessments of the probable impact of the firm's innovative activities on changing industry-wide entry barriers, buyer and supplier power, substitution threats and rivalry forces. Sound competitive strategy by the firm 'can lead to two broad types of competitive advantage: lower cost or differentiation (uniqueness)' (ibid., p. 4). The firm, when developing a technology strategy, is, however, dealing with technical, economic and other kinds of phenomena that have well-known varying uncertainty characteristics over the life cycles of its products.

Organisational behaviour of the new-technology-based firm

At this time it is pertinent to ask: how does a new-technology-based firm, as an organisation, behave in response to the changes in its business environment brought about by such factors as those associated with technical innovation and competitive structure of its industry? For the purpose of this discussion it is useful to differentiate between routine and non-routine behaviour by 'fallible' firm decision-makers. The fallibility of these decision-makers is frequently manifested, for example, when a new business situation facing the firm is assessed as requiring 'routine' instead of 'non-routine responses'; or when incorrect information and methods are used in making a decision which affects the future of this type of firm. Decision-makers may work hard to reduce their fallibility, but it seems safe to assume that they will not succeed in eliminating this most human of attributes they possess.

Regular and predictable behaviour by the firm may be viewed as 'routine' behaviour. When firms encounter new problems or situations with which they have had no experience and about which they have no information, they face conditions of complete uncertainty. Such a situation would be encountered by a firm faced with a decision as to whether or not it should undertake the process of transforming a primary invention into a commercially successful 'radically new' product innovation. Responses to various kinds of problems encountered by firms are developed under varying degrees of uncertainty, in terms of the nature of the responses and their implementation. Problems which firms believe are not appropriate to deal with in a regular and predictable fashion may be viewed as requiring non-routine responses. This chapter is primarily concerned with non-routine behaviour in firms engaged in the process of technical change in an industry with a dynamic competitive structure.

Of the conceptual frameworks that provide guidance and assistance when attempting to explain the behaviour of firms, the framework articulated by Nelson and Winter (1982) seems to have the greatest flexibility and scope for dealing with firms in innovative new-technology industries. Their framework is also compatible with Schumpeter's concept of behavioural competition and an integral key component in the conceptual foundation for an evolutionary theory for economic change and development.

Briefly, the crucial elements in the Nelson–Winter framework are the three concepts *organisational 'routine'*, *'search'* and *'selection'* or *'decision environment'*. Organisational 'routine' represents the set of routines and procedures that, at any time, firms have developed to provide ways of doing things and also determining what to do. When dealing with non-routine business problems, under conditions of uncertainty, established organisational routines are an inadequate source of guidance to the firm when determining what to do. In such situations, firms tend to adapt or change their routines and procedures to take into account, as best they can, the nature and business implications for the firm of the perceived conditions of uncertainty related to the problem. In so doing, firms frequently risk their future survival on attempts to adapt their organisational routines.

Organisational 'search' denotes all those firm activities associated with the evaluation of current routines and the processes whereby 'routines' are modified or replaced. The firm's organisation 'selection environment' is the whole collection of considerations which affects its viability and need to change. The 'selection environment' is defined by conditions both inside and outside the firm's industry (Nelson and Winter, 1982).

INNOVATION: SELECTED PERSPECTIVES AND DIMENSIONS

Definitions

Innovation, in the form of advancing technology, is clearly regarded as a major explanatory factor in the process of evolutionary economic development at the level of the firm, industry and economy. It is, however, a complex concept with many meanings. To fulfil our current purposes, there is considerable merit in providing at this juncture working definitions of technology, innovation and technological change. Attention is focused primarily on the technological and economic aspects of these concepts.

We will begin by defining *technology* as consisting of society's pool of knowledge concerning the industrial, mechanical and practical arts: 'It is made up of knowledge concerning physical and social phenomena, knowledge regarding the application of basic principles to practical work, and knowledge of the rules of thumb of practitioners and craftsmen' (Mansfield *et al.* 1982). Recently, Dosi (1984) has stressed that 'theoretical' as well as the 'practical' pieces of knowledge together make up the set or pool of knowledge which we define as technology. These pieces of knowledge in the set may also be viewed as including know-how, methods, procedures, experience of successes and failures and also, of course, physical devices and equipment.

Commercial products and processes represent various combinations of pieces of knowledge in a specific technology set. The first commercial production of a 'new combination' of pieces of knowledge in a new technology set may be defined as a *'radical' technical innovation* and the beginning of the commercial phase of a life cycle for a specific product. *Incremental innovation* is the result of carrying out further successful innovative activities on the radical product and the process related to it. The intra- and inter-firm and industry diffusion of radical and incremental innovations, over time and space, represents technical change.

The technical innovation life cycle may usefully be viewed as having a pre-commercial and a commercial phase. Conceptually, the pre-commercial, or formulation and gestation, phase for a specific radical product begins when inventions or sets of inventions establish the level of *technical feasibility* which induces firms or a firm to decide to explore the technical possibilities of eventually producing a radical product (or process). This action represents the making of a non-routine decision by the firm. If the R&D activities which follow establish the acceptable level of *economic feasibility* for the embryonic radical product, then the firm tends to make another non-routine decision to produce the radical product innovation commercial. The commercial production or the exploitation phase of the radical innovation signals a discontinuous change in the path of technical progress and a future for the innovation that is fraught with both technical and commercial uncertainties (Clark, 1983). The discontinuity in the path of technical progress generated by a radical innovation 'may lead to serious dislocations, economic perturbations and adjustments for the firms in a particular sector' (Freeman, 1986, p. 103). The semiconductor, or radical innovation, had such an adverse impact on electronic computer-sector firms which used vacuum tubes in their computers.

Innovation — a technical perspective

Innovation — namely the process of creating and developing new technical possibilities — has attracted considerable theoretical and empirical study over the last quarter of a century. Nevertheless, we are far from having a full understanding of either the nature of or the economic, technical, spatial, social and other dimensions of this complex process. This discussion, however, is restricted to a few tentative ideas and perspectives concerning the technical and economic dimensions of the process of technical innovation in firms primarily found in the so-called 'new technology' industries. As compared to other firms, these 'innovative' or 'new technology'-based firms spend more on R&D relative to their sales, and employ a higher proportion of technology- and science-oriented workers. In other words, they manifest a relatively strong emphasis on activities related to the process of technical innovation.

Technological paradigm or industry technology life cycle

There are a number of ways of conceptualising the processes of radical and incremental innovation from a technological perspective. In this articulation the innovation life cycle of a radical product (process) is viewed within the context of a *technological paradigm*. A technological paradigm may be thought of as both 'a model and a pattern of solution of *selected* technological problems, based on *selected* principles derived from natural sciences and on *selected* material technologies' (Dosi, 1984, p. 83). In this definition of a technological paradigm there is no implied suggestion that there exists only a uni-directional deterministic sequence of 'science–technology–production'. Solution sequences for selected technological problems may originate from production or technology as well as from science. The nature and influence of the complex relationships among science, technology and production represent topics subject to considerable contemporary debate (Rosenberg, 1974; Freeman, 1979; Price, 1984; Walsh, 1984).

Dosi (1984, p. 88) suggests that:

the emergence of new technological paradigms is contextual to the explicit emergence of economically defined 'needs'. In other words, the supply side determines the 'universe' of possible modalities through which generic 'needs' or productive requirements (which as such do not have any direct economic significance) are satisfied.

51

The technology of a specific technological paradigm may, for example, be related to generic 'needs' or 'tasks' such as transporting people and commodities; providing electrical power; and switching and amplifying electrical signals. Thus, for example, the latter generic 'need' is, among others, related to the semiconductor set of technologies. Despite empirical support for the notion of the technological paradigm and its utility by such eminent researchers on the innovation process, further development and testing of the concept are necessary. At present we find these major researchers using very similar concepts to Dosi's technological paradigm, but they are known by different names such as 'technological imperatives' (Rosenberg, 1976), 'technological regime' (Nelson and Winter, 1977), and 'technological guideposts' (Sahal, 1984).

New technological paradigm: selected characteristics

The emergence of a technological paradigm appears to depend on a new synthesis of a great many proven established ideas or, in other words, inventions. This creative symbiosis, however, materialises infrequently, but when it does, the consequences tend to be striking. In effect they represent a technical break with the past in an otherwise evolutionary system of technical progress. The birth of a new technological paradigm or a specific new-technology-based industry represents the creation of new technical possibilities. As these possibilities are developed and applied commercially, they achieve the defined status of either radical or incremental product or process innovations.

A change in paradigm seems to induce strongly or require the industrially relevant firms to start immediately in the technical problem-solving activity within the new paradigm. Know-how transferability from one paradigm to another, or even within a paradigm from one trajectory pathway to another, is not smooth and it is costly to bring about successfully.

A new-technology industry

Conceptually, the birth of a new-technology industry begins with the first commercial production of a radical product innovation by an innovator firm. This first radical innovation may also be viewed as the first innovation produced within the new technological paradigm. The first radical product establishes both the first product life cycle in a specific product industry and the commercial birth of a new technological paradigm's *technology life cycle* — for example, solid-state electronics.

Unfortunately, this conceptual classification scheme of product and technology life cycles may not, however, duplicate the classification schemes for products and industries found in national and international Standard Industrial Classification manuals. A broadly defined, robust 'new technology' such as solid-state electronics provides the technology base for the creation of many Standard Industrial Classification-type industries — for example, solid-state computers and semiconductors. Conceptually, the narrower set of semiconductor technologies may be viewed both as a specific technological paradigm and as a subset of technologies within the broader solid-state electronics technological paradigm. The new technological paradigm and the new radical product may also be viewed as ushering in a 'revolutionary' design. Design here means a revolutionary 'adaptation of means to some preconceived end' (Layton, 1972). Nevertheless, although design in general is the central activity of technology, 'it remains far closer to art or craft than science' (Alic, 1986, p. 256). The commercial launch of the new product is quickly followed by the production of similar products by firms whose technologies belong to the same technology paradigm as the innovator firm. Imitator firms which use legal and illegal means, with various degrees of commercial success, for obtaining the 'radically new' design or some other similar design(s), are also part of the growing matrix of competitive firms in the early development phase of this new-technology industry.

Another characteristic that serves to identify the creation of a technological paradigm is the associated creation and presence of a significant technique with greater adaptability to its task environment. Further advances and technical progress usually take place in each new technique. These creative technical advances which indicate technical progress in a technique may be viewed as incremental innovations. Some of these are process innovations and others are product innovations.

It seems that positive and negative *heuristics* exist within specific dynamic sets of technologies associated with particular technological paradigms. These heuristics embody strong prescriptions on the directions of technical change which should be pursued or neglected. The use of heuristics, however, does not guarantee either desirable or unique outcomes. Product innovation, it seems, involves a great deal of trial and error and emphasis on scaling and learning processes by the innovative firm as it attempts to cope with the state of *technological uncertainty* associated with innovation. A direction of technical change that is common to a wide range of technologies is the increasing mechanisation of operations that have been done by hand (Nelson and Winter, 1977).

Selected technical problems associated with specific material technologies are usually discussed in relation to a set or cluster of technologies such as bio-technical, organic chemistry, and semiconductor technologies. Normal technological progress within a specific paradigm, for example, the semiconductor technological paradigm, may be defined by its *technological trajectory*. In other words, the pattern of 'normal' problem-solving activity within a technological paradigm, characterised by incremental innovation, defines the paradigm's aggregate *technological trajectory*. This trajectory, for example, may be specified by a semi-logarithmic form of the technometric function as used by Sahal (1984) in the case of the US computer industry.

Economic as well as technical variables define the various dimensions and form of the technological trajectory's pattern of 'normal' problem-solving activity. The trajectory may be thought of as: 'the movement of multi-dimensional trade-offs among technological variables that the paradigm defines as relevant. Progress can be defined as the improvement of these trade-offs. One could imagine the trajectory as a 'cylinder' in the multi-dimensional space' (Dosi, 1984, p. 85). Individual firms tend to have their own pathway within this 'cylinder' or aggregate trajectory. These firms attempt to profit as long as possible by keeping confidential or protecting their economic control over firm-specific plant and product system-specific technology, as well as their organisational and economic expertise (Thomas, 1987).

Rejuvenation and industry technology life cycle

If we apply the technological trajectory to long-established industries, such as the American automobile and machine-tools industries, we find that under certain conditions, major changes may be effected in their technological trajectories. This 'rejuvenation' or 'de-maturity' may occur in particularly robust technological paradigms. In such industries, firms may be stimulated by intense and growing foreign competition, or because major technical advances are made in industries which produce key components used in their products and/or in their manufacturing processes. They begin to conduct exploratory research and discover new productive directions in which their industry technology may develop.

Once the directional change is made in the industry's trajectory, sources of 'normal' problem-solving activity then tend to generate a burst of incremental innovation. The pattern is reminiscent of the early development phase for new-technology industries. Subsequently, however, there is a resumption of a less rapidly paced 'normal' technological process (Dosi, 1984). Clark (1983), for example, suggests that a process of 'rejuvenation' in the American automobile industry began in the early 1970s. There are also indications that the early 1980s witnessed the beginning of a 'rejuvenation' phase in the American machine-tools industry (Friar and Horwitch, 1985).

Decline in the industry technology

Eventually older technologies lose their dominance or are largely overthrown by the entry of newer technologies initially characterised by their revolutionary design. In the recent past this was the case when a specific cluster of technologies — for example, those embodied in reciprocating engines in commercial aircraft — vacuum tubes and mechanical calculators were 'overthrown' by new radical innovations such as jet engines, solid-state electronics and electronic computers (Abernathy and Clark, 1985). Such displacements of older technologies render much technical and human capital obsolete. Furthermore, resultant adverse human and economic costs are not always offset by the substitution of the new technologies (Freeman, 1986).

INNOVATION: SELECTED TECHNICAL AND ECONOMIC RELATIONSHIPS

The conceptualisation of innovation within the context of a technological paradigm brings into focus a number of important technical and economic relationships. There are, for example, significant connections between innovations and new technologies as well as between the embodied and disembodied characteristics of technologies at different stages in their life cycles. Furthermore, the conceptualisation suggests that the competitive relationships between new and older technologies serving a common market, over time, tend to result in the growth of industries embracing newer and more robust technologies and the decline of the older technology industries. Some of these relationships and their implications are now examined within a competitive firm and industry framework. A particular type of industry technology cycle is used as a framework for carrying out an examination of these relationships. This type of industry technology cycle is called a 'Component Generation' or 'Characteristic' Technology Cycle.

Component Generation Technology Cycle

It is useful, at this time, to view an industry as an 'industry system' whose final product is composed of parts or components produced by its subsystem industries. The components therefore represent vital integral parts of a *technologically interdependent final product system*. Such a conceptualisation facilitates an understanding of why technological progress in 'component' industries normally contributes to technological progress in the final product industry system.

Early in the commercial life of a 'new product innovation' industry system, there is considerable fluidity in product design. There also tends to be an active search for a set of technologies with widespread market appeal. The search for promising technological trajectories and strategies is influenced by technical and economic constraints. Within the new product industry's technological paradigm, technological advances are initially associated with improvements of core components or aspects thereof (Nelson and Winter, 1982).

Product design evolution tends to be dominated by a core component which determines fundamental product functions and performance. A major change in the core component requires significant change in most other technical aspects of the product. The competitive life of a core component may be associated with a generation of products. The evolution of the underlying set of product (and process) technologies defines the Component Generation Technology Cycle (CGTC).

The CGTC concept underscores the critical nature of the evolutionary interdependent relationships between technology and product. Unfortunately, at this time, we do not have an adequate metric for deciding clearly and accurately how novel an innovation must be to be classified as incremental or radical to permit one to identify readily and without doubt the family members of a product line. The Component Generation concept intuitively suggests a specific set of product lines which represents a component or product generation. How technologically new does a product have to be to begin a new generation of a particular product and signal the technological decline of the previous generation? Clearly, there are still many unresolved conceptual and empirical problems related to the use of the CGTC in examining the nature and implications of important dynamic technical and economic relationships during the commercial phase of the life cycle of radical product (component) innovation.

Notwithstanding these problems Sahal (1984) presents intriguing evidence in support of his contention that one may identify, in the period 1951–79, four CGTCs within the US electronic computer industry.

These particular technology cycles are evidenced by so-called 'component generations' of approximately 8–12 years duration as distinguished from product life cycles of approximately 3–4 years duration. Component generations, however, vary in duration among industries as well as within the same industry.

Each new generation, on average, effected a ten-fold increase in speed, a twenty-fold increase in memory capacity, and a ten-fold increase in reliability, while reducing the component cost ten-fold and the industry system cost 2.5-fold (Hodges, 1977). The four CGTCs for computers are identified as the 'vacuum tube cycle', 1951–8; 'transistor cycle', 1959–63; 'small-scale integrated circuit cycle', 1964–9; and 'large-scale integrated circuit cycle, 1969–79 (Sahal, 1984, p. 160). A fifth CGTC — namely, the 'very large-scale integrated circuit cycle' — was initiated in the early 1980s. This technology in 1986 had still not demonstrated significant proof of its commercial viability. It would appear that the vacuum tube, transistory and small-scale integrated circuit cycles represent three types of radical product (component) technologies. In contrast, although the small-scale, large-scale and very large-scale integrated circuit cycles represent dramatic advances in chip complexity, each step up in scale represents only a step up within the existing integrated-circuit industry technology.

Perceived potential and limits of technology

We may also discuss, at this time, another set of dimensions which are related to Sahal's CGTCs. These dimensions, which are described here in summary form, are more fully articulated in Foster (1986). This set of specific dimensions provides information concerning the nature of the relationship between technical performance and research effort over the life of a technology cycle. Such information is relevant when discussing innovation, competition and technology strategy at firm and industry levels.

The particular technology associated with a specific CGTC, for example the 'transistor cycle', has theoretical and practical limits. The R&D mission of firms in the 'transistor' technology industry is to advance towards these limits. The current 'state of the art' determines how much advancement is possible. The difference between what is possible and the technical limit may be called the *technical potential*. When a firm's technical potential is high, as it seems to be in contemporary 'new technology'-based industries, technology is likely to be an important element in the firm's business strategy. By the same token, if its technical potential is low, then other business functions such as marketing and cost accounting are likely to loom larger for the firm.

Early in the commercial life of a particular technology, R&D programmes in firms within the technology industry build knowledge bases, draw and test lines of engineering, identify problems and discard unworkable approaches (Rosenberg 1982, pp. 120–40). Progress initially, towards the technical limits of the technology, tends to be slow. Subsequently the pace increases and the maximum rate of progress is typically reached when approximately half the potential has been achieved. Thereafter, the technology begins to be constrained as technical limits are reached and there is a slowing down in the rate of performance improvement. In other words, diminishing rates of return accrue to R&D inputs. This pattern of relationship between research effort and technical performance over the technology cycle is referred to as the S-*curve phenomenon* because it tends to have a log normal form.

R&D productivity may be defined as the improvement in the performance of the product or process divided by the incremental effort required. Thus, the relationship between technical progress and R&D investment determines R&D productivity at various stages of development along the *S* curve. For competitive firms the end objective is not R&D productivity but the rate of profit earned from the R&D investment, i.e. the *R&D return*. Another useful variable is the *R&D yield*, which represents the profit derived from a particular technical advance (innovation). R&D yield, however, is a function of the competitive structure of the technology industry: supply/demand conditions, firm strategies, substitute products, relative power of suppliers and buyers, and other external influences (Hakansson and Laage-Hellman, 1984; Pappas, 1984).

Within firms, controlling and improving R&D productivity is primarily the responsibility of the R&D department; whereas R&D yield is the result of competitor strategies and market conditions and these matters are traditionally the responsibility of 'business units' within the firms. Both dimensions should be analysed independently but ultimately they need to be coupled if they are to be used successfully by firms in providing guidance in the development of their technology strategies (Foster, 1986; Graham, 1986).

TECHNOLOGY STRATEGIES IN NEW-TECHNOLOGY FIRMS AND INDUSTRIES

Strategy alternatives

This is an opportune time to explore briefly, tentatively and suggestively, a number of relationships which have been identified between competitive firms and technology-based strategies in young and in mature technology industries that have emerged in the United States during the last 30 years (Cooper, 1973; Utterback and Abernathy, 1975; Abernathy and Utterback, 1978; Bollinger *et al.*, 1983; Rothwell, 1984; Friar and Horwitch, 1985; Macdonald, 1985). Before discussing these relationships, however, there is merit in focusing attention briefly on selected dimensions related to the evaluation of the new technology industries that emerged during this recent period in US industrial history. Industry origins and the patterns of change in internal and external selection environments of firms over industry technology life cycles represent a number of the dimensions that are examined.

Industry origin

If we examine the origins of these new-technology industries, we observe a number of similarities and differences. This is also the case when we compare the origin of specific industries in the United States with their counterparts in other countries. We find, for example, that the commercial origin of the semiconductor industry in the United States was, in the early 1960s, dominated by small entrepreneurial firms; whereas in the United Kingdom, Western Germany and Japan this industry in each case was launched by a few large firms. Our understanding of the processes which underlie the birth of contemporary new technology industries and firms is unfortunately incomplete. This is especially the case with respect to the roles 'spin-offs' and incubator firms play in the birth of new-technology firms (Beesley and Hamilton, 1984; Senker, 1985).

Be that as it may, considerable interest in the critical role of these small entrepreneurial firms in the early growth of new-technology industries in the United States was again stimulated in the latter half of the 1970s by the entrepreneurially launched personal computer industry. The true spark for this industry came from an entrepreneurial small-firms environment that was made up of hobbyists, publicists and promoters, technological champions, and entrepreneurs (Friar and Horwitch, 1985). In the 1980s, there seems to be a growing consensus in the United States, Canada and Western Europe that innovation by small 'new'-technology entrepreneurial firms is exceptionally important in the birth of new industries (Freeman et al., 1982), and they could well serve as important vehicles for the regeneration of economic development in regional and national economies (Rothwell, 1982; Steed, 1982).

Firm size and innovation

The relationship between firm size and innovation is a topic that has been intensely debated over the last decade and a half. On the one side are those who stress the behavioural and organisational strengths of small firms in this innovation process; on the other side are those who argue that large size and monopoly power are prerequisites for economic progress via technical change (Rothwell, 1984). Unfortunately, the debators have not been sufficiently aware of sector differences and thus the need to conduct their debate on a sector-by-sector basis. In addition, neither side has given due consideration to the high probability that the relative contributions of large and small firms to the innovation process in a particular industry might well depend on the technological age of that industry. Recent studies also suggest that we can expect the relationship between firm size and innovation to vary between the different phases of not only the component industry technology life cycle (such as that for the integrated-circuit industry) but also the different phases of the Kondratiev-type 'long waves' (Freeman *et al.*, 1982; Kaplinsky, 1983, Clark *et al.*, 1984).

During the 1980s, however, there has been a growing emphasis in the literature on the dynamic complementary roles of small and large firms in technical innovation activities. To some extent this trend represents the explicit recognition of an important relationship between innovation and firm strategy which has been identified in studies of a number of narrowly defined new-technology-based industries (Kaplinsky, 1983; Rothwell, 1984, Friar and Horwitch, 1985; Macdonald, 1985; Doz *et al.*, 1986).

The marked growth in the development and use of technology as a strategic competitive factor in recent years has also served to focus more sharply the interest of both academics and the firms' key decision-makers on the dynamic complementarities of small and large firms over the component technology life cycle (Friar and Horwitch, 1985).

Since the rejuvenated 'bio-technology industry' came into being with successful cloning of the first gene in 1973, its emerging phase has exemplified this close dynamic relationship between small and large firms. There has also been considerable diversity in the form and nature of these relationships. At present bio-technology represents a set of techniques with potential application and strategic impact in a number of established industries, some of which will doubtless experience major restructuring in the next few decades. The question as to whether or not a new 'bio-technology industry' will emerge cannot be answered at this time (Hamilton, 1985).

61

Selection environment and strategy

In essence, firms and their environment are relatively unstructured at start-up in an emerging industry. Examples are provided in the United States by the small 'entrepreneurial' integrated-circuits-producing firms in the early 1960s and by the new set of vendors for artificial intelligence models. The production characteristics in an emerging radically new product industry are characterised as: unco-ordinated and vague; loose and unsettled relationships between process elements; high rate of change; process is composed of unstandardised and manual operations and it is fluid and adaptable; production capacity is flexible; product innovation generates simple process innovation; and the introduction of a new technology composed of elements diffused from other industries (Kaplinsky, 1983). The sector characteristics at start-up in an emerging industry are characterised by: a diversity of unstandardised products; ambiguous performance requirements; a rapid rate of product change; demand is not known, or is uncertain; ill-defined product market; new technologies that adapt to emergent needs in the market; and the unco-ordinated state of product, administrative, and production process developments (Macdonald, 1985).

Within the emerging new-technology industry, rivalry tends to be limited by hesitant demand growth, and a relatively small number of early starters. In addition, the industry-wide rather than firm-specific effect of marketing effort tends to limit rivalry within the emerging industry. Technical specifications rather than price provide the bases for competition among firms. Entry is relatively easy for new arrivals which do not have to recover any special expenses beyond financing the most recent business intelligence on the new industry! Where R&D and capital costs are relatively high, however, entry is more difficult (e.g. in biotechnology).

During the dynamic early growth phase in emerging industries, when entry barriers are relatively low, the new, small, autonomous entrepreneurial firms are joined by the new ventures established by firms from other industries. These, usually larger, firms possess superior production or marketing expertise that has applicability in a growing industry (Littler and Sweeting, 1983; Doz et al., 1986). Initially, the small and 'larger' firms remain more or less distinct. Even so there fairly quickly develops a vital interplay between the two types of firms. People, technology, technique and relevant managerial knowledge percolate through the system. The rates and effectiveness of the percolation of proprietary technical knowledge do vary between industries, however, largely because patents do not provide uniformly sound protection. Nevertheless, for various reasons many of the small entrepreneurial firms do not survive this early industry development phase. Even relatively large start-up firms in the personal computer industry were unable to create sustainable businesses: for example, MITS, IMSAI and Processor Technology, which together accounted for a 50 per cent share of the US market in 1976, failed in 1977 (Friar and Horwitch, 1985).

The growth phase in a new-technology industry cycle is usually characterised by the trend to economic concentration. In some of these industries, however, where firms produce small batches or individualised products to customers' specification, the firms may remain small. In 1972, for example, 83 per cent of firms in the British scientific instruments industry had less than 100 employees (Rothwell, 1984). Firms in a new-technology industry concentrate as products and processes become standardised. They become fewer in number and larger in size and they tend to extend their range of applications programmes to provide comprehensive cover to the broadening limits of the industry market (Kaplinsky, 1983). During this expansionary phase, aggregate industry growth rates can be very high, necessitating raising substantial financial resources. The US computer-aided design (CAD) industry growth rate, for example, was approximately 80 per cent per annum during the period 1974–80 (ibid.). Industry environment during this phase tends to be conducive to the emergence of 'predators' amongst established industry firms. In other words, larger multiregional or multinational firms from outside the industry as a speculative investment often take over, or take a substantial share of, firms already established in the industry.

A number of the post-World War II new-technology industries have reached or are approaching maturity — for example, the CAD and semiconductor industries. In this phase of constrained market development in the CAD industry we observe two divergent trends — a continued tendency to concentration and an opposing tendency for the entry of new small firms selling microprocessor-driven, limited-capability dedicated systems (Kaplinsky, 1983).

Technology strategy

Contemporary literature in the field of strategic management provides evidence of the recognition of technology as a top-level strategic concern in new-technology-based industries. This is especially the case within the large firms in these industries. Technology strategy is also of increasing interest to key decision-makers in the more commercially progressive and successful new entrepreneurial firms in currently emerging industries such as bio-technology (Friar and Horwitch, 1985).

In nascent industries with ambivalent or even amorphous structure, some three broad strategy options have been identified by Macdonald (1985) as being used implicitly if not explicitly by new entrepreneurial firms. Some start-up firms dedicate organisational effort to serving a market in which the demand is too small for a late or larger entry to have a significant advantage. In other words, these high-technology firms develop small volume niches as protection. They will as a result, however, remain technically static as they age as organisations and eventually become 'low tech' firms.

Another group of start-up firms seems to exercise the option of exiting from the industry as more powerful firms enter. These firms exploit risk as a shelter and as a barrier to competition. To remain viable such firms must be technologically versatile and well managed. To be successful, entry and exit behaviour also demands a high level of sensitivity to industry signals.

Firms that take the third strategy option tend to aspire to both pushing the new technology to its extreme practical limit and to becoming a large successful firm. Key decision-makers in these firms need a great deal of luck and skill in conjecture because they need to make the right moves before their competitors. These decision-makers must gain experience rapidly in lessening expectations and risking more in order to accelerate events in the lives of their firms. Firms attempt gradually to establish a series of protective barriers, abandoning some like windows along the industry life cycle and maintaining others that eventually converge on the structure of the growing industry or on that of a strategic group within the industry (Macdonald, 1985). Strategies pursued reflect increasing commitment to more focused programmes over time (Hamilton, 1985).

In his study of the CAD industry in the United States, Kaplinsky (1983) found that the key to the discussion of firm size and technical change lies in the barriers raised against new entrants. The incentives to new entrants into the industry are substantial because investment in the CAD sector is a relatively profitable activity. Nevertheless, the industry continues to be dominated by a small number of firms, which suggests that existing barriers to entry must be effective. Kaplinsky found the primary barrier to entry in the CAD industry to be technology.

The scale of software inputs necessary to offer a competitive package of applications programmes was the major source of protection for existing producers against new entrants into the industry. The CAD sector, in comparison with the US manufacturing industry in general, still invests a very large proportion of sales in R&D. Most CAD suppliers employ more than 100 software writers each year and the number continues to increase. Nevertheless, a number of firms were able to detail their vast stocks of software. The study also revealed that the critical protective factors for existing firms were that software development occurred in a relatively specialised industry in the context of a general shortage of software writers, and necessary software development was sequential in nature. It was also evident that existing firms in the CAD industry had developed effective ways of protecting their proprietary information. The ruling by the US Supreme Court in 1981 that *firmware*, i.e. software incorporated in the hardware, could be patented has contributed significantly to this protection (Kaplinsky, 1983).

The vital importance of technical innovation to the development of technology-based firms and industries is widely accepted. There is also a growing realisation that it is increasingly crucial to establish strategic linkages between firms and to develop varied structures for encouraging innovation. Since the mid-1970s there has been considerable experimentation in the use of externally orientated strategic practices for acquiring new technology. Firms use such methods as: licensing; contracting the development of new technology; joint ventures or the acquiring of a share or all of another firm for monitoring or buying technology. This trend reflected greater co-operation among competitors and a possible lessening of the use of technology *per se* as a purely competitive tool (Friar and Horwitch, 1985).

There is tentative evidence, however, that this trend has peaked and now there is renewed focus on internal methods of creating new technology — i.e. firms tend increasingly to rely on their own R&D staff at divisional and corporate levels and/or rely on the establishment of internal ventures or entrepreneurial units to innovate. This incipient trend suggests that the pursuit of external methods for obtaining new technology generated an unacceptably high level of organisational complexity for firms. It seems that there is also a growing perceived need by firms to regain total proprietary control over all activities directed towards technical innovation (ibid.).

Technological transition

The question concerning the relative effectiveness of externally and internally orientated strategic practices for acquiring new technology will probably be one of increasing interest to firms whose technology has begun to be constrained by its practical limits and whose rate of economic performance consequently begins to slow down. Such firms, if they focus their R&D activities completely on improving the performance of current technology, may well face commercial disaster in the not too distant future as they vainly attempt to make a transition to a more profitable new product technology.

In the mid-1950s, for example, when the transistor replaced the vacuum tube, the ten leading producers of vacuum tube components in the United States were caught without any new-technology alternatives. Only four of these ten producers belatedly attempted to secure an entry into the new solid-state technology field. All four failed and not one of the large and powerful vacuum tube-producing firms is a force in today's $10 billion semiconductor industry (Foster, 1986).

At present the leverage in computer development is shifting from hardware to software. There are indications that major changes will accompany the transition if it continues to gain momentum. The question is already being asked as to who will be most likely to survive such fundamental changes — will it be the large hardware manufacturers like IBM, Siemens, and Fuijitsu, in which manufacturing is an entrenched and powerful corporate function, or the smaller companies that now dominate the software industry? (ibid.)

For top management, *technological transitions* represent extremely disruptive challenges. Evidently these discontinuities are now facing contemporary new-technology-based firms in a growing number of industries. Technological transition, it seems, is emerging as a complex multifaceted research problem of great practical importance and academic interest.

CONCLUDING SECTION

In the articulation of the first heuristic conceptual framework, theoretical notions developed by Schumpeter, Nelson, Winter and Porter were found to be especially useful. The framework identified key elements in the dynamic process within which firm behaviour patterns and market outcomes are generated over time. Attention was especially focused on the diversity of firm characteristics, experience and capabilities and on how this diversity interacted over time with industry structure.

Firms face uncertainties of outcome when they make decisions which are related to the process of innovation. The Nelson–Winter framework composed of the three concepts 'organisational routine', 'search' and 'selection environment' is especially useful in conceptualising the nature and implications of the process involved in making non-routine decisions.

The second heuristic conceptual framework focused attention on the uncertainties of technological outcome related to the process of innovation. Innovation was shown to be a very complex concept with many meanings. The conceptualisation of the innovation process was carried out within both the innovation life cycle, and technological paradigm frameworks. The evolutionary nature of innovation and technical change and the uncertainties, discontinuities and continuities associated with the technical dimensions of these processes were revealed, and their importance underscored, by the use of these evolutionary frameworks. These exploratory conceptualisations also indicated that our understanding of the process of innovation is still relatively minimal.

Work carried out for this essay suggests that future conceptualisation of innovation would benefit greatly from greater agreement with respect to the definition and classification of key concepts used in the conceptualisation of the process of technical innovation. Unfortunately, we still do not possess an acceptable metric for deciding clearly and accurately how 'radical' or how economically or technologically important a particular innovation may be. It would also be most helpful if we were able to agree as to how we should measure the 'breadth' and 'robustness' of the

various technologies associated with products, component generations, and industry systems.

The third and fourth heuristic frameworks focused attention on
selected dimensions of the uncertainties of both economic and
technological outcomes related to the process of innovation in
new-technology firms and industries. In effect, these frameworks
provided a set of conceptualisations which represented both a
synthesis and the further development of key elements from the
first two heuristic frameworks.

The frameworks also presented a number of insights concerning certain selected relationships between innovation and competition at firm and industry levels. Life cycle models were shown to
be useful in identifying important technological and economic
dimensions of the role innovation plays in the development
patterns of new-technology firms and industries. The perspectives
provided were especially illuminating in the examination of
technology strategy as a major subject of growing concern to top-
level management in new-technology industries. This is a subject
that is attracting attention from an increasing number of
researchers in a variety of academic disciplines.

This chapter has identified an important and challenging
research agenda which is connected to the role innovation plays
in the process of economic development at the level of the firm
and industry in a competitive framework. It also provided a
number of suggestions as to how some of these research problems
might usefully be addressed.

REFERENCES

Abernathy, W. J. (1978) *The productivity dilemma*. Johns Hopkins
University Press, Baltimore.
—— and K. B. Clark (1985) Innovation: mapping the winds of
creative destruction. *Research Policy, 14*, 3–22.
—— K. B. Clark and A. M. Kantrow (1983) *Industrial renaissance:
producing a competitive future for America*. Basic Books, New York.
—— and J. M. Utterback (1978) Patterns of industrial innovation.
Technology Review, 80, 40–7.
Alic, J. A. (1986) The federal role in commercial technology development. *Technovation, 4*, 253–67.
Beesley, M. E. and R. T. Hamilton (1984) Small firms' seedbed role and
the concept of turbulence. *Journal of Industrial Economics, 33*,
217–31.
Bollinger, L., K. Hope and J. M. Utterback (1983) A review of

literature and hypotheses on new technology based firms. *Research Policy*, *12*, 1–14.

Clark, J., C. Freeman and L. Soete (1984) Long waves, inventions, and innovations. In C. Freeman (ed.), *Long waves in the world economy*. Frances Pinter, London.

Clark, K. B. (1983) Competition, technical diversity, and radical innovation. *Research on Technological Innovation Management and Policy*, *1*, 103–49.

Cooper, A. C. (1973) Technical entrepreneurship: what do we know? *R & D Management*, *3*, 59–64.

Dosi, G. (1984) Technological paradigms and technological trajectories. The determinants and directions of technical change and the transformation of the economy. In C. Freeman (ed.), *Long waves in the world economy*. Frances Pinter, London.

Doz, Y., R. Angelmar and C. K. Prahalad (1986) Technological innovation and interdependence: a challenge for the large, complex firm. *Technology in Society*, *7*, 105–25.

Foster, R. N. (1986) Timing technological transitions. *Technology in Society*, *7*, 127–41.

Freeman, C. (1979) The determinants of innovation. *Futures*, *11*, 205–15.

—— (ed.) (1986) *Design, innovation and long cycles in economic development*. Frances Pinter, London.

—— J. Clark and L. Soete (1982) *Unemployment and technical innovation*. Greenwood Press, Wesport, Connecticut.

Friar, J. and M. Horwitch (1985) The emergence of technology strategy: a new dimension of strategic management. *Technology in Society*, *7*, 143–78.

Graham, M. B. W. (1986) Corporate research and development: the latest transformation. *Technology in Society*, *7*, 179–95.

Hakansson, H. and J. Laage-Hellman (1984) Developing a network R & D strategy. *Journal of Product Innovation Management*, *4*, 224–37.

Hodges, D. A. (1977) Microelectronic memories. *Scientific American*, September, 130–45.

Kaplinsky, R. (1983) Firm size and technical change in a dynamic context. *Journal of Industrial Economics*, *32*, 39–60.

Layton, E. (1972) Technology as knowledge. *Technology and Culture*, *15*, 31–41.

Littler, D. A. and R. C. Sweeting (1983) New business development in mature firms. *Omega*, *6*, 537–45.

Macdonald, R. J. (1985) Strategic alternatives in emerging industries. *Journal of Product Innovation Management*, *3*, 158–69.

Mansfield, E., A. Romeo, M. Schwartz, D. Teece, S. Wagner and P. Brach (1982) *Technology transfer, productivity, and economic policy*. Norton and Co., New York.

Nelson, R. R. and S. G. Winter (1977) In search of a useful theory of innovation. *Research Policy*, *5*, 36–76.

—— (1982) *An evolutionary theory of economic change*. The Belknap Press of Harvard University Press, Cambridge, Mass.

Pappas, C. (1984) Strategic management of technology. *Journal of*

Product Innovation Management, *1*, 30–5.

Porter, M. E. (1980) *Competitive strategy: techniques for analyzing industries and competitors*. The Free Press, New York.

—————— (1983) The technological dimension of competitive strategy. *Research on Technological Innovation, Management and Policy*, *1*, 1–33.

Price, D. (1984) The science/technology relationship, the craft of experimental science, and policy for the improvement of high technology innovation. *Research Policy*, *13*, 3–20.

Rosenberg, N. (1974) Science, invention, and economic growth. *Economic Journal*, *84*, 90–108.

—————— (1976) *Perspectives on technology*. Cambridge University Press, Cambridge.

—————— (1982) *Inside the black box: technology and economics*. Cambridge University Press, Cambridge.

Rosenbloom, R. S. (1981) Technological innovation in firms and industries: an assessment of the state of the art. In P. Kelly and M. Kranzberg *et al.* (eds) *Technological innovation: a critical review of current knowledge*. San Francisco Press, San Francisco.

Rothwell R. (1982) The role of technology in industrial change: implications for regional policy. *Regional Studies*, *16*, 361–9.

—————— (1984) The role of small firms in the emergence of new technologies. *Omega*, *12*, 19–29.

Sahal, D. (1984) The innovation dynamics and technology cycles in the computer industry. *Omega*, *12*, 153–63.

Schumpeter, J. A. (1934) *The theory of economic development*. Harvard University Press, Cambridge.

—————— (1939) *Business Cycles*. McGraw-Hill, New York.

—————— (1950) *Capitalism, socialism and democracy*. Harper and Row, New York.

Senker, J. (1985) Small high technology firms: some regional implications. *Technovation*, *3*, 243–62.

Steed, G. P. F. (1982) *Threshold firms*. Canadian Government Printing Centre, Hull, Quebec.

Thomas, M. D. (1987) The innovation factor in the process of microeconomic industrial change: conceptual explorations. In B. van der Knaap and E. Wever (eds) *New technology and regional development*. Croom Helm, London.

Utterback, J. M. and W. J. Abernathy (1975) A dynamic model of process and product innovation. *Omega*, *3*, 639–56.

Walsh, V. (1984) Invention and innovation in the chemical industry: demand-pull or discovery-push? *Research Policy*, *13*, 211–34.

4

The Role of Innovative Small and Medium-sized Enterprises and the Revival of Traditionally Industrial Regions

Denis Maillat

THE GENERAL CONTEXT: RISK-TAKING

SMEs (small and medium-sized enterprises) have today become essential factors in the revival of production systems in industrial regions. Not only do they create new jobs, but they are also considered as major channels of innovation and technological change (Storey, 1982; Aydalot *et al.*, 1986; Keeble and Wever, 1986; Nijkamp, 1986). SMEs have certain characteristics which make them suitable for initiating changes in the production system. At the regional level, they contribute by their creativity and, especially, by their local foothold.

Current developments have reduced the relative importance of enterprises with complex organisational structures and reinforced the role of small enterprises and small entrepreneurs capable of rapid adjustment. Efforts to promote and stimulate the entrepreneurial spirit have never been as numerous as they are today (Martin, 1986). There is an increasing emphasis on risk-taking and economic stimulation at the local level. Indeed, 'although industrial revival requires technicians, it also calls for entrepreneurs. By organizing productive resources, entrepreneurs become the catalysts of economic redeployment' (Louard, 1983).

This process is particularly crucial in traditional industrial regions where production systems have been disrupted by international competition and the emergence of new technologies. Only through innovation and the creation of new enterprises will these regions succeed in replacing the jobs they have lost. There is no doubt that many traditional industrial regions are currently stagnating, yet many have resources which are conducive to economic development. Examples are found particularly in regions such as the cradle of the Swiss Jura Arc region (Maillat *et al.*, 1984; Maillat, 1986), the Franche-Comté, the Alsace, the Rhône-Alpes (Pottier, 1984), St-Etienne (Peyrache, 1986) and the Nord-Pas-de-Calais (Cunat, 1986). This chapter discusses regions such as these.

An examination of recent economic change highlights the role played by SMEs. Since 1974, the combined effects of the recession and the emergence of new technologies have triggered technological change and the transformation of production systems. A number of experts have defined the current economic situation as equivalent to the turning-point between the descending and ascending phases of the Kondratiev cycle — that is, halfway between a recession and a revival. This means that production is no longer stimulated by demand and that innovation is therefore the only means of creating new goods, services and production processes. This period is marked by a degree of uncertainty stemming from unsuitable technologies and markets. Many new products are in the first or at the beginning of the second phase of their life cycles. Moreover, according to expert estimates, most of the products of the year 2000 have yet to be conceived. Opportunities for innovation are therefore still wide open.

This explains why a number of experts believe that the best solution to the prevailing crisis is economic liberalism, not in the sense of a mere *laissez-faire*, but as a method, a *modus operandi* and a means of controlling an economy characterised by decentralised decision-making. The advantage of this method over economic planning resides in its ability to withstand uncertainty (Saint-Etienne, 1986). To mitigate the risks engendered by this uncertainty, there is a current need to stimulate creative processes and multiply innovative opportunities. The proliferation of SMEs would meet this need since their founders take risks, innovate, and experiment through trial and error. Their pioneering, path-breaking spirit meshes with the concept of competition as a stimulus to economic development.

The myriad of combinations offered by new technologies enable SMEs to find new outlets and infiltrate new markets. Moreover, entrance barriers are still relatively surmountable. SMEs are thus able to penetrate a world in which the beaten path must be avoided at all costs. Traditionally large enterprises were viewed as having a predominant role in economic development and they were also considered to mitigate uncertainty. Large enterprises, particularly parent companies, were seen as indispensable to the economic vitality of industrial systems. They were considered as virtually solely capable of setting in motion the process of regional and national development. Their role began to be questioned at the onset of the recession, not only because they laid off scores of employees, but also because they experienced difficulty in reviving innovation. Their overly complex and bureaucratic organisational structures are not conducive to sufficiently rapid adaptation. Strategically, it can be to their advantage to remain observers of technological change for a certain period of time.

In any event, many large enterprises have not only stopped creating new establishments, but have instead begun to disinvest. Their expansion policies place greater emphasis on takeovers rather than on organic growth. The point is not to denigrate the contribution of large enterprises which in fact continue to dominate most local economies. However, the role of SMEs has become increasingly strategic from the regional point of view, enabling regions to complement the filtering down process, and thus to reconstitute their production systems.

THE CHARACTERISTICS OF INNOVATIVE SMEs

SMEs as a group are characterised by heterogeneity:

> These enterprises are extremely different from one another. They operate under a great variety of market conditions, involve a wide spectrum of products and employ considerably diverse means of production ranging from piece by piece, quasi-cottage systems to highly automated, assembly-line systems. This diversity embraces, in particular, recently created 'infant' enterprises as well as 'stunted' enterprises which have no growth potential. It includes highly productive enterprises as well as barely surviving, obsolete establishments lacking the financial and intellectual resources necessary to adapt to new market and technological conditions (Léo, 1986).

Moreover, the number of SMEs (enterprises of less than 200 employees) is high. In the industrialised countries, they constitute more than 90 per cent of all enterprises and employ more than 50 per cent of the total labour force (OECD, 1982).

An analysis of the revival process should take into account the fact that 'some firms are more important for the regional economy than others. A firm making products for export cannot be compared with a new bar or disco' (Wever, 1986). A choice must therefore be made, and attention paid to what are known as innovative enterprises. The potential of a region is largely dependent on its proportion of innovative enterprises (Boulianne and Maillat, 1983; Meyer-Krahmer, 1985), although that proportion rarely surpasses 10 per cent of the total number of enterprises (OECD, 1984). The definition of an innovative enterprise varies. In traditionally industrial regions, innovative enterprises are considered to be those capable of technological change, either through the internal development of new products and production processes or through the purchase of new machines, licences, and so on, which incorporate the latest technology. These enterprises have profiles which distinguish them from others mainly as management and development strategies are concerned (Boulianne and Maillat, 1983; Pellenbarg and Kok, 1985).

The personality of the entrepreneur

The vitality of SMEs (especially small ones) depends largely on the personality of the entrepreneur. This chapter will not attempt to draw a typical portrait of the dynamic entrepreneur. However, it should be underscored that among the qualities required are economic know-how (detection of opportunities, development of strategies, identification of resources) and relational know-how (with regard to human beings and the environment) (according to A. Shapero, cited by Louart, 1983). These aspects of the entrepreneurial personality were considered important enough in the United States to teach such specific know-how to persons displaying entrepreneurial potential. This know-how is often acquired through professional experience. Thus, in a survey carried out by Maillat and Vasserot (1986), the founders of all the enterprises studied had been professional employees before establishing their own enterprises. They were typically engineers or technicians, about 39 years old on average, with professional experience in an industrial enterprise. Their previous activities were as follows: salaried engineer (35·1 per cent), manager (21·1 per cent), salaried technician (17·5 per cent), administrative executive (15·8 per cent), other (3·5 per cent). These figures are supported by existing literature on this subject, indicating that most new firm founders have previously worked in small and medium-sized enterprises (Storey, 1982). In these enterprises, employees acquire the experience necessary for the development of entrepreneurial skills. This experience is not only likely to encourage employees to start their own businesses but may also reduce their risk of failure (Keeble and Wever, 1986).

However, experience is not necessarily a guarantee of success. In a study concerning the Netherlands, Wever (1986) even points out that, 'contrary to expectations, entrepreneurs who had previously owned or managed a firm were somewhat less successful'. In fact,

> the more important differences between successful and less successful entrepreneurs have to do with their behaviour as businessmen. The successful ones prepare the launch more systematically and give special attention to market orientation. Successful firm founders are more oriented to external markets and to a larger clientele.

The emergence of entrepreneurs also depends upon the environment: most entrepreneurs start activities with which they are already familiar. In that way a relationship arises between the industrial composition of new firms and the existing firms in a region (Wever, 1986). The probability of the emergence of new enterprise founders seems greater in regions with many SMEs than in regions where large firms predominate. Indeed,

> industrial concentration deprives the environment, it destroys the spirit of enterprise while decreasing the number of firms and increasing the distance between workers and management. It moreover transforms the risk-taking necessity inherent in every form of firm creation into a planned procedure of risk minimization (Aydalot, 1985).

The internal organisation of innovative enterprises

The organisational structure of SMEs is no less important than the personality of the entrepreneur. The relationship between the innovative capacity of an enterprise and the proportion of tertiary staff it employs has often been demonstrated. This proportion is indicative of the increase in activities which are not directly productive. It is a well-known fact that the innovative capacity of an enterprise depends to a large extent on the amount of funds it allocates to R&D, the creation of prototypes, project studies, quality control, sales and marketing. It is the staff involved in all of these areas, and not just in R&D alone, which constitutes the human capital and thus the specific know-how of the enterprise (Bailly and Maillat, 1986).

It is important to to underscore the fact that enterprises in which innovations take the form of entirely new products have a high proportion of extremely qualified staff (university graduates, engineers) (Maillat and Vasserot, 1986). Moreover, the distribution of this qualified staff within the various sectors of the enterprise is of considerable importance. A study by Boulianne and Maillat (1983) demonstrated that the most innovative enterprises were those which concentrated staff in the following areas.

— from the logistical point of view, purchase, supply, personnel management and production management (including technical offices).
— from the strategic point of view, management, financing and research.

The organisation of change and the use of external resources

Innovative SMEs are characterised by their determination to confront and work with technological change. Their organisational structure reflects this determination. The most dynamic enterprises are those in which development policy depends on more than one person (contrary to most family enterprises) and in which external input is welcome (Boulianne and Maillat, 1983). In an effort to assess the ability of enterprises to absorb external know-how, Meyer-Krahmer (1985) drew distinctions between large, medium and small degrees of openness to external input. Enterprises with a large degree of openness always managed to obtain necessary information, regardless of their location, through formal contacts with experts, consultants, research laboratories, and so on. Such was the case, for instance, with technologically sophisticated enterprises whose location was independent of information factors (footloose enterprises). Enterprises with a medium degree of openness showed a preference for solving their problems internally and had only occasional, informal contacts with outside sources of information. However, the local availability of experts, universities, technical schools, and so on increased the likelihood that these enterprises would resort to external input. Enterprises with a small degree of openness were impervious to the local availability of information owing to their inherent reluctance to use external resources (resistance to outside interference).

SMEs and export

SMEs were long viewed as subcontracting firms and therefore as relatively minor exporters. Their markets were considered local by definition. These assumptions no longer hold true, at last in so far as innovative SMEs are concerned. Innovative SMEs are exporting enterprises which are open to foreign markets. They often have a particular area of specialisation over which they hold a virtual monopoly. Clearly, the greater their specialisation, the more international their markets tend to be. Thus, it appears that one of the major differences between innovative and non-innovative firms is the geographical scope and the degree of internationalisation of their markets (Meyer-Krahmer, 1985).

THE LOCAL FOOTHOLD AND INTEGRATION OF INNOVATIVE SMEs

The fact that innovative SMEs are essentially export-orientated does not mean that they have no local foothold. However, they often paradoxically consider themselves as footloose. Thus, on the one hand, they present themselves as free from local ties, yet on the other, they are seen to be established in a specific region. Their choice of site can in large part be traced to the local origin of their founders: for example, close to 50 per cent of enterprise founders in the Jura Arc region are of local origin (Maillat and Vasserot, 1986). However, similar rates can be found in regions without industrial traditions. Thus, a rate of 40 per cent was recorded in the tourist and tertiary Tessin region (Ratti and Di

Stefano, 1986). The local origin of SME founders is therefore an unsatisfactory explanation. In fact, the local foothold of SMEs is dictated by the environment within which they are integrated. By environment is meant the set of interrelated factors which provide potential innovators with all the different inputs necessary for the various stages of the innovative process (Planque and Py, 1986). In traditionally industrial regions, this environment usually generates specific know-how.

Know-how

The existence of specific know-how is an important element in the revival of traditional industrial regions. This is particularly true in cases in which traditional know-how can be updated and adapted to new technologies (for example, the transfer from micromechanics to microelectronics in the watch-making and machine industries). In other words, the revival of traditional industrial regions is in large part determined by their know-how and their potential ability to adapt this know-how to new technologies. This ability determines to what extent a region is likely or not to generate innovative enterprises. A survey we carried out asking enterprises to assess the importance and iden- tify the origin of know-how generated three types of answers. A first group of enterprises considered that know-how depended primarily on the environment (labour force qualifications, tradi- tion); a second group that the only source of know-how was the enterprise itself; and a third group that know-how did not exist. A comparison of the answers with the characteristics of the enter- prises surveyed showed that the vast majority of innovative enter- prises considered know-how to be environment-related. For these enterprises, know-how rested on the quality of the labour force: its professional conscientiousness, experience and sense of respon- sibilities (Boulianne and Maillat, 1983).

Know-how is obviously not a quality which is acquired once and for all. It is accumulated through learning and experience, and must be maintained and developed. It is not easily transferred owing to its relation to time and experience. It also depends on the characteristics of the enterprise, the circulation of instructions and information and the work atmosphere. Moreover, know-how is a mixed blessing in the sense that some acquired habits must be overcome with respect to new technologies. On the whole, know-how can be said to be an essential environmental factor resulting from a multitude of interactions between enterprises and host regions. It constitutes the distinctive trait of a region, and undoubtedly represents a comparative advantage. In order to benefit from specific know-how, an enterprise must therefore be established in a particular environment.

Services to enterprises

One of the major reasons that innovative enterprises consider themselves as footloose is that their immediate surroundings rarely provide them with the specialised services they need. This constitutes a real impasse for regional development in theoretical as well as in practical terms. It is very difficult to determine whether or not a certain degree of proximity should exist between innovative SMEs and specialised services.

Research carried out so far has not provided a unique and definitive answer. Some research has concluded that a lack of proximity presents no real handicap for innovative SMEs, while other research has implied that service activities are essential to the smooth operation of territorial production systems. To break this impasse, it is necessary to look at the regional production system as a whole, rather than at the individual needs of each enterprise in isolation.

Current transformations in production systems are increasing the interconnections between service and manufacturing activities (Bailly and Maillat, 1986). Thus, 'today, the production of special machines implies a permanent contact between customers and manufacturers. Manufacturers do not just produce and sell machines; they design and sell a whole system of production' (Pottier, 1984). Reference is increasingly made to products and services rather than to products alone. This means that the acquisition of an industrial product implies the purchase of an increasing proportion of research, enterprise consultancy, customer service, training, and so on.

This evolution prompts two observations. First of all, a well-rounded production system must encompass a certain number of backward and forward linkages. Recognition of the connection between this new organisation of the production system and the need to maintain and update regional know-how leads to the hypothesis that these activities call for a certain proximity if regional know-how is to be updated. This evolution reflects the need to establish ties between the informational and physical aspects of production.

> Information is giving structures to physical elements in the production system, combining, coordinating and controlling relations. It plays an integrative role, integrating for example the process in the environment of a firm with its internal (physical) operations. Therefore, professional services form an intermediary or interface between the internal 'hardware' of a firm — the sphere of production — and the external world. (Lambooy and Tordoir, 1985)

The development of this tertiary ability and know-how should not escape industrial regions as otherwise their production systems may remain incomplete.

Secondly, it is well known that SMEs are unable to internalise all the staff they need and are therefore consumers of integrated external services (professional services). In view of this, the demand for such services can only grow. This growth is further spurred by the fact that SMEs must constantly renew their products and remain dynamic in order to endure. Consequently, the size of the market area within which specialised services can be cost effective is progressively shrinking. This of course presents enterprises with the problem of the location of these service activities. It has often been observed that service and secondary activities develop within different spatial parameters. Although the service activities of enterprises were for a long time located mainly in large cities, today this is no longer invariably the case. These services can develop within other levels of the urban hierarchy (Bailly *et al.* 1984; Cappellin, 1985).

Ultimately, in order to promote their own revival, traditional industrial regions must establish complete production systems, including service enterprises (professional services) and production (manufacturing) enterprises in a series of linkages ranging from backwards (innovations) and forwards (markets) (Maillat, 1984). This poses the problem of choosing an appropriate policy.

REGIONAL POLICY AND STIMULATIVE MEASURES

The revival of traditional industrial regions depends on their ability to develop coherent and complete production systems including both manufacturing activities and services to enterprises. The two major types of measures outlined below serve this end.

(1) A degree of economic liberalism is necessary to stimulate both technological change and the creation of new enterprises. In other words, enterprises must be granted a certain operational margin. This implies the reduction of a number of transactional costs which large enterprises are in a position to support but which are too costly for small enterprises (Lambooy, 1986; Martin, 1986).

Martin suggests cost reductions in the following areas:

— Government regulations interfering in the function of markets in which SMEs operate (for example, minimum wage legislation).
— Expensive legal transactions required to conclude and carry out the terms of a contract.
— Dissemination of information concerning the economic situation, technological advances, etc.
— Transactions with government services (internal revenue, social security, etc.) which force SMEs to resort to costly consultants.

A study carried out in Switzerland showed that government regulations entailed considerable costs for SMEs. The study recorded 35 federal laws and regulations having a considerable impact on SMEs. These range from business accounting regulations to the law limiting the number of foreigners exercising a lucrative activity and include a whole range of intermediate legislation concerning vocational training, environmental protection, labour, pollution, road traffic, economic surveys, accident insurance, social benefits, and so on. The study showed that in 1983, the enterprises questioned (all of which had under 200 employees) devoted an average of nine weeks to the processing of such administrative matters at a mean cost of 23,400 Swiss francs. This added up to 1.3 billion francs for all SMEs, or 7 per cent of total investments in plant and equipment in Switzerland. Such red tape needs to be pared down to a bare minimum. Its reduction would pave the way for a climate more conducive to innovations and to the creation of new SMEs. Of course, this deregulation would have to go hand in glove with a reorientation of regional policy.

(2) Regional policy aimed at promoting the revival of traditional industrial regions should employ stimulatory measures designed to increase the motivation and ability of SMEs to take new initiatives. Emphasis must be placed on measures capable of energising SMEs — that is, on the acquisition of know-how, discovery of new outlets, training, management counselling, technical assistance, access to capital markets, and so on. The objective should be the creation of a territorially self-sufficient production system (including backward and forward linkages). For this purpose, emphasis should be placed on the development of activities tending to:

— improve the access of enterprise to scientific and technical information;
— ensure ties between SMEs and research institutions (technological interfacing);
— provide support for technological assessment (evaluation of payments, feasibility studies, etc.);
— provide enterprises with assistance in sales and marketing (market studies, research of partners, etc.);
— find solutions to mitigate the lack of shareholders' equity (for example, venture capital);
— encourage the recycling and in-service training of managers, cadres and workers.

The above-mentioned measures can, of course, be carried out by private enterprises, especially those providing production services (professional services). Nevertheless, regional government institutions can contribute to the emergence and development of these service enterprises. In order to be effective, government institutions should strive to create a relationship of exchange between the agency responsible for implementing a measure and its beneficiaries. This exchange can take place in the following three different ways:

(1) by closely involving SMEs in the conception and implementation of the measure;
(2) by allowing SMEs a degree of financial and decision-making participation within the agencies responsible for the implementation of the measure; and
(3) by charging a fee for the implementation of the measure and thus making the SME the purchaser of a service and

the client of an agency whose performance must give satisfaction or be rejected.

Such an approach makes regional policy the responsibility of all participants in the regional economy.

REFERENCES

Aydalot, P. (1985) Some comments on the location of new firm creation. Paper presented at the VIᵉ Conferenza Italiana di Scienze Regionali, Genova.
—— et al. (1986) *Milieux innovateurs en Europe*. GREMI, 90 rue de Tolbiac, F-75634, Paris.
Bailly, A. and D. Maillat (1986) *Le secteur tertiaire en question*. ERESA, Geneva.
——, D. Maillat and M. Rey (1984) Tertiaire moteur et développement régional: le cas des petites et moyennes villes. *RERU*, 5.
Boulianne, L. and D. Maillat (1983) *Technologie, entreprises et régions*. Editions Georgi, Saint-Saphorin, Switzerland.
Cappelin, R. (1985) *The development of service activities in the Italian urban system*. Commission of the European Communities, Brussels, 16–18 October.
Cunat, F. (1986) Stratégies d'adaptation d'entreprises du Nord-Pas-de-Calais. Table ronde du CREUSET, St-Etienne.
Keeble, D. and E. Wever (1986) *New firms and regional development in Europe*. Croom Helm, London.
Lambooy, J. G. (1986) The complementarity of SMB and the professional services. Table ronde: Les PME innovatrices et leur environnement local et économique, 4–5 July, CER, Aix-en-Provence.
—— and P. P. Tordoir (1985) Professional services and regional development: a conceptual approach. FAST-Conference, Brussels.
Léo, P. Y. (1986) Les milieux régionaux des PMI, une approche statistique et régionalisée des choix stratégiques des PMI à partir de l'E.A.E. Table ronde du CREUSET, St-Etienne.
Louart, P. (1983) Les PME au coeur du renouveau industriel Américain. *Revue française de gestion*, September–October.
Maillat, D. (1984) De-industrialisation, tertiary-type activities and redeployment: the 'Arc jurassien Case'. 24th RSA European Congress, Milan.
—— (1986) New technologies from the viewpoint of regional economics: the example of Neuchâtel. *Dossiers de l'IRER*, 9. Université de Neuchâtel.
—— and J. Y. Vasserot (1986) Les milieux innovateurs, le cas de l'Arc jurassien. In P. Aydalot et al., *Milieux innovateurs en Europe*, GREMI.

————— et al. (1984) *La nouvelle politique régionale: le cas de l'Arc jurassien*. EDES, Neuchâtel.

Martin, F. (1986) L'entrepreneurship et le développement local: une évaluation. *Revue canadienne des sciences régionales*, *IX*(1).

Meyer-Krahmer, F. (1985) Innovation behaviour and regional indigenous potential. *Regional Studies*, *19*(6).

Nijkamp, P. (1986) *Technological change, employment and spatial dynamics*. Springer Verlag, Berlin.

OECD (1982) *L'innovation dans les petites et moyennes entreprises*. OECD, Paris.

————— (1984) *Rapport analytique sur la recherche, la technologie et la politique régionale*. OECD, Paris.

Pellenbarg, P. H. and J. A. Kok (1985) Small and medium-sized innovative firms in the Netherlands' urban and rural regions. *Tijdschrift voor Economische en Sociale Geografie*, 76.

Peyrache, V. (1986) Mutations régionales vers les technologies nouvelles, le cas de la région de Saint-Etienne. In P. Aydalot *et al*. *Milieux innovateurs en Europe*, GREMI.

Planque, B. and B. Py (1986) *La dynamique de l'insertion des firmes innovatrices dans leur environnement*. CER, Aix-en-Provence.

Pottier, C. (1984) The adaptation of regional industrial structures to technical changes. Paper presented to RSA Congress, Milan, August.

————— (1985) The adaptation of regional industrial structures to technical changes. *Papers of the Regional Science Association*, 58.

————— and P. Y. Touati (1984) *L'adaptation des industries régionales aux mutations technologiques et ses incidences sur l'emploi*. INEREC.

Ratti, R. and A. di Stefano (1986) L'innovation technologique au Tessin. In P. Aydalot *et al.*, *Milieux innovateurs en Europe*, GREMI, Paris.

Saint-Etienne, C. (1986) *La France et l'incertain, programme économique pour l'avenir*. Economica.

Storey, D. J. (1982) *Entrepreneurship and the new firm*. Croom Helm, London.

Wever, E. (1986) New firm formation in the Netherlands. In D. Keeble and E. Wever (eds) *New firms and regional development in Europe*. Croom Helm, London.

5

Business Formation and Regional Development: Some Major Issues

Manfred M. Fischer

INTRODUCTION

Quite recently research on small firms and business formation has become an increasingly important focus of academic and policy discussions in most advanced economies. With the declining mobility of industry, the emphasis in regional policy in recent years has shifted towards developing the indigenous potential of the regions.

One major reason for the interest in the small-firms sector is the clear empirical evidence of a substantial increase in the numbers of new and small firms in most advanced economies since the early 1970s. This trend is well documented, especially in Great Britain, the Netherlands and France (see, for example, Storey, 1982; Aydalot, 1986; Keeble and Wever, 1986a; Korte, 1986; Wever, 1986) and is largely due to a considerable growth in the rate of new independent businesses. Various attempts to explain this phenomenon can be found in the literature. The most widely recognised explanatory approaches are the recession push theory, the technological change theory and the income growth theory. The basic arguments of these approaches will be briefly outlined in what follows.

The recession push theory, advocated, for example, by Gudgin (1984) and others, hypothesises that new business resurgence is primarily an impact of deepening economic recession. The theory is based upon two arguments. Firstly, the increasing levels of unemployment and recession-induced blocking of promotion prospects push individuals into business formation. Secondly, corporate strategies and withdrawals of large business organisations from less profitable activities leave market niches in which more flexible small firms with lower overhead costs may operate profitably (see Keeble and Wever, 1986b).

The second major explanatory approach is technological change theory. This theory views the growth of new small firms as an impact of the radical change in microelectronics and new information technology. It is argued that the speed and nature of this technological change opens a wide variety of new product, process and market opportunities. These opportunities are especially suited for exploitation by small flexible businesses established by highly skilled or research-based entrepreneurs.

The major argument of the third approach refers to substantial income growth during the last decades (particularly in northern Europe) and is closely related to the growth in demand for more sophisticated goods. Both trends have induced a wide range of market niches for new small businesses. No doubt each of these three theories provides essential and convincing elements which certainly have to be integrated in any broader explanation of the multidimensional nature of the phenomenon.

This chapter does not attempt to give a comprehensive review of small business research and new business formation in regional science or related disciplines: the intention and purpose is much more modest. In the next section several forms of business formation are defined. In the subsequent two sections some major aspects of the business formation process and the two major hypotheses accounting for spatial differences in business formation are examined. In the penultimate section the role of new small businesses for regional development as well as the role of public policy in stimulating the creation of new small firms are discussed. Finally, some suggestions for future research are made.

DIFFERENT FORMS OF NEW BUSINESS FORMATION

In any discussion concerning the creation of new businesses the definition of new business formation is an obvious and important starting point. With this term a wide range of diverse phenomena is covered.

Figure 5.1 provides a basic typology of different forms of new business formation and is based upon two dimensions. The first dimension represents a differentiation of newly established firms in terms of the dependence or independence of an already-existing

Figure 5.1: A basic classification of different forms of business formation

	Independent	Dependent
Genuine	Creation of a new business set up by the initiative of an independent entre-preneur only	Establishment of branch plants of already existing companies
Derivative	Franchising networking, take-overs	Splitting up of larger business organisations into smaller units, management buyouts

company. Independence is understood here in a purely legal sense. The second dimension distinguishes whether the creation is genuine or derivative. The classification leads to four major categories of new business formation (see Steinle, 1986):

(1) independent genuine business formation;
(2) independent derivative business formation;
(3) dependent genuine business formation; and
(4) dependent derivative business formation.

The first category concerns the creation of new firms set up by the initiative of independent entrepreneurs in both the formal and informal economy. *Independent genuine business formation* in the informal economy (mainly in labour-intensive service industries) has become increasingly significant in most advanced economies during the past decade, even if it is rather hard to measure this phenomenon exactly (especially at the regional level). Major factors which enforced the growth of this type of business forma-tion are increasing levels of insurance contributions, tax, and other dues to the state. In addition, the establishment of co-operative businesses (i.e. businesses owned and controlled by those who work therein) is subsumed under this category.

The second category, *independent derivative business formation*, covers various forms of independent business formation such as, for example, franchising and networking. The major distinguishing feature to the first category is the derivative nature of the process. Franchising consists of a business organisation (the so-called franchiser) with a market-tested package centred on a product or a service setting up contractual relationships with franchisees who establish their own legally independent business but operate under the franchiser's trade name and market the franchiser's product or service in accordance with precisely specified procedures. Typical examples of franchising are independently owned petrol service stations operating with a major oil company. More recent franchising can also be found in fast-food retailing and car rentals. The major attraction of franchising to the franchiser is the rapid achievement of a wide national or even international coverage of their product or service where most of the capital is invested by the franchisees. From the point of view of the franchisee, franchising minimises many of the risks associated with self-employment (Mason and Harrison, 1985; see also Taylor and Thrift, 1983).

In comparison with franchising networking is a relatively new form of business formation. This system offers selected managers a guaranteed, and, for a certain area, exclusive, consultancy contract if they leave the company payroll and become self-employed. IBM and Rank Xerox, for example, practice this system which brings substantial cost saving to the company. There are various forms of networking. Rank Xerox in the UK, for example, offers a two-year renewable contract for a minimum of two days per week, pays the market price for the service and allows the networkers to work for other clients as well. According to Mason and Harrison (1985), the networkers in the UK are usually working at home and are linked via terminals with their former company. This form of new business formation may have significant spatial impacts in the long run.

Dependent genuine business formation refers mainly to the creation of branch plants of a company already operating elsewhere. From a logical point of view plants established by foreign companies should also be subsumed here even if they are registered as independent firms in company law.

The last category is *dependent derivative business formation*. This type of business formation is generally the outcome of corporate strategies of larger companies. Major examples are the splitting up of larger companies into several smaller, legally independent units and the creation of new businesses on the basis of management buyouts. Management or staff buyout is a very recent form of new business formation. It refers to the purchase of divisions of companies by their staff which maintains viable product lines or services of firms otherwise being closed or running down as part of a wider corporate restructuring.

Business formation now plays an increasingly important role in regional policy, even though the attraction of branch plants is a more traditional concern. Since the policy of stimulating the creation of branch plants in depressed or backward regions has become less and less successful in the 1970s, increasing attention has been paid to promoting the indigenous potential of disadvantaged areas. Essentially, two major approaches are used to achieve this objective. The first one is directed towards stimulating innovation within existing plants. The second aims to assist the creation of independent genuine business, where particular emphasis is laid on small new firm formation.

In the next section some major aspects of the process of small business formation in the formal economy are considered. Hereby a small business is defined as an enterprise which has a rather small share of its market, is managed by its owner(s) and is not part of a larger enterprise.

THE PROCESS OF BUSINESS FORMATION

New business formation is a complex process which is influenced by a wide range of factors. In particular personal motivations and aspirations on the one hand and regional economic conditions on the other have been identified as playing a central role.

From a regional policy viewpoint there are several important questions which have to be addressed in order to arrive at a deeper understanding of the process:

(a) which factors motivate an individual to set up his or her own business?
(b) which conditions favour the creation of new businesses and which factors impede new business formation?

(c) which planning, organisational and financial problems occur in the process of business formation?

(d) what are the causes of failure of newly established firms and under which conditions new businesses are successful?

Figure 5.2, based on Keeble and Wever (1986b) and Steinle (1986), offers a useful framework to discuss the process of business formation in some more detail. Hereby particular focus is laid on the four key questions mentioned above. Five stages are distinguished: idea generation and motives to set up a new business (Stage 1), validation and conceptualisation of business ideas (Stage 2), preparation on start (Stage 3), initial implementation (Stage 4), and stabilisation (Stage 5). These stages will be briefly discussed below. Naturally, they have different requirements and exhibit different difficulties and bottlenecks.

In the **first stage** the idea of starting a business is generated. Speculations about possible new products, processes or services are undertaken. A number of case studies have analysed the motivations and attitudes of new firm founders. Two types of motivation factors are usually distinguished: push and pull factors. Push factors (displacement factors in the sense of Shapero, 1983) refer to situations in which individuals are pushed into business formation.

An extreme but illustrative example is provided by refugees who are often forced to become self-employed in the service sector or in the informal sector because otherwise they have no chance to survive. This could be observed in Portugal after the revolution in 1974 when large numbers of refugees from the former colonies Angola and Mozambique had to be integrated. Furthermore, unemployment or an insecure job position can be push factors. Storey's (1982) study of new firm formation, based on a sample of 159 firms in the county of Cleveland in north-east England (1972–7), indicates that 26 per cent of the new firm founders were unemployed immediately prior to establishing their firms. In addition, the frustration of working in a large company may be an important push factor. Cross (1981) has found that 17 per cent of the founders in the manufacturing sector in Scotland (1968–77) were for this reason pushed into establishing a new firm.

Displacement factors are certainly important. However, several surveys of firm founders show that pull factors or positive motives such as the desire to be one's own boss, profit

Figure 5.2: The process of business formation

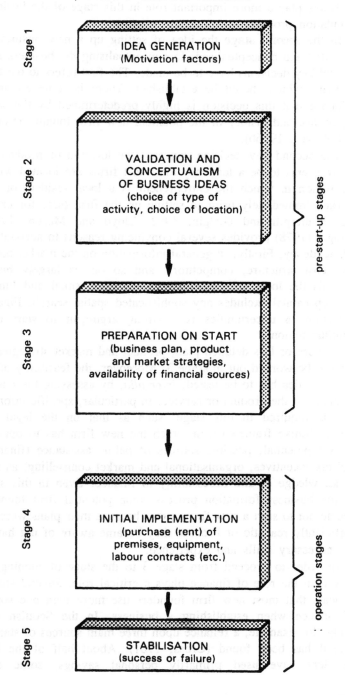

Stage 1 — IDEA GENERATION (Motivation factors)

Stage 2 — VALIDATION AND CONCEPTUALISM OF BUSINESS IDEAS (choice of type of activity, choice of location)

Stage 3 — PREPARATION ON START (business plan, product and market strategies, availability of financial sources)

Stage 4 — INITIAL IMPLEMENTATION (purchase (rent) of premises, equipment, labour contracts (etc.)

Stage 5 — STABILISATION (success or failure)

pre-start-up stages

operation stages

expectations and the ambition to be fully responsible for one's decisions play a more important role in this stage of the business foundation process.

In the **second stage** the idea of setting up a new business is validated and conceptualised. In conceptualising the business idea several key decisions have to be made. The first refers to the type of firms which should be established. There is some empirical evidence that this decision is highly predetermined by the work experience and history of the potential new firm founder (Keeble and Wever, 1986b).

The second key decision concerns the location of production. There seems to be a tendency that most firms are located within the region in which the entrepreneur is a local resident or had worked immediately prior to setting up the firm (see, for example, Fothergill and Gudgin, 1982; Lloyd and Mason, 1984). Gudgin (1978) provides several convincing reasons to account for this tendency. Firstly, in general information on the market potential, cost structure, competitors, and so on, is largely biased towards the local area. Secondly, quite often small and limited start-up capital excludes any sophisticated spatial search. Finally, reduction in uncertainties is a strong argument to start in a familiar region.

A more or less detailed plan, product and market strategies all have to be worked out in **stage 3**. Moreover, the feasibility of the business idea has to be tested, *inter alia*, by assessing the market potential of the product or service. In particular, specific information is required in this stage, such as that on the legal and administrative framework in which the new firm has to operate, market potential, possible sources of public assistance (financial and tax incentives, organisational and market counselling) as well as knowledge of and accessibility to finance. Even in this stage of the business formation process some potential firm founders decide not to start a new firm, either because their plans were not sufficiently realistic or because they became aware of not having the necessary skills and experience.

In order to proceed from stage 3 to the stage of running the new firm the role of finance plays a critical role. Several studies indicate that most new firm founders use more than one source of finance when establishing a business. In the Scottish case study, for example, a reliance upon three main sources of start-up capital has been found (Cross, 1981). About half of the firm founders have used primarily personal savings, some even exclusively, for setting up a new manufacturing enterprise, about 18 per cent loan facilities at commercials banks, and approximately 9 per cent governmental loans. Finance from relatives and friends had only been of minor importance. A heavy reliance on personal resources has also been found in case studies of Greater Manchester, Merseyside and South Hampshire (Lloyd and Mason, 1984) as well as in the Cleveland case study (Storey, 1982).

It is interesting to note that quite often only small amounts of finance have been used for the start-up (see, for example, Cross, 1981; Lloyd and Mason, 1984). In the Scottish study, for example, more than half of the firm founders invested less than £5,000. This certainly points to finance as one of the major problems a potential entrepreneur is facing in setting up a new business. The banks require security against loans. In order to be able to obtain a loan the potential entrepreneurs need to demonstrate a track record, but they cannot achieve a track record without one.

In **Stage 4** the new business will be established. Premises and equipment have to be purchased or rented. Labour contracts as well as a series of financial commitments to complete taxation and administrative documents have to be made. Working experience in key managerial positions or previous experience in setting up a new firm may be extremely useful in this stage in which the entrepreneur becomes more and more engaged in four major business functions, the commercial, financial, production and social function — even if he works alone or only with family work (see Keeble and Wever, 1986b).

The problems arising in this stage differ widely from the pre-start ones. Storey (1985) shows that the major problems in the first year of operation which new business in the 1970s in northern England faced were shortages of highly skilled labour and of demand, followed by supply shortages and high labour turnover. Increasing rates of unemployment since this time, however, might have reduced the problems of labour shortage and high labour turnover, even if new small business are usually paying lower wages than larger companies.

A large proportion of the new businesses close during the first years of operation. In the Netherlands, for example, nearly 50 per cent of the firms founded in 1970 had disappeared (i.e. closed or relocated to another region) within a five-year period (Wever, 1986). Gudgin's (1978) study on Leicestershire shows that 25 per cent of all new manufacturing plants established between 1947 and 1957 had closed by 1957, and 55 per cent by 1970. There is evidence that the closure rates are generally lower in times of economic growth, and there are also sectoral variations. Those sectors with low entry barriers are often characterised by higher death rates.

Most new, especially indigenous, firms start at a very low scale of employment. In some cases the entrepreneur even works alone or only with family help. When the initial problems of opening a business have been overcome and the stage of establishing output, employment and profitability (**Stage 5**) is reached, the entrepreneur has to decide whether to expand or not. There is empirical evidence that only very few small firms succeed in growing in employment terms. Based on the Cleveland sample, Storey (1982), for example, estimates a probability of $0 \cdot 5$–$0 \cdot 75$ per cent that these firms would employ more than 100 employees by the end of a ten-year period. Case studies have found, for example, an average size of 12 at the end of a ten-year period in East Anglia (Gould and Keeble, 1984) or an average size of 15 for new manufacturing firms in Leicestershire at the end of an eight-year period (Fothergill and Gudgin, 1982). Even if a strict comparison between the various studies is hampered by differences in data sources, survey methodologies and the time period concerned there exist clear sectoral variations in growth rates. In particular, new technology-based firms (especially in the computer electronics industry) seem to show a much faster rate of growth in employment and also in turnover than other new firms (see Keeble and Kelly, 1986).

In the final stage running costs are important and efficient use of labour and routinisation are crucial for success. Storey (1985) finds that the fast-growing new firm is much more likely to experience problems than the new firm with more conventional growth rates. The nature of the problems is also different. Expanding firms were primarily concerned with shortages of skilled labour, supply and financial problems whereas non-expanding new firms were concerned with shortage of demand.

SPATIAL VARIATION IN NEW BUSINESS FORMATION

A relatively large number of studies have examined spatial varia-tions in new manufacturing business formation. They predominantly focused on the role of conurbations and large cities in generating new businesses (see, for example, Firn and Swales, 1978). Only limited work has been done on the nature of new manufacturing business formation in rural areas (see, for example, Gould and Keeble, 1984) and virtually no research was undertaken on spatial differences in service business formation. There is a general agreement that there are significant regional differences in terms of the numbers of small firms and firm foundation rates.

Based on empirical evidence provided in these studies, Keeble and Wever (1986b) draw three broad generalisations. Firstly, the larger diversified conurbations tend to show high new business creation rates, in both the service and manufacturing sectors. Secondly, high formation rates, but lower total volumes can also be found in rural areas. Thirdly, the old industrialised regions specialised in mining, textiles, heavy engineering and shipbuilding have the lowest rates and small volumes of new businesses. Naturally, there are several exceptions from these rather broad generalisations: for example, extremely peripheral rural regions such as the Mezzogiorno and the Greek islands are characterised by low firm birth rates. Moreover, there are wide differences in formation rates both between and within conurbations.

British case studies provide strong empirical evidence that business formation is significantly higher in rural areas than in conurbations and larger cities. The greater importance of new manufacturing firm creation in rural areas of Scotland has been documented by Cross (1981) whereas Gudgin (1978) has established similar results for the East Midlands, and Gould and Keeble (1984) for East Anglia. The rural areas of East Anglia, for example, experienced a business creation rate of $6 \cdot 3$ in the time period 1971–81, which is much higher than that of the large town category with $2 \cdot 2$.

No agreement can be found with respect to the explanation of such spatial differences. There are two major conflicting hypotheses. The first, and perhaps more widely accepted one, considers the size-structure of the region's factories to be the key determinant (see, for example, Fothergill and Gudgin, 1982). Business formation rates are directly related to employment in small businesses. Hereby it is assumed that large firms are poor incubators for new firm founders compared with small businesses. Cross (1981), for example, has found that new firm manufacturing founders in Scotland have most likely worked for a company with less than ten employees prior to setting up their own business. This evidently supports the hypothesis. Forthergill and

Gudgin (1982), using data for the East Midlands and for northern England, also find empirical support for this view.

The second major hypothesis, especially advocated by Gould and Keeble (1984), recognises the occupational structure of the resident labour force as the major determinant. This hypothesis states that the higher the proportion of the regional labour force with managerial, professional, technical and other non-manual qualifications is, the higher will be the business formation rate in the region. Here, it is assumed that non-manual employees are better equipped to set up a new business. Indeed Cross (1981) and Storey (1982) have found that managerial expertise and educational qualifications of potential firm founders have a direct effect on their propensity to start a new business. The East Anglia case study (703 new independent manufacturing firms, 1971–81) also supports this hypothesis (Gould and Keeble, 1984).

Naturally, there are also other, usually minor, influences on the spatial variation of business formation rates, such as the composition of the economic structure or the residential attractiveness of the regions. Storey (1982) made an attempt to arrive at a comprehensive set of eleven indicators thought to influence entrepreneurship and took the average of these indicators to produce a ranking of entrepreneurship for each region in Britain. The indicators included in the construction of the index were the percentage of the labour force employed in manufacturing plants with less than ten employees, the percentage of the labour force employed in manufacturing plants with more than 500 employees, the percentage of school leavers going to degree courses, the percentage of school leavers without qualifications, the percentage of the labour force in administrative or managerial occupations, the percentage of the labour force in manual occupations, savings per head of population, owner-occupied dwellings as a percentage of all dwellings, the average dwelling price, a composite index representing regional barriers to entry and disposable income per head. Naturally, a major statistical problem in constructing this or similar indices of regional entrepreneurship is the problem of multicollinearity of the variables included (Whittington, 1984).

SMALL BUSINESSES, REGIONAL DEVELOPMENT AND POLICY

The potential of small firms for the development of national and regional economies has become an important but certainly a controversial issue since the release of the Birch Report findings (Birch, 1979). Some view small firms as a source of competition, innovation, diversity and employment; others like Keeble and Wever (1986b), for example, come to a negative assessment on this question, based on evidence and arguments concerning the small size and share of output and employment of new firms. Certainly, there is empirical evidence that new firms generally do not have the prospect of significant direct employment effects in the short run.

Naturally, it is necessary to aim at a more differentiated evaluation in taking the diversity within the small firm sector into account. Firstly, Keeble and Wever's (1986b) negative judgement is largely based on new manufacturing firms. In the case of the service sector, however, there are plausible reasons to suggest — although detailed empirical research is missing — that new small businesses are generating a quite considerable number of jobs in producer-related and market consumer services, even in the short run.

Secondly, the multiplier effects of new firm formation are largely dependent upon the types of new firms. In broad terms, the effects of a new high-tech firm in microelectronics are likely to be much greater than those of a new retail outlet, pub or café. Certainly, new firms in a sector with a finite regional demand may merely lead to the displacement of existing firms and, thus, have only rather small direct effects on the regional economy.

Thirdly, even if a new firm employs only relatively few workers and, thus, has only small direct employment effects, the indirect multiplier effects may be substantial. Many small businesses have subcontracting arrangements and induce indirect employment effects through these arrangements. An illustrative, though certainly extreme example in this respect, reported in Keeble and Kelly (1986), is a leading new firm in the computer industry in Cambridgeshire which has claimed to have created indirect to direct employment in the ratio of more than 20:1. A newly established firm may not only yield indirect employment effects through subcontracting arrangements, but may also stimulate the provision of producer-related and market consumer services in a regional economy. The establishment of new high-tech firms in New England in the US, for example, has largely promoted the creation of such service sector jobs, with market consumer jobs mainly being due to the substantial spending power of the workers in the high-tech sector. In an assessment of the role of business start-ups for regional development, such important effects have to be taken into account.

Finally, the role of small high-tech firms in technological and regional development merits some attention. This issue is also controversial. Some studies have claimed that new firms play only a minor role in technological development. Gould and Keeble (1984), for example, note that new high-tech manufacturing firms do not have a significant job-creating potential. Even in the highly successful Cambridge region this type of small firm has created only about 800 jobs in the period 1971–81. Furthermore, Lloyd and Mason (1984) are rather sceptical about the role of small high-tech firms in technological and regional development.

This contrasts with Oakey (1981, 1984a, 1984b), Rothwell and Zegveld (1982) and others. In a rather detailed analysis on this issue Rothwell and Zegveld (ibid.) come to the conclusion that small firms tend to be more flexible and can perceive and adjust more rapidly to new technologies than large organisationally and technologically more rigid corporations. As a consequence, technology-based new small businesses may play an important role in the emergence of new technologies and in economic growth. This view on the significance of small firms in innovation and regional development is also confirmed by several other studies, especially Oakey's (1984a) work on high-tech small firms in the instrument and electronics industries in Britain and the US (see also Oakey *et al.*, 1980, 1982; Oakey, 1981; Nijkamp, 1986, *inter alia*). Small firms are certainly playing a particularly important role in the development of the sunrise industries, such as information technology and bio-technology where R&D departments of large business organisations are relatively rarely major sources of completely new innovations.

All these arguments indicate the complex and multidimensional nature of the question, but also point to the fact that much more detailed empirical work, especially in the form of impact studies at the micro level, has to be undertaken in order to arrive at a more differentiated and realistic assessment on the role of new small businesses for regional development.

Over the last few years, there has been a substantial increase in public policy concern with new business formation in various European countries, especially in the UK, Ireland, the Netherlands, the FRG and France. Impressive efforts have been undertaken to promote the creation of new and small firms. The main emphasis has been laid on financial assistance, in the form of fiscal incentives, loans, grants and investment schemes.

In Great Britain, for example, a loan guarantee scheme was introduced in 1981–2 in order to encourage participating banks and finance institutes to make additional loan facilities available to new and existing small businesses which appear to have a good chance of success. Under this scheme 80 per cent of medium- to long-term loans (2–7 years) up to a maximum of £75,000 were guaranteed to the bank in the event of default (see Mason and Harrison, 1986, for more details of this scheme). In several European countries (Austria, the UK, the FRG, Switzerland, *inter alia*), investment schemes have been established to assist small firms to undertake investments in certain types of advanced capital equipment, especially numerically controlled and computerised numerically controlled machine tools, and to strengthen their innovative capacity by assisting them to introduce new products and process technologies. In the UK an Enterprise Allowance Scheme was introduced to encourage more unemployed individuals to become self-employed. Under this scheme a payment of £40 per week for up to 52 weeks is provided to supplement their earnings in the early stage of opening a new business (see Mason and Harrison, 1986).

Only very recently, the provision of inexpensive or free business information and advice has been regarded as an important element of a policy aiming to facilitate the small firm formation process. Moreover, certain deregulations (for example, in the UK) have been made in order to reduce the legislative and administrative burden of new founders.

There are several attempts to evaluate such nationally available policy measures, but only very few studies analyse the regional operation and impacts of such measures. Mason and Harrison's (1986) study is one of the few exceptions. One of the major conclusions drawn in this study is the recommendation to introduce a regional dimension to nationally available schemes of assistance in order to strengthen the indigenous sector in peripheral regional economies.

OUTLOOK: SOME TOPICS FOR FUTURE RESEARCH

Spatial research on the new firm formation process has been largely restricted to manufacturing firms but manufacturing firms represent only a rather small proportion of all new businesses. Storey's (1982) work on new firms in Cleveland is one of the few exceptions which cover both manufacturing and non-manufacturing sectors.

Future research activities have to pay more attention to start-ups in the service sector for several reasons. Firstly, the service sector, especially producer-related and market consumer services, have shown the greatest increase in job opportunities in nearly all more advanced economies since 1970 (see Fischer and Nijkamp, 1987a, b). Secondly, barriers to establishing a new business, such as capital and information requirements, are generally lower in the service than they are in the manufacturing sector. Thirdly, new forms of small businesses such as franchising and networking have been primarily developed in the service sector (Mason and Harrison, 1985). Fourthly, the present rapid developments in information processing technologies can be expected to have a major impact on the new business formation process in the service sector. All these arguments emphasise that we need to know more about the role of new businesses in the service sector.

In contrast to the recent and increasing interest in the nature and spatial variations of the (manufacturing) firm formation process, research on the performance and closures of small (manufacturing and service) firms in different spatial environments is largely lacking up to now.

A third topic which evidently needs further and more detailed attention is the interaction between small and large firms. Admittedly, there is some evidence that small (especially manufacturing) firms mainly act as subcontractors and suppliers of components and special services to large business organisations and, thus, heavily depend directly or indirectly for their performance and survival upon large firms. However, detailed empirical information is still missing. Taylor and Thrift (1983), moreover, suggest that large business organisations also depend to some extent on small firms. Nevertheless, further research is necessary to gain deeper empirical knowledge on the mutual relationship between small firms and large firms.

Finally, the spatial outcomes and the evaluation of the operation of policy measures recently introduced in several countries to assist small firms warrants more detailed analysis, but here several methodological problems still have to be solved.

REFERENCES

Aydalot, P. (1986) The location of new firm creation: the French case. In D. Keeble and E. Wever (eds), *New firms and regional development in Europe*. Croom Helm, London, pp. 105-23.

Bade, F.-J. (1986) The economic importance of small and medium-sized firms in the Federal Republic of Germany. In D. Keeble and E. Wever (eds), *New firms and regional development in Europe*. Croom Helm, London, pp. 256-74.

Birch, D. L. (1979) *The job generation process*. MIT Program on Neighbourhood and Regional Change, Cambridge, Massachusetts.

Brusco, S. (1986) Small firms and industrial districts: the experience of Italy. In D. Keeble and E. Wever (eds), *New firms and regional development in Europe*. Croom Helm, London, pp. 184-202.

Cross, M. (1981) *New firm formation and regional development*. Gower, Westmead, Farnborough.

Dokopoulou, E. (1986) Small manufacturing firms and regional development in Greece: patterns and changes. In D. Keeble and E. Wever (eds), *New firms and regional development in Europe*. Croom Helm, London, pp. 299-317.

Firn, J. R. and J. K. Swales (1978) The formation of new manufacturing enterprise in central Clydeside and West-Midlands conurbations, 1963-1972. *Regional Studies, 12*, 199-214.

Fischer, M. M. and P. Nijkamp (1987a) Current trends in regional labour markets. In I. Gordon (ed.), *Unemployment regions and labour markets; reactions to recession*. Pion, London.

——— (eds) (1987b) *Regional labour markets: analytical contributions and cross-national comparisons*. North-Holland, Amsterdam.

Fothergill, S. and G. Gudgin (1982) *Unequal growth: urban and regional change in the UK*. Heinemann, London.

Frank, C. E. J., R. H. C. Miall and R. D. Rees (1984) Issues in small firms research of relevance to policy making. *Regional Studies, 18*, 257-66.

Giaoutzi, M. (1986) Factors affecting the capacity of technological change. The case of less-developed countries. *Papers of the Regional Science Association, 58*, 73-82.

Gould, A. and D. Keeble (1984) New firms and rural industrialisation in East Anglia. *Regional Studies, 18*, 189-201.

Gudgin, G (1978) *Industrial location processes and regional employment growth*. Saxon House, Farnborough.

——— (1984) *Employment creation by small and medium sized firms in the U.K.* Department of Applied Economics, University of Cambridge.

——— and Fothergill, S (1984) Geographical variation in the rate of formation of new manufacturing firms. *Regional Studies, 18*, 203-6.

Harrison, R. T. and M. Hart (1983) The process of new business formation: some evidence from Northern Ireland. *Environment and Planning A, 15*, 1395-412.

Hendriks, A. J. (1986) Local entrepreneurial initiatives and central government. In P. Nijkamp (ed.), *Technological change, employment and spatial dynamics*. Springer, Berlin, pp. 280–98.

Keeble, D. and T. Kelly (1986) New firms and high-technology industry in the United Kingdom: the case of computer electronics. In D. Keeble and E. Wever (eds), *New firms and regional development in Europe*. Croom Helm, London, pp. 75–104.

Keeble, D. and E. Wever (1986a) *New firms and regional development in Europe*. Croom Helm, London.

—— (1986b) Introduction. In D. Keeble and E. Wever (eds), *New firms and regional development in Europe*. Croom Helm, London, pp. 1–34.

Korte, W. (1986) Small and medium-sized establishments in Western Europe. In D. Keeble and E. Wever (eds), *New firms and regional development in Europe*. Croom Helm, London, pp. 35–53.

Lambooy, J. G. and P. H. Renooy (1986) Informal economy and the labour market; relations with the economic order. Paper presented at the 18th Annual Conference of the Regional Science Conference, British section, Bristol.

Lloyd, P. E. and C. M. Mason (1984) Spatial variations in new firm formation in the United Kingdom: comparative evidence from Merseyside, Greater Manchester and South Hampshire. *Regional Studies, 18*, 207–20.

Mason, C. M. and R. T. Harrison (1985) The geography of small firms in the UK: towards a research agenda. *Progress in Human Geography, 9*, 1–37.

—— (1986) The regional impact of public policy towards small firms in the United Kingdom. In D. Keeble and E. Wever (eds), *New firms and regional development in Europe*. Croom Helm, London, pp. 224–55.

Nijkamp, P. (ed.) (1986) *Technological change, employment and spatial dynamics*. Springer, Berlin.

Oakey, R. P. (1981) *High technology industry and industrial location: the instruments industry example*. Gower, Aldershot.

—— (1984a) *High-technology small firms: innovation and regional development in Britain and the United States*. Frances Pinter, London.

—— (1984b) Innovation and regional growth in small high technology firms: evidence from Britain and the USA. *Regional Studies, 18*, 237–51.

—— P. A. Nash and A. T. Thwaites (1980) The regional distribution of innovative manufacturing establishments in Britain. *Regional Studies, 14*, 235–53.

Oakey, R. P., A. T. Thwaites and P. A. Nash (1982) Technological change and regional development: some evidence on regional variations in product and process innovation. *Environment and Planning A, 14*, 1073–86.

O'Farrell, P. (1986) The nature of new firms in Ireland: empirical evidence and policy implications. In D. Keeble and E. Wever (eds), *New firms and regional development in Europe*. Croom Helm, London, pp. 151–83.

—— and R. Crouchley (1984) An industrial and spatial analysis of new firm formation in Ireland. *Regional Studies, 18,* 221–36.

Pomazi, I. (1986) Regional differences in the distribution of small enterprises in Hungary. Paper presented at the 26th European Regional Science Conference, Krakow.

Rothwell, R. and W. Zegveld (1982) *Innovation and the small and medium sized firm: their role in employment and in economic change.* Frances Pinter, London.

Shapero, A. (1983) *New business formation.* Enschede.

Steinle, W. (1986) Policy instruments to facilitate the creation of small and medium-sized companies. Interim Report for the Commission of the European Communities, Bonn.

Storey, D. J. (1982) *Entrepreneurship and the new firm.* Croom Helm, London and Canberra.

—— (1984) Editorial. *Regional Studies, 18,* 187–8.

—— (1985) The problems facing new firms. *Journal of Management Studies,* 22(3), 327–45.

Taylor, H. J. and N. J. Thrift (1983) Business organisation, segmentation and location. *Regional Studies, 17,* 445–65.

Wever, E. (1986) New firm formation in the Netherlands. In D. Keeble and E. Wever (eds), *New firms and regional development in Europe.* Croom Helm, London, pp. 54–74.

Whittington, R. C. (1984) Regional bias in new formation in the UK. *Regional Studies, 18,* 253–6.

6

High Technology, Small Firms and Regional Economic Development: A Question of Balance?

Neil Alderman, Pooran Wynarczyk and Alfred T. Thwaites

INTRODUCTION

Throughout Europe the recently observed growth in the numbers of new, small firms (Keeble and Wever, 1986) together with the need to achieve economic regeneration of depressed regions by means of indigenous mechanisms, has encouraged policy-makers to place an increasing reliance upon assistance to small and medium-sized firms. Similarly the acknowledged importance of industrial innovation, in the form of high-technology product and process development, for economic growth (Mansfield, 1968; Rosenberg, 1974; Freeman, 1982) has led to an emphasis upon specific developments in new technological systems such as microelectronics and bio-technology. Consequently, the new small high-technology manufacturing or service firm, possessing both attributes, has a very high profile in policy terms. This chapter draws upon research undertaken at the Centre for Urban and Regional Development Studies at the University of Newcastle and elsewhere to question some of the assumptions underlying these particular policy emphases and to draw attention to potential implications for regional economic development.

WHAT CHARACTERISES THE HIGH-TECHNOLOGY FIRM?

It must be implicitly assumed that the definition of precisely what constitutes high technology is meaningful in terms of the policies which employ it. A consideration of the various definitions of high technology used by either academics or practitioners reveals that this issue is problematic. So far there is no agreed definition and particular applications usually have recourse to a subjective and pragmatic classification at varying levels of industrial disaggregation.

Harris and McArthur (1985) have identified three approaches to the definition of high technology: purely subjective, drawing a distinction between product and process innovation, and using surrogate measures of innovativeness. Most commonly found are those definitions in the latter category. They typically assume that high technology is related to research and development (R&D) effort. Ellin and Gillespie (1983) used both R&D expenditure and the proportion of scientists and technologists as a surrogate for those employed in R&D in order to define high technology. These criteria gave rise to a slightly broader spread of industries than usually included in more subjective classifications, although the authors were constrained by data availability. In the US context, Armington (1984) used similar criteria and arrived at a wide range of product areas, including many mature products.

Wiess (1985) has argued that it is often the assumption that high-technology industries are associated with not only R&D, but also a high growth in output and sales, yet this can be true of industries that are not considered high-technology. Alternatively, the emphasis may be placed upon employment growth or employment composition, which, it is suggested, is also an unreliable indicator (Langridge, 1984). The consequence of using sectoral indicators is that they give rise to a definition of high technology that is product-based. McQuaid and Langridge (1984) argue that there is a need to maintain a distinction between product and process innovation, the second type of definition noted above. Such sectorally based definitions ignore the fact that within each sector or product group there will be a range of technological levels. A machine-tool company may be producing modern sophisticated computer-controlled lathes or manual ones, the design of which has changed little in 100 years. To talk about the prospects for regional economic development on the basis of apparently high-technology sectors assumes that each region will have a share of the high-technology end of the spectrum of firms.

Similarly, definitions that concentrate upon production in the 'new' technologies such as microelectronics fail to acknowledge that much of their impact will be felt as inputs to the production of other products, many of which fall within what are traditionally low-technology sectors. Indeed, microelectronics are seen by some (for example, Freeman, 1985) as one of the driving forces behind the next economic long wave and it may be argued that employment prospects and hopes for economic regeneration lie less with the actual producing industries, and more with the opportunities for revitalising and changing existing areas of activity through the diffusion of such technologies.

Some support for this is provided by figures published by the British Engineering Industry Training Board, which show that between 1978 and 1984 employment in the electronics industry contracted by over 60,000 and all regions except Wales shared in this decline (Lawson, 1985).

This leads to the notion that the application of high-technology in more than just the firms' products will be an important factor in stimulating economic development. This appears to be widely recognised as firms are exhorted to invest in advanced manufacturing technology (ACARD, 1983; NEDO, 1985), and in a recent newsletter the Commission of the European Communities records the need for the 'modernisation of traditional industries'. The justifications for this are phrased in terms of improved productivity, the ability to respond to customer demands or market conditions and the reduction of inventory, which in turn releases capital for further investment (*British Business*, 1986). Whilst these conditions apply to the individual establishment or enterprise, the same is likely to be true for the regions, with those that lag in terms of technological change experiencing shrinking markets and falling income and employment prospects (Thwaites, 1982).

It is not sufficient, however, to argue that all that needs to be done is to remove the distinction between the production and application of new technology, because as Harris and McArthur (1985) argue, on the basis of the findings of Northcott and Rogers (1984) concerning the use of microelectronics, this will lead to a definition that covers most of manufacturing. Instead, it is necessary to consider what may be termed the total technological capability of the firm. This is reflected not only in the technological sophistication of its products, but also in its use of advanced process technology, computerised aids in the design function or drawing office and the application of integrated management information systems to control and monitor the company's commercial and manufacturing activities. These aspects of high technology are applicable to many traditional sectors and have received particular attention in the context of small-batch engineering (see, for example, Blackburn et al., 1985, Chapter 6).

Considering high technology in the proposed fashion implies moving away from a sectorally based definition towards a perspective that is centred upon the competence of the individual enterprise or establishment. Such a perspective also breaks down the often artificial distinction between manufacturing and services. Competence in the application and use of new technology opens up possibilities for the firm to diversify into new product areas and even service activities. Thus, for example, successful experience in developing computer-aided design systems for their particular product range has been turned by some companies into a new software product or design service. Although the producer industries may not be exhibiting the anticipated employment growth, the expansion of new service-related activities arising from applications of electronics in particular offers prospects for employment generation. This is of particular importance to those regions which do not have a strong base of the new-technology producers.

REGIONAL VARIATIONS IN TECHNOLOGICAL CAPABILITY

In 1981 a survey was undertaken in CURDS of establishments in nine engineering industries (see Thwaites *et al.*, 1982). From returns to this survey it is possible to identify those establishments that were manufacturing products incorporating microprocessors, had computer equipment on site for commercial activities, such as accounts and sales, and were either using computerised numerically controlled (CNC) machine tools on the shop-floor or microprocessors in other forms of process control, or were using computer systems in other ways to control and monitor their production operations.

Of the establishments from which complete responses were received 86, or 11 per cent, were engaged in all three aspects of technological activity — product, process and commercial applications. Not surprisingly, the majority were large establishments, since the economies of scale that may be achieved and the amount of investment needed in relation to high-technology process control in this sample were intrinsically related to the size of the establishment. Only 16 per cent had fewer than 100 employees in this instance. Furthermore, 40 per cent were establishments with multi-site organisations that exercised some degree of control over other establishments in the company group. Independent firms were least likely to display this level of technological capability, their average size being somewhat lower than those in the corporate sector. These 86 establishments were also observed to be concentrated within particular industries, the dominant one being metal-working machine tools, largely due to the opportunities for incorporating microprocessor controls in machine tools. However, the pumps, valves and compressors, the mechanical handling equipment and the general mechanical engineering sectors were also above average.

In spatial terms a significant difference was observed between a group of 'core' regions (the South East, East Anglia, the East and West Midlands and the North West), where 13·6 per cent of establishments had these technological attributes, and a group of 'peripheral' regions (the South West, Yorkshire and Humberside, the North, Wales and Scotland), where only 8 per cent had all three attributes. Moreover, this distinction could not be entirely accounted for by factors such as industrial structure, external control or even the distribution of on-site research and development, which is strongly related to the introduction of microprocessor-based products (ibid.).

Taking the Northern region of Britain as a good example, if the overall level of technological capability in sectors which dominate its economy is lower than in areas such as the South East, there may be scope for building up this capability through policy measures, particularly as the small-firms sector, as illustrated above, is likely to be particularly weak in this respect. The impact of policies that consider high-technology to refer to sectors such as electronics itself are likely to be less, simply because in the Northern region, despite substantial contraction, the machinery sector in 1984 still employed almost twice as many people as the electronics sector (Laslett and Laidlaw, 1986). Other research undertaken within CURDS into the strengths of the electronics sector (Williams and Charles, 1986) has revealed how the generation of new firms has not compensated for losses of 23,000 jobs in branch plants since 1970. They identified 99 small electronics firms (i.e. employing fewer than 250) in the region, the majority of which could be classified as employing 'intermediate or traditional technology'. These findings serve to reinforce the statements about the limitations of product-based definitions.

The implications, then, are that in looking at economic development there is a need to broaden the enquiry beyond these

Table 6.1: Sectoral distribution of new firms in East Anglia and Northern England (ranked by number of firms)

	East Anglia			Northern England	
Rank	Industry	% of all new firms	Rank	Industry	% of all new firms
(1)	Mechanical engineering	22·2	(1)	Mechanical engineering	19·7
(2)	Paper & printing	17·8	(2)	Metal goods n.e.s.	14·1
(3)	Timber & furniture	11·0	(3)	Timber & furniture	13·2
(4)	Metal goods n.e.s.	10·2	(4)	Paper & printing	10·6
(5)	Electrical engineering	8·1	(5)	Clothing	7·4
(6)	'Other' manufacturing	7·8	(6)	Electrical engineering	6·4
(7)	Instrument engineering	4·8	(7)	'Other' manufacturing	4·4
	TOTAL	81·9			75·8

Note: n.e.s. = not elsewhere specified
Source: Storey (1985, Chapter 9)

restrictive definitions of high technology to consider all technologically competent firms irrespective of sector. These firms will be those using the appropriate technology in all aspects of their operations, from products and the production process, to management and communications. These are the companies that can be expected to have the best potential for development in both high- and low-technology sectors, however defined.

HIGH-TECHNOLOGY SMALL FIRMS

A second fundamental assumption underlying current policy emphases concerns the role of high-technology small firms. By implication most of the industries encompassed by popular definitions of high technology are new industries and therefore many new small businesses are to be found in these sectors. A great deal of faith has been placed in the ability to generate new businesses in these high-technology sectors within the depressed regions and for these to be significant providers of new jobs and a key instrument in the redressing of economic imbalances between regions.

There are a number of reasons for casting doubt upon these ideas. For a start, the prosperous regions are not dominated by new firm formation in high-technology sectors. Storey (1985) demonstrates that in East Anglia — an area regarded as a key location for high-technology growth (Gould and Keeble, 1984) — and the Northern region, the sectoral distribution of new firms has been broadly similar. In neither case are sectors such as electrical engineering and instrument engineering as important as sectors such as mechanical engineering (see Table 6.1). Similarly, in the United States, Armington (1984) found that high-technology employment was not concentrated in the faster-growing regions. Moreover, as identified above, a lot of the opportunities for new firms are occurring in new service activities arising from technological advancement, the best example perhaps being software services, and the distinction between manufacturing and service sectors starts to break down.

SMALL-FIRM GROWTH AND PERFORMANCE

Having questioned the relationship between high technology and regional new-firm formation, another assumption that may be questioned is that it is in the high-technology sectors that the firms with the best growth performance will be found. Recently some new analyses of the performance of small firms in the north-east of England have been undertaken and the results of these are used in this section to support this argument.

Data on financial and qualitative aspects of 636 single-plant independent manufacturing companies, which traded at some stage between 1965 and 1981 in one of the counties of Durham, Cleveland, and Tyne and Wear is provided in Storey *et al.* (1987). From the data base a group of companies with high-performance characteristics in the form of 'fast growth' has recently been identified and compared with other companies in the data base.

The fast-growth independent companies were defined in terms of employment growth because this would be directly relevant to the prospects of them providing significant new jobs and employment opportunities in the future. It also avoided the problem of defining performance in financial terms in a period of rapid inflation. Rapid-growth independent companies were thus defined as those that were incorporated after 1965 and achieved an employment of at least 50 employees within five years of start-up. On the basis of this definition information was available for 24 companies.

It is apparent from Table 6.2 that the majority are to be found

Table 6.2: Industrial sector composition of companies

	'Fast growth' No.	%
Other manufacturing	6	25·0
Mechanical engineering	5	21·0
Textiles	4	17·0
Timber furniture	3	13·0
Food and drink	2	8·0
Paper and print	1	4·0
Instruments engineering	1	4·0
Shipbuilding and allied	1	4·0
Metal goods not elsewhere specified	1	4·0
Electrical engineering	0	0
Other sectors	0	0
TOTAL	24	100·0

Source: derived from Storey *et al.* (1987)

111

Table 6.3: Employment growth by age of company

	Non-fast growers			Fast growers		
	Mean	Median	N	Mean	Median	N
Year 2	10·1	8·0	88	44·9	24·5	10
Year 3	12·2	10·0		70·7	34·0	
Year 4	12·3	11·0		89·8	55·5	
Year 5	14·6	11·0		97·5	61·0	

Note: Only ten fast growers and 88 non-fast growers provided employment for all the years. To include companies providing data for only occasional years leads to difficulties in estimating whether differences in values are due to presence of different companies.

Source: Storey et al. (1987)

in the 'traditional' sectors of 'other' manufacturing, which includes product groups such as rubber, plastics and toys, etc., mechanical engineering and textiles. Moreover, these sectors contain a higher proportion of fast-growth companies than expected, given their share of all independent companies (Storey et al., 1987). It is notable that the high-technology sector of electrical engineering had no fast-growth companies at all whilst instrument engineering had just one. The median employment of those other companies not growing rapidly appeared to have stabilised at eleven employees by five years after incorporation, whereas the median employment of fast-growth companies had increased in each year up to the fifth year (Table 6.3). The failure rate of these fast-growth companies is also considerably lower than for new businesses generally (Ganguly, 1985).

These results shed doubts upon the notion that high-technology sectors are the major generators of high employment growth companies, at least in a peripheral region such as the North of England. A crude comparison is provided by 1984 employment figures published by Segal, Quince and Partners (1985, p. 29) for 61 high-technology companies established in the Cambridge area between 1974 and 1978 (i.e. they were at least five years old, although some were not independent companies), which show that the median employment was 13, only marginally higher than the non-fast growth companies in the North East sample.

The empirical evidence presented thus far provides some support for the view that high-technology companies are not necessarily going to be the major source of rapid job growth and suggests instead that traditional sectors, such as mechanical engineering, still offer potential when it comes to promoting economic regeneration, particularly in those areas heavily dependent upon such industries. Given that many depressed regions show little sign of successfully transforming their economies into ones based upon the new-technology industries as popularly defined, the realisation of technological potential within firms regardless of industrial sector may offer improved prospects for regional growth. It is this perspective on technological capability or competence that helps to provide a more balanced view of regional economic development and needs to be built upon in research and policy initiatives.

TECHNOLOGICAL TRANSFORMATION

The development of a high technological capability within manufacturing companies along the lines described above is seen by many as part of a more general transformation from a mechanical era to an electronic one, the microelectronics revolution, and a rapid change in this direction is predicted (Orme, 1979; Forrester, 1980). However, it should not be anticipated that the implementation of such technology is going to be a straightforward process, particularly where the current technological capability is comparatively low, and this may be one reason why relatively few establishments are identified in the CURDS 1981 survey, referred to earlier, as having a high overall level of technological competence.

In order to investigate the extent of this transformation and the ease with which it is being effected, a recent study undertaken in CURDS for the Engineering Industry Training Board (EITB) of Great Britain set out to examine the experiences of engineering establishments within the Northern region. The study involved in-depth interviews at some 30 engineering establishments, covering 15 product groups, and detailed case studies at six of the sites. Some 60 per cent of these establishments fell within the mechanical engineering sector. Although the study was not concerned specifically with small and medium-sized enterprises, more than two-thirds of the sample were establishments with less than 500 employees and one-third employed less than 250. The majority were not independent enterprises, however, but this would have been unrepresentative otherwise, given the Northern region's high level of external control.

Although the principal remit of the study was with identifying the training implications of new-technology introduction, the investigations also attempted to identify the extent to which companies were moving towards the establishment of integrated manufacturing systems, based upon microelectronic control and computerised information systems, and the extent to which such developments were part of strategic planning decisions. Previous studies have considered the separate components of such systems (for example, Arnold and Senker, 1982; Senker and Beasley, 1985), but have paid rather less attention to the issue of integration.

Whilst the survey revealed a considerable amount of new technology adoption, particularly during the immediately preceding five years, there were few cases identified where truly integrated systems could be said to have been achieved. Even in these cases it was either found that certain parts of the company's operations (such as design) still lay outside the system, or that full integration had only been achieved in particular areas of the plant (such as with machining cells). It became apparent that, despite the fact that many establishments exhibited the necessary basic components of an integrated manufacturing system, linking them together in such a way as to transform their production system remained highly problematic. The smaller establishments in particular experienced considerable difficulties and the next section considers some of these problems.

THE IMPLEMENTATION OF NEW TECHNOLOGY

The main characteristic underlying a move into a high-technology state is that it requires decisions to be made on a long-term or strategic basis (Gold, 1982; Senker, 1984). Hence, it was found that the successful introduction of such technology was being hampered by adherence to existing methods of investment appraisal that placed an emphasis upon short-term profit motives. Of course, one of the difficulties facing small firms in particular is the high cost of much of the technology. Thus, a single CNC machining centre could constitute a major investment for the small firm. Not surprisingly, perhaps, the introduction of new technology tends to be piecemeal, leading to subsequent stumbling blocks caused by equipment incompatibility when the time comes to hook components of the system together.

Such problems can be alleviated through appropriate strategic planning that identifies the needs of the company and leads to the design of the complete system in advance of its installation. This was the case at one of the most successful companies visited during the survey. The complete system requirements had been defined at the outset, even though the implementation was to be necessarily gradual over a period of some years. The justification for such investments was also made differently, relating more to long-term survival and growth prospects of the company than to short-term pay-back.

Even given appropriate planning and the ability to make the necessary investment, the evaluation of competing new technologies is itself not a straightforward issue. Of particular concern to many people was a lack of impartial advice. A lack of information was not a problem: in fact, if anything, firms are apt to be inundated with sales literature and the like. It is the sifting of this that is sometimes a problem, particularly as salesmen and their literature have a vested interest in persuading the potential purchaser that their equipment is the best and will meet all the buyer's requirements. Small firms can be at a greater disadvantage than their larger counterparts in this respect, because they are often too small to support the relevant specialist departments, particularly in the field of management information systems and data processing. Even where a senior manager or director has the relevant background they may be so busy with day-to-day running of the company that they are unable to devote sufficient time to technology development strategies.

At a number of establishments in the survey the need had arisen for a feasibility study into some aspect of the new technology to be commissioned. In one case the consultants' recommendations concerning the feasibility of a computer aided design and manufacturing system (CADCAM) had to be rejected on the grounds that the productivity gains predicted by the consultants were found to be based upon unrealistic assumptions concerning the flow of work and the quantitative aspects of the operation of the drawing office. The problem of communication between the client and the consultants is likely to be a recurring one. In this particular case it would seem that the consultants were attempting to answer the question 'which system?', rather than the one relevant to the company of 'is such a system needed?'. The provision of grant aid for feasibility studies is

115

already a policy in operation in Britain, and one or two establishments had made successful use of this. Nevertheless, these studies often presuppose that the basic question has been answered and that the company has decided it requires a particular application and simply needs the details filling in.

In attempting to make the transition to a high-technology state various pressures for change and flexibility in terms of work organisation are being experienced. In engineering firms the most contentious of these are occurring on the shop-floor. Increasingly for small engineering firms the inherent flexibility of CNC machine tools makes them an attractive proposition (Dodgson, 1985). Inevitably, however, this means the microprocessor control is taking over a lot of the operations that the traditional craftsman was required to carry out. In two small companies the expansion of CNC was creating problems of boredom on the part of the machine operators. A number of solutions were being tried involving, among other things, multi-machine operation, extending operator responsibility to include some on-machine programming or broadening the range of tasks carried out by the operator. All these options implied an increased flexibility on the part of the individual in terms of skills and in terms of work organisation.

The achievement of this flexibility is not immediate, however. Such changes may imply the removal of traditional craft demarcations that are jealously guarded by the shop-floor trade unions. Cross (1985), observing changing demands in the process industries giving rise to the development of what he termed the 'flexible craftsman', predicted that such changes would follow in the engineering industry. The evidence suggests that these developments are very slow at present. Small firms, however, often have an advantage in that the tradition of unionisation (if it exists at all) tends to be less strongly rooted and agreements for flexible working are more easily reached, a view that was generally borne out by the survey.

Whether or not collective agreements are possible, the individual is still required to adapt. This can be usually only be achieved through extensive preparation and considerable training. In order successfully to implement an integrated manufacturing system with a common data base for real-time monitoring of operations, a greater number of people have to assume responsibility for entering data on to the system, often at computer terminals throughout the factory. The importance of accuracy and promptness is often not fully understood, yet the consequences are serious. It is not only those on the shop-floor who have to adapt: managers may have to become used to working in reduced time-scales because information can be provided more frequently. Such adaptations in ways of thinking and working are not achieved overnight.

The smaller company, just as with the large company, is faced with a need for considerable retraining of its work-force. Typically, it is too small to support a full-time training officer or training department. In areas with only a limited engineering base small firms do not themselves generate sufficient demand for training provision. Whereas the large company can often afford to have a training programme designed and implemented for part of its work-force by a local technical college or other educational institution, the small firm has to make do with what is already on offer. Frequently, this may be inadequate and a number of companies mentioned the high cost of sending individuals away to attend the relevant courses.

The overall picture emerging from the survey was that while the best prospects for manufacturers lie with high-technology applications, whether in the form of products or in the production or management processes, the transformation to a high-technology state within traditional sectors will be a slow and turbulent one. Small companies can be expected to face particular problems.

REGIONAL ECONOMIC DEVELOPMENT: A QUESTION OF BALANCE

The empirical evidence presented in this paper suggests that if small-firm performance in the North of England is similar to that in other peripheral regions, then high-technology small firms are unlikely to be the panacea for regional economic regeneration that some commentators have claimed. It has demonstrated that, in the British case at least, the major generators of new small firms are the traditional manufacturing sectors, and that sectors such as mechanical engineering are also the source of those with the best employment growth performance. Broadening out the definition of high technology to include those companies with a high technological capability in terms of their application of microelectronics-based technology enables one to identify areas of activity that may offer improved prospects for regions that are currently unsuccessful in transforming their economies into ones based upon the new high-technology sectors.

This is not to completely reject the role of policy in encouraging high-technology production in depressed areas. Indeed, this may assume greater importance at a regional level as more companies turn to 'just-in-time' or Japanese 'Kanban' methods of production that reduce inventory to a minimum and rely on very tight scheduling of component delivery where local sourcing is an obvious advantage. Nevertheless, it may be suggested that policy needs to maintain a broad scope, since there is clearly potential for encouraging diversification within the existing stock of establishments.

Policy should not be directed simply at keeping old industries alive, but should attempt to assist in the technological transformation that will make them more competitive. The introduction of high-technology process control and so on will inevitably be seen as a threat to existing employment opportunities within the region. However, the evidence suggests that, faced with severe recession, it is those companies that have taken steps to improve productivity, and maintain their competitiveness by harnessing the technology, which possess the best prospects for long-term survival. Indeed, seen in the context of the longer term growth of the company, job prospects are likely to be positive. One small engineering company in the CURDS survey had experienced recent employment growth and attributed this directly to the results of investment in CNC machine-tool technology.

The ability to effect the necessary transformation at a regional level is going to depend upon a number of factors. A conducive infrastructure of R&D, training provision and skilled labour needs to be fostered, together with an availability of impartial advice and sound consultancy assistance for the evaluation and implementation of new technological systems. A lot of organisations and agencies are jumping on to the high-technology bandwagon. The turbulence of the transformation will be such that a co-ordinated strategy involving all interested parties needs to be developed. This strategy needs to maintain a balance between those industries normally considered to be high-technology and more traditional industries. It also needs to strike a balance between the needs of small independent firms and the externally controlled branch plants, since these are usually important in employment terms and will be at greatest risk if they remain with an unrealised technological potential. Above all a concerted effort is required to encourage people to think strategically about new technology, to involve everyone affected from the outset and to change the parameters used for judging and evaluating the options open to them.

These conclusions raise issues about the way regional economic development is researched. They point to the need to consider the totality of technology as it is applied and integrated at the level of the individual enterprise or establishment and how the implementation of the technology produces impacts and interactions through broader organisational and institutional contexts (Harris and McArthur, 1985) in particular localities. Much research has focused upon particular pieces of the puzzle; small firms or large firms, telecommunications or computers, and so on. An adherence to categorisations of this nature will be insufficient to provide an understanding of the totality of the role of technology in economic development. There is thus a need for a research approach that accommodates some of the issues raised here.

REFERENCES

Advisory Council for Applied Research and Development (ACARD) (1983) *New opportunities in manufacturing: the management of technology.* HMSO, London.

Armington, C. (1984) *The changing geography of high technology business.* Applied Systems Institute, Washington, D.C.

Arnold, E. and P. Senker (1982) Designing the future — the implications of CAD interactive graphics for employment and skills in the British engineering industry. *Occasional Paper 9*, Engineering Industry Training Board, Watford.

Blackburn, P., R. Coombs and K. Green (1985) *Technology, economic growth and the labour process.* Macmillan, Basingstoke.

British Business (1986) AMT—the way ahead for machine tools. 8 August.

Cross, M. (1985) *Towards the flexible craftsman.* Technical Change Centre, London.

Dodgson, M. (1985) New technology, employment and small engineering firms. *International Small Business Journal, 3*(2), 8–19.

Ellin, D. and A. E. Gillespie (1983) High technology product industries and job creation in Great Britain. *Working Note*, CURDS, University of Newcastle upon Tyne.

Forrester, T. (ed.) (1980) *The microelectronics revolution.* Blackwell, Oxford.

Freeman, C. (1982) *The economics of innovation*, 2nd ed. Frances Pinter, London.

——— (1985) The role of technical change in national economic development. In A. Amin and J. B. Goddard (eds) *Technological change, industrial restructuring and regional development*. Allen and Unwin, London.

Ganguly, P. (1985) *UK small business statistics and international comparisons*. Harper and Row, London.

Gold, B. (1982) CAM sets new rules for production. *Harvard Business Review*, *60*(6), 88–94.

Gould, A. and D. Keeble (1984) New firms and rural industrialisation in East Anglia. *Regional Studies*, *18*, 189–201.

Harris, F. and R. McArthur (1985) The issue of high technology: an alternative view. *Working Paper 16*, North-West Industry Research Unit, University of Manchester.

Keeble, D. and E. Wever (eds) (1986) *New firms and regional development*. Croom Helm, London.

Langridge, R. J. (1984) Defining 'high-tech' for locational analysis. *Discussion Paper 22, Series C*, Department of Economics, University of Reading.

Laslett, R. E. and C. J. Laidlaw (1986) *Regional profile: trends in engineering manpower and training in the Northern Region from 1978*. Engineering Industry Training Board, Watford.

Lawson, G. (1985) *Sector profile: manpower in the electronics industry*. Engineering Industry Training Board, Watford.

McQuaid, R. W. and R. J. Langridge (1984) Defining high-technology industries. Paper presented at the Regional Science Association, British Section, Annual Conference, University of Kent at Canterbury, 5–7 September.

Mansfield, E. (1968) *The economics of technical change*. W. W. Norton, New York.

National Economic Development Office (NEDO) (1985) *AMT: the impact of new technology in engineering batch production*. NEDO, London.

Northcott, J. and P. Rogers (1984) *Microelectronics in British industry: the pattern of change*. Policy Studies Institute, London.

Orme, M. (1979) *Micros: a pervasive force*. Associated Business Press, London.

Rosenberg, N. (1974) Science, invention and economic growth. *Economic Journal*, *84*, 90–108.

Segal, Quince and Partners (1985) *The Cambridge phenomenon*. Segal, Quince and Partners, Cambridge.

Senker, P. (1984) The implications of CAD/CAM for management. *Omega*, *12*(3), 225–31.

—— and M. Beasley (1985) Computer-aided production and inventory control systems: training needs for successful implementation. *Occasional Paper 13*, Engineering Industry Training Board, Watford.

Storey, D. J. (ed.) (1985) *Small firms in regional economic development*. Cambridge University Press, Cambridge.

—— K. Keasey, R. Watson and P. Wynarczyk (1987) *The performance of small firms*. Croom Helm, London.

Thwaites, A. T. (1982) Some evidence of regional variations in the introduction and diffusion of industrial products and processes within British manufacturing industry. *Regional Studies*, *16*, 371–81.

—— A. Edwards and D. C. Gibbs (1982) *Interregional diffusion of production innovations in Great Britain. Final Report to the Department of Industry and Commission of the European Communities.* Centre for Urban and Regional Development Studies, University of Newcastle upon Tyne.

Wiess, M. A. (1985) High-technology industries and the future of employment. In P. Hall and A. Markusen (eds) *Silicon landscapes.* Allen and Unwin, London.

Williams, H. and D. Charles (1986) The electronics industry in the North-East: growth or decline? *Northern Economic Review, 13,* 29–38.

The Regional Development Potential of Small and Medium-sized Enterprises: A European Perspective

Peter Nijkamp, Theo Alsters and Ronald van der Mark

REGIONAL DEVELOPMENT POLICY IN TRANSITION

The economies of most industrialised countries show clear signs of structural change processes: the stagnation phenomena which hit our economies in the seventies have induced a process of economic restructuring, in which efficacy of public policy efforts and self-generating revitalisation efforts of the private sector play a dominant role. Technological progress, research and development (R&D), innovation of production and management functions, and flexible adjustment to new circumstances are at present regarded as key forces for the enhancement of productivity and competitiveness (cf. Nelson and Winter, 1982; Stoneman, 1983).

This re-orientation in economic policy has also gradually exerted a profound impact on regional planning. Until the mid-seventies regional planning was mainly caught in the dilemma of efficiency versus equity. In order to find a compromise between these two conflicting policy objectives, regional development policy was usually based on attempts at favouring large-scale investments in fixed capital, the use of unskilled or idle labour, the exploitation of low-cost natural resources, and the production of medium-quality commodities, so that in less advanced regions price was the main factor for competition (cf. also OECD, 1986).

In the 1980s, however, the context and contents of regional policy have dramatically changed. A first reason is the increase in *knowledge orientation* of modern production technology. The necessity to manufacture sophisticated products that not only compete on a local market, but also on a world market, has called for an 'intellectualisation' of all phases of production (ranging from product design to after-sales services). This rise in R&D

intensity is in turn induced by new technological developments in areas like computer science telecommunication and informatics. Consequently, the development potential of a region is co-determined by its access to and use of this modern knowledge network (cf. Giaoutzi and Nijkamp, 1987).

Another reason for a re-orientation has to be sought in the changing production structure of our economies. In contrast with the trend towards mass production and industrial concentration, we nowadays observe a new evolution towards *small production units*. This is partly due to the fact that the economic stagnation has triggered off the emergence of a small-scale innovative entrepreneurship, and partly due to the decentralisation tendencies which have been made possible by modern information technologies (cf. Nijkamp, 1986). In any case, small- and medium-sized enterprises (SMEs) are likely to play a crucial role in the economic revitalisation of lagging regions, as such firms in particular exhibit the features of a Schumpeterian entrepreneurial spirit. This is also reflected in a conclusion of Webster, quoted by Detomasi (1985, p.7):

> . . . it is now generally acknowledged that employment growth is primarily generated by small firms, not large ones and that the overwhelming majority of net job creation in communities and regions is the product of net firm births, deaths, expansions and contractions rather than the one product of firms migrating from one region or community to another. Hence, the old conventional wisdom (upon which much public policy was based) which perceived employment creation and economic growth in regions to be a product of luring firms to a region from another location has been empirically and theoretically negated.

A final point regards the *seedbed function* of a region in generating new developments (cf. Beesley and Hamilton, 1984). Economic growth does not take place at a nation-wide scale: specific regions provide a specific incubator function for specific new activities. Research on the incubator hypothesis already has a long history since the early attempts of Hoover and Vernon (1959) (for a review, see Davelaar and Nijkamp, 1987). A related question here is the identification of favourable locational conditions that act as attractors of new (preferably innovative) activities. In this framework, a regional profile analysis may be a

123

useful analytical tool in order to identify by means of a strength–weakness analysis which regions are favourable candidates for stimulating the rise of promising enterprises, given the locational requirements of new firms (for example, the regional entrepreneurial vitality, the industrial diversity, the available infrastructure, and so on). Clearly, the locational behaviour of many firms exhibits a certain bias towards areas in which the entrepreneurs live, but new locations will only become a success if they are realised in favourable regions.

From the previous remarks the conclusion can be drawn that successful regional policy is increasingly focusing attention on the revitalisation of indigenous regional resources which may trigger off the creation of new, preferably knowledge-based activities, particularly in the SME sector (see also Storey, 1983; Keeble and Wever, 1986).

In the light of the context outlined above, the present chapter aims at analysing in more detail the regional development potential offered by the SME sector. The chapter is organised as follows: The next section will outline the principles of a multidimensional locational profile analysis, while in the subsequent section the features and regional relevance of the SME sector will be discussed. Special attention will be given here to the factors determining the regional production environment of the SME sector. The fourth section then describes the methodology of the study, based on a step-wise multi-criteria analysis, in which the attributes of a regional development potential are related to the specific regional importance of a set of SME branches. Finally, in the penultimate section a case study, based on 18 regions of the Common Market, is presented, and the chapter is concluded with some brief retrospective comments.

A MULTIDIMENSIONAL LOCATIONAL PROFILE ANALYSIS

In the current phase of the industrial life cycle, SMEs play an important role in the recovery, restructuring and improvement of a regional economy (cf. de Smidt, 1981). In the framework of an economic revitalisation, new and innovative SMEs also provide a stimulus for economic growth in less favoured regions (cf. Aydalot, 1984). An extremely relevant question — from both a regional policy and a sectoral policy viewpoint — is: which regional conditions are favourable for the emergence and expansion of SMEs? In other words, which specific regional conditions act as seedbeds for the creation of new SMEs? Clearly, various regional conditions are fixed — at least in the short run — and cannot be directly adjusted to the locational demand profile of SMEs. Examples are: physical and climatological conditions, the locational position of a region, the socio-demographic structure, the employment situation, and so forth.

> In fact, regional resources are relatively spatially fixed and some basic characteristics of single regional environments such as the quality of the labor force, the level of technical and management know-how and the social and institutional structures are relatively stable. Therefore, regional growth as well as sectoral location are largely determined by the endowment and productivity of the stock of regional resources rather than by the external flow of resources (Cappellin, 1983, p. 460).

In view of the fact that SMEs in symbiosis with larger firms, are usually regarded as activities with a high innovation potential (see also Rothwell and Zegveld, 1982), it is clear that the SME sector may act as a driving force for a regional revitalisation. SMEs are essentially regional resources with a great potential. Consequently, a regional innovative policy should have an open eye for the locational conditions of the SME sector and for specific ways of improving these conditions through the provision of suitable social overhead capital. Consequently, a thorough analysis may make a distinction between the *actual* and the *potential* location of a firm (cf. Pellenbarg and Kok, 1986). The potential location refers to the suitability of places or regions for new or innovative activities. This distinction implies that new SMEs will not necessarily be located at places where in the past existing SMEs have already found a location.

The assessment of a locational *supply* profile (the multidimensional profile of attributes characterising the locational conditions of a region for specific activities like the SME sector) requires a detailed geographical analysis of the regional availability of all relevant existing location factors; while the assessment of a locational *demand* profile (the multidimensional profile of attributes which are regarded as important attractors that reflect the location of existing and new activities like the SME sector in a certain region) requires regional entrepreneurial information.

In this framework, it is usual to make a distinction of

locational profiles into the regional production structure (RPS) and the regional production environment (RPE). An RPS is composed, *inter alia*, of the sectoral structure, the industrial size classes, the number of innovative firms, the availability of R&D infrastructure, and so on. An RPE includes exogenous location factors like accessibility, availability of industrial sites, agglomeration economies, residential climate, educational infrastructure, and so on.

Both the RPS and the RPE are supply factors, so that an improvement of the regional development potential would require a more efficient use of these available resources or a tailor-made adjustment of these resources to locational requirements of promising new activities, in order to enhance the competitive position of a region. Various empirical studies have in recent years been made in order to assess the development potential for a set of regions, based *inter alia* on multiple-criteria methods, quasi-production function approaches, or logit analyses. In all these studies, it was taken for granted that concepts like regional development and development potential are not unidimensional. It is thus evident that a multidimensional profile analysis is a necessary vehicle in order to take into account the diversity of locational factors in a regional development study. In our chapter, an attempt will also be made to take into account the relative importance (i.e. priority) attached to the locational factors for the SME sector, so that one may arrive at an evaluation of the regional production potential for SMEs. Thus, for instance, if a specific locational factor for an SME activity is well represented in a given area and if this factor is attached a high priority, then the area concerned may be a favourable location for the SME activity concerned. This may lead to a strength–weakness analysis which may be used for both peripheral development areas and central restructuring areas. Before presenting the formal methodology of our study, we will in the next section pay more explicit attention to the SME factor *per se*.

THE SME SECTOR

The interest in the SME sector is a result of a new industrial spirit, in which the self-generating employment capacity of the industrial sector is emphasised. In this context, it is assumed that the SME sector contains many growers and renewers, which may favour technological innovation (Rothwell and Zegveld, 1982). Furthermore, the SME sector has in the recent past demonstrated a remarkable capability to achieve a relatively stable employment level (cf. Hamilton, 1985). Thus, the SME sector is a potentially effective vehicle for creating new jobs, for stimulating a regional revitalisation based on indigenous development resources and on greater flexibility, and for favouring industrial innovation. Small size appears to generate significant economies, especially in case of a favourable RPS and RPE (including an open communication infrastructure — see Duché and Savey, 1985).

In the framework of our chapter SMEs will be defined as enterprises (industry, handicraft) with less than 500 employees. These firms can be further subdivided into:

- very small   ($\leqslant$ 10 employees)
- small   (10–100 employees)
- medium-sized   (100–500 employees)

Clearly, the SME sector as a whole is very heterogeneous.

The advantages of the SME sector are quite diverse, and may be judged on the basis of the following criteria derived from Alsters and van der Mark (1986):

(a) *Employment impacts*: in many European countries the rise in the number of jobs in the SME sector has to some extent compensated for the loss of jobs in the large industrial sectors. In addition, the quality of labour in the SME sector (including various spin-off effects) and the relatively lower wage rates have meant a significant stimulus to the rise of the SME sector.

(b) *New firm creation*: besides the growth of existing firms, new establishments also contribute to the employment growth in the SME sector. It is noteworthy, however, that in various cases new establishments are reflecting a branch plant strategy of a large mother company. Finally, it has been noted that not only the birth rate, but also the death rate of SMEs is in general high.

(c) *Innovation potential*: the flexible manufacturing in SMEs leads to a high innovativeness of SMEs, especially in central favourable locations. New ventures based on large spin-off effects and various buyouts induce an innovative climate in areas with a good knowledge and R&D infrastructure.

(d) *Flexibility*: in contrast with bureaucratic management of large-scale companies, SMEs have a high degree of flexibility, so that they can easily adjust themselves to new management and organisation patterns, new production methods, new scale techniques or new marketing strategies, mainly because of their low overhead infrastructure.

(e) *Variation in production systems*: SMEs are able to operate on small and specialised markets by providing competitive tailor-made goods.

The above mentioned list of potential advantages of SMEs in a regional development strategy will be fully realised only if the region concerned has an optimal development potential. The elements in the RPE which favour the specific regional development potential geared to the SME sector are the following (see Alsters and van der Mark (1986) for details):

(1) *Accessibility*: the regional availability of an efficient communication and transportation infrastructure is of crucial importance for SMEs, in particular because SMEs in general need backward and forward linkages with other firms and/or markets.

(2) *Centrality*: the centrality (or peripherality) of a region refers to its relative position in a larger set of regions. The distance (including transport costs and lagged innovation diffusion) to the economic heartland(s) of these regions determines to a large extent the development potential of a region, as is also demonstrated by the economic position of various regions in the Common Market.

(3) *Agglomeration size*: up to a certain critical threshold level, large agglomerations do provide economies of scale for the SME sector, due to close functional linkages and direct access to relevant information systems.

(4) *Institutional and policy framework*: in this context, various forms of financial support for SMEs (including venture capital), various policy measures fostering innovations and new technologies in the SME sector (by favouring R&D infrastructure, for example), and information and advice to SMEs (via technology transfer points or science parks, for example) may be mentioned.

(5) *Educational facilities*: educational facilities and specialised personnel are extremely important locational conditions for new SMEs. Bottlenecks in terms of skilled employees reduce

the regional development potential with respect to the SME sector.

(6) *Residential climate*: various studies have demonstrated the relevance of a favourable residential climate, especially for highly skilled employees in the SME sector.

(7) *Energy costs*: low regional energy costs favour the creation of SMEs in those regions.

(8) *Wage rates*: low wage rates may give a region a stronger (interregional or international) competitive position.

(9) *Labour force*: the composition and growth of the regional labour force (especially in the economically active age) are two important determinants of its development potential.

(10) *Employment perspectives*: unacceptable unemployment levels may be coped with by means of effective migration policies, educational programmes, reductions in labour time, specific industrial sector policies, participation policies for the labour market, and so on.

(11) *Regional opportunities for SMEs*: this element refers both to the contribution of the SME sector to promising industrial activities and to the benefits of promising industrial activities for the SME sector.

The above-mentioned eleven attributes of an RPE will be used in the next section in order to assess an operational multidimensional profile for the development potential of a set of regions in regard to the SME sector.

METHODOLOGY

In the present section the analytical framework for assessing the profiles of RPEs will be described.

Firstly, the concept of an RPE matrix will be introduced. This matrix denoted by E contains the numerical values of the above mentioned eleven attributes (see previous section) across all regions (R) under study. Thus, this matrix can be represented as:

$$E = \begin{bmatrix} e_{11} & \cdots & e_{1R} \\ \vdots & & \vdots \\ e_{11} & \cdots & e_{1R} \end{bmatrix}$$

where $I = 11$. The assessment of the values of e_{ir} $(i = 1, \ldots, I;$ $r = 1, \ldots, R)$ requires an operational definition of each of the successive development potential factors, which is consistent and comparable across all regions via appropriate standardisations. Thus, E represents the multidimensional profiles of each of the R regions concerned.

In addition to the RPE matrix, we construct a so-called RSE (regional sector evaluation) matrix. This matrix denoted by S represents for each relevant branch (sub-sector) of the SME sector the relative importance of each of the factors included in the RPE matrix. Thus, this matrix has the following shape:

$$S = \begin{bmatrix} s_{11} & \cdots & s_{1J} \\ \vdots & & \vdots \\ s_{I1} & \cdots & s_{IJ} \end{bmatrix}$$

where J is the number of relevant branches in the SME sector. Each entry s_{ij} $(i = 1, \ldots, I; j = 1, \ldots J)$ represents the relative weight attached to factor i for branch j. These weights are regarded as score points and satisfy the usual additivity condition:

$$\sum_{i=1}^{I} s_{ij} = 1 \quad , \quad \text{for each } j \tag{1}$$

In the framework of this study, the following branches of the industrial SME sector are distinguished, based on a distinction between final-market orientated, intermediate, export-orientated, innovative and high-tech firms (for more details, see Alsters and van der Mark, 1986):

(1) final-market orientated

(2) intermediate

(3) intermediate innovative

(4) final-market export orientated

(5) intermediate export orientated

(6) intermediate high-tech orientated

(7) final-market export orientated and innovative

130

(8) intermediate, export orientated and innovative
(9) intermediate, innovative and high-tech orientated
(10) final-market innovative
(11) intermediate, export orientated, innovative and high-tech orientated

It is clear that firms in each of these branches will attach a different priority to the factors of the locational profile in the RSE matrix. These priority weights can in principle be assessed by means of expert judgements of persons who are familiar with the SME sector.

The resulting problem is essentially a multi-criteria evaluation problem. We have a set of performance scores (incorporated in the RPE matrix) and a set of weights (incorporated in the RSE matrix). For the sake of simplicity, we will employ here only the simplest multi-criteria techniques available, namely the weighted summation technique. Clearly, other more sophisticated techniques may also be used, but for illustrative purposes we prefer here the use of the weighted summation technique.

This technique provides, then, an evaluation of the regional development potential of each of the branches of the SME sector in three steps. Firstly, for each region r $(r=1, \ldots, R)$ a compound sector evaluation matrix C_r can be constructed which is defined as follows:

$$C_r = \begin{bmatrix} e_{1r}s_{11} & \cdots & e_{1r}s_{1J} \\ \vdots & & \vdots \\ e_{Ir}s_{I1} & \cdots & e_{Ir}s_{IJ} \end{bmatrix}$$

Each ith row of C_r represents the weighted regional development potential for factor i with respect of all J branches, while each jth column represents the weighted regional development potential across all attributes for SME branch j.

Next, one may calculate the total regional development potential across all SME branches in region r by means of the following J-dimensional profile:

$$c_r = \left[\sum_{i=1}^{I} e_{ir}s_{i1} \quad \cdots \quad \sum_{i=1}^{I} e_{ir}s_{iJ} \right]^T \tag{2}$$

131

In the final step, the overall growth potential of region r (in terms of the weighted development potential of all relevant attributes for all SME branches) is calculated as:

$$c_r = \sum_{j=1}^{J} \sum_{i=1}^{I} e_{ir} s_{iJ} \qquad (3)$$

The various elements c_r can for all regions r $(r=1,. . .,R)$ be included in an $R \times 1$ multiregional profile vector c. The results from these steps can be used to make a systematic typology of the development potential for the SME sector in a system of regions.

Finally, we will use a regional performance indicator (RPI) matrix, which comprises for each region a set of relevant growth indicators. This matrix denoted by G has the following shape:

$$G = \begin{bmatrix} g_{11} & \cdots & g_{1R} \\ \vdots & & \vdots \\ g_{K1} & \cdots & g_{KR} \end{bmatrix}$$

where K is the number of performance indicators. The following indicators will be used here:

(1) relative change in gross regional product
(2) relative change in value added
(3) relative change in regional unemployment
(4) relative change in industrial employment
(5) relative change in employment share of SME sector (by size of establishment).

It is of course an interesting analytical question whether the RPI matrix bears a correspondence with the multiregional profile vector c. In the next section, the above-mentioned analytical framework will be further clarified on the basis of a study in the development potential for the SME sector in various regions of the Common Market.

A CASE STUDY

In the present case study 18 different regions from the European

Community will be taken into consideration. These regions are standard regions (so-called level II regions), except Greece (level I) and Twente (level III). These 18 regions are:

(1) Greece
(2) Sicily
(3) Puglia
(4) Ireland
(5) Midi-Pyrénées
(6) Aquitaine
(7) Languedoc-Rousillon
(8) Northern Ireland
(9) Cleveland, Durham, Cumbria, and Tyne and Wear (North)

(10) Yorkshire and Humberside
(11) Lorraine
(12) Luxembourg
(13) Saarland
(14) Twente
(15) Liège
(16) Limburg
(17) East-Flanders
(18) Nord-Pas de Calais

Regions (1)–(7) from this list are peripheral areas, while the remaining regions are restructuring areas. For each of these regions the data on the eleven profile elements making up the regional development potential (accessibility, centrality, and so on — see the third section) have been gathered. Instead of presenting all details we will present here only the main trends in the form of a strength–weakness table (see Table 7.1).

If we were to be interested in the overall development potential of these regions alone, without regard to the specific relevance of these factors for the SME sector, we might calculate the unweighted average of the eleven RPE factors (see Figure 7.1).

The next step of the analysis is the assessment of the RSE matrix for each of the eleven SME branches (see previous section) and for all eleven profile factors (see third section). Based on expert judgements this weight matrix could be quantified (see Table 7.2).

Next, by using the methodology outlined in the previous section the regional development potential can be gauged. The main results for each type of SMEs is given in Table 7.3.

It is interesting to see that from the peripheral regions (1)–(7) only Aquitaine and Languedoc-Roussillon have a slightly more favourable development potential. The perspectives of all others are relatively unfavourable. On the other hand, Northern Ireland is the only restructuring area from the list (8)–(18), which has less than average favourable perspectives.

It is also noteworthy that the SME branches (2), (6), (8), (10)

133

Table 7.1: A strength–weakness table for 18 regions in terms of eleven factors representing the regional production environment (RPE)

Regions	RPE factors

Regions	(1)	(2)	(3)	(4)	(5)	(6)	(7)	(8)	(9)	(10)	(11)
(1)				x				x			
(2)				x	x			x			
(3)				x	x			x			
(4)				x				x	x		x
(5)				x	x	x				x	x
(6)			x		x	x				x	
(7)			x		x	x				x	
(8)								x	x		x
(9)		x	x					x	x	x	x
(10)		x	x	x	x			x	x	x	x
(11)		x	x		x	x			x	x	
(12)		x			x	x			x	x	
(13)	x	x		x	x	x	x				
(14)	x	x	x					x			x
(15)	x	x							x		
(16)	x	x					x	x	x		
(17)	x	x			x	x			x		
(18)	x	x			x				x		

Legend: x = higher than average value.

Figure 7.1: Unweighted representation of the development potential of 18 regions

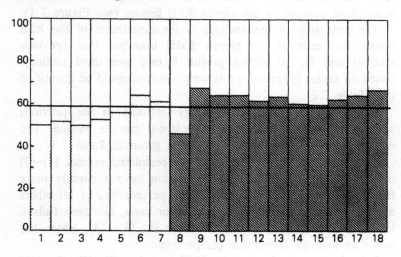

Table 7.2: Expert assessment of the RSE matrix

SME branches						RPE factors					
	(1)	(2)	(3)	(4)	(5)	(6)	(7)	(8)	(9)	(10)	(11)
1	·2	·03	·3	·03	·1	·04	·04	·1	·1	·04	·02
2	·2	·1	·2	·05	·08	·03	·08	·1	·1	0	·05
3	·08	·03	·1	·1	·2	·1	·06	·08	·1	·04	·1
4	·2	·2	·2	·03	·06	0	·05	·1	·1	·03	·03
5	·2	·2	·1	·04	·05	·04	·07	·1	·1	·03	·07
6	·08	·04	·1	·04	·2	·01	·03	·04	·2	·06	·2
7	·2	·2	·1	·06	·1	·02	·04	·04	·1	·04	·1
8	·1	·1	·09	·06	·2	0	·04	·1	·1	·1	·1
9	·08	·1	·08	·06	·2	·04	·04	·04	·1	·05	·2
10	·1	·02	·2	·03	·2	·02	·03	·05	·1	·06	·2
11	·06	·08	·06	·08	·2	0	·03	·02	·2	·06	·2

Table 7.3: A strength–weakness table of the development potential of 18 regions with respect to eleven SME branches

Regions						SME branches					
	(1)	(2)	(3)	(4)	(5)	(6)	(7)	(8)	(9)	(10)	(11)
1	O	O	O			O		O			O
2	O		O			O		O		O	O
3			O			O		O			O
4	O	O	O	O		O					O
5			O			O		O	O		O
6	X		X			X		X		X	X
7	X		X					X		X	X
8		O	O	O	O	O					O
9			X			X			X	X	X
10	X	X		X		X				X	X
11	X		X			X		X			X
12			X			X		X	X		X
13			X	X		X					X
14	X	X		X	X	–X	X				X
15	X	X		X	X		X				
16		X		X	X	X	X				X
17	X	X		X	X		X				
18	X	X		X		X					X

Legend: X = higher than average value over all regions and higher than average SME value in own region.
O = higher than average SME value in own region.

and (11) do not have a strong position in the peripheral regions. Only category (9) has a slightly higher score in peripheral areas. Besides, branches (5) and (7) appear to perform relatively well in all regions (except in Belgium). Finally, branches (8) and (10) appear to have a strong position almost exclusively in Belgian and Dutch regions.

The overall development potential of all regions (see previous section) can now also easily be calculated (see Figure 7.2).

A comparison of the results from Figure 7.2 with those from Figure 7.1 shows that both figures to a large extent present a similar pattern. However, from the peripheral areas only Aquitaine now scores higher than average, while from the restructuring areas — besides Northern Ireland — Liège and Luxembourg also have a less than average score.

Finally, we may confront the results from Figure 7.2 with the RPI matrix. This confrontation is given in Table 7.4.

The overall picture from Table 7.4 is extremely interesting. Peripheral areas [categories (1)–(7)] appear to have a relatively fairly favourable regional performance in terms of: growth in gross regional product, growth in gross value added, less growth in unemployment, and rise in industrial employment. Furthermore, the SME sector appears to perform relatively well in peripheral areas, for almost all size classes.

The restructuring areas do in general not show favourable results in terms of regional product, gross value added, unemployment, and

Figure 7.2: Weighted representation of the development potential of 18 regions for the aggregate SME sector

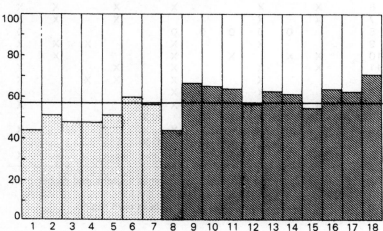

Table 7.4: Confrontation of regional development potential with regional performance indicators

Regions	1	2	3	4	5				Cr
1	−	−	−	+	+	−	+		−
2	+	+	−	+	−	+	+	−	−
3	+	+	−	+	−	+	−	+	−
4	+	+	−	+	+	+	+	−	−
5	+	+	−	+	+	−	+	−	−
6	−	+	−	+	+	−	+	−	+
7	+	−	−	+	+	−	−	−	−
8	+	+	+	−	−	+	−	+	−
9	+	+	+	−	−	+	−	+	+
10	+	+	+	−	−	+	−	+	+
11	−	−	−	−	+	−	+	−	+
12	−	−	+	+	−	+	+	+	−
13	−	−	−	+	−	−	+	−	+
14	−	−	+	−	+	−	+	−	+
15	−	−	−	−	+	+	−	+	−
16	−	−	+	−	−	+	+	−	+
17	−	−	−	−	+	+	−	+	+
18	−	−	−	−	−	+	−	+	+

Legend: − less than regional average
+ more than regional average

industrial employment. Various SME size classes appear to perform slightly better, while especially, the size class with more than 500 employees leads to better results than those in the peripheral areas. The conclusion from this analysis is that — despite a relatively lower development potential of peripheral European areas — the relative growth performance of these areas, especially for the SME sector, is fairly favourable in comparion with other European restructuring areas.

RETROSPECT

This study has aimed at analysing the indigenous development potential of SMEs for a regional revitalisation, based on global regional data and expert views on the SME sector. Problems of perception and image (cf. Pellenbarg, 1986) were not taken into consideration, as this would require survey techniques or interviews. Clearly, the results obtained in this study are co-determined by the geographical scale of the analysis. Another limitation of this study is that the impact of the whole regional sectoral mix upon the SME sector could not be taken into account due to lack of input–output data. The approach adopted in this chapter has focused attention mainly on the locational supply side and less on the requested demand profile of SMEs. This would no doubt be a fruitful area for future research. Despite these limitations, however, the present study has revealed — by means of a strength–weakness analysis — the importance of a diversity of locational factors for enhacing the regional development potential of the SME sector in various European regions. Moreover, the method of multiple-criteria analysis has proven to provide an operational research tool for industrial locational analysis.

REFERENCES

Alsters, T. F. A. and R. C. van der Mark (1986) *Giving way — or putting up? The development potential of small and medium-sized enterprises.* Report DG XVI/109/86, Commission of the European Communities, Brussels.

Aydalot, P. (1984) Questions for regional geography. *Tijdschrift voor Economische en Sociale Geografie, 75,* 4–14.

Beesley, M. E. and R. T. Hamilton (1984) Small firms' seedbed role and the concept of turbulence. *Journal of Industrial Economics, 33,* 217–31.

Cappellin, R. (1983) Productivity growth and technological change in a regional perspective. *Giornale degli Economisti ed Annali di Economia, 42,* 459–82.

Davelaar, E. J. and P. Nijkamp (1987) The urban incubation hypothesis: old wine in new bottles? *Gesellschaft, Wirtschaft, Raum* (M. M. Fischer and M. Sauberer, eds.), AMR-Info, Vienna, 198–213.

Detomasi, D. (1985) Toward a generic policy for community economic vitality. In *Public policy and regional development. Proceedings of the Second Conference.* School of Public and Environmental Affairs, Indiana University, Bloomington, pp. 1–9.

Duché, G. and S. Savey (1985) Nouvelle Organisation de la Production et PME. *Bulletin de la Societé Languedocienne de Géographie, 19,* 21–42.

Giaoutzi, M. and P. Nijkamp (eds) (1987) *Informatics and regional development planning.* Avebury, Aldershot.

Hamilton, I. F. E. (1985) Les systèmes industriels. *Bulletin de la Societé Languedocienne de Géographie, 19,* 5–19.

Hoover, E. M. and R. Vernon (1959) *Anatomy of a metropolis.* Harvard University Press, Cambridge.

Keeble, D. and E. Wever (eds) (1986) *New firms and regional development in Europe.* Croom Helm, London.

Nelson, R. R. and S. G. Winter (1982) *An evolutionary theory of economic change.* Harvard University Press, Cambridge.

Nijkamp, P. (ed.) (1986) *Technological change, employment and spatial dynamics*. Springer Verlag, Berlin.

OECD (1986) *Aide-mémoire* for the implementation of technological innovation programmes at local level. Technical co-operation services, Paris (mimeographed).

Pellenbarg, P. (1986) Ruimtelijke cognitie. Unpublished PhD dissertation, Department of Geography, State University, Groningen.

Pellenbarg, P. H. and J. A. A. M. Kok (1986) Economische Vernieuwing in Ruimtelijk Perspectief: De Randstad en Overig Nederland. *K.N.A.G. Geografisch Tijdschrift*, *20*(1), 84–100.

Rothwell, R. and W. Zegveld (1982) *Innovation and the small and medium sized firm*. Frances Pinter, London.

Smidt, M. de (1981) Innovatie, industrialisatiebeleid en regionale ouduikkling. *Geografisch Tijdschrift*, *15*(3), 228–38.

Stoneman, P. (1983) *The economic analysis of technological change*. Oxford University Press, Oxford.

Storey, D. J. (ed.) (1983) *The small firm*. Croom Helm, London.

Wever, E. (1984) *Nieuwe Bedrijven in Nederland*. Van Gorcum, Assen.

8

The Role of Small and Medium-sized Enterprises in European Job Creation: Key Issues for Policy and Research*

David J. Storey

INTRODUCTION

For those politicians, economists and industrialists interested in the question of firm size, the prime question until the early 1970s was whether there was an inevitable trend towards increasing size and concentration. This was of key importance for the efficiency of a market because, although larger firms were often able to obtain scale economies at the plant level, and were able to marshal sufficient resources to undertake R&D, they were also often able to influence market price by variations in their own output. Of perhaps even greater concern was that large firms could both discourage the entry into the market of potential competitors and, by their advertising expenditure, influence in an unacceptable manner the purchasing patterns of consumers.

From the 1920s onwards there seemed to be an inevitable tendency towards an increasing share of employment and output being concentrated in larger firms. Hull (1987), for example, reports the long period results of Stockmann et al. (1983) who show that in Germany in 1907, firms with less than ten workers provided 41.8 per cent of employment and those with more than 1,000 workers provided 13.8 per cent. By 1970 matters had changed fundamentally, so that firms with less than ten employees

*This chapter is an abridged version of Chapter 2 of *Job creation in small and medium-sized enterprises*, Programme of Research and Actions on the Development of the Labour Market, DGV, Commission of the European Communities, 1987. The permission of the EEC to reproduce this chapter is gratefully acknowledged.

provided 22 per cent of employment and those with more than
1,000 employees provided 31·2 per cent. Similar trends are likely
to have been apparent in other countries. In the United Kingdom,
for example, the proportion of total manufacturing employment in
firms with less than 200 workers fell from 38·0 per cent in 1935
to 22·6 per cent in 1976 (Storey, 1982).

During the 1960s, and for some of the 1970s, there appeared
to be little doubt that large firms would take an increased share
of output and employment. The policy questions which were
discussed in that period were the extent to which these
developments were desirable. The broad consensus which was
apparent amongst European governments was that the growth of
large firms had mixed benefits and that it was appropriate to
impose controls upon them. Many governments often felt
threatened by the presence of multinational companies within their
borders, especially when, world-wide the company was more
powerful than the government and within its borders the company
was a major, often strategic, employer.

The outcome of these considerations was that in most countries
a code of competition was drawn up (under a variety of different
names), the objective of which was to ensure that the large firm
did not exploit its strength within the market-place, either to
provide a poorer quality product or charge an overly high price
for the product. On the other hand there were relatively few cases
where large firms were required to become smaller since it was
felt that such policies could seriously damage the competitive
position of the firm. The major policy initiatives in this area
covered merger and acquisitions, where large firms were often
prevented from becoming even larger.

THE CHANGES IN THE 1970s

During the 1970s these developments came to an abrupt halt. In
the 1970s not a single major OECD country for which data is
available experienced the type of interrupted decline in importance
of small firms and increasing concentration which had so
characterised most of the previous three decades.

In Table 8.1 data for the twelve OECD countries is taken and
plotted on a time series. For each country the upper row provides
an indication of the percentage of employment in manufacturing
enterprises in the smallest size of enterprise (generally with less

141

Table 8.1: Employment in different-sized enterprises: manufacturing in OECD countries

		1970	1971	1972	1973	1974	1975	1976	1977	1978	1979	1980	1981	1982	1983	COMMENT
Australia	1–19						11·6			11·3	11·2	11·8	11·8	12·6	12·1	General increase in small
	500+						49·6			50·2	50·8	49·5	49·7	48·6	41·3	
Austria	1–19				15·8								17·4			
	500+				40·7								38·2			
Belgium	1–19									11·8	11·9	11·8	12·1	12·5	12·1	Very small and very large have grown
	500+									40·7	41·8	41·7	41·6	41·6	41·3	
Denmark	1–19				6·8	7·5	8·4	7·9	8·7	8·6	8·5	8·7	9·3	9·1	9·2	Increase in small
	500+				37·0	38·1	37·0	35·6	35·4	36·8	37·0	37·2	36·6	36·1	35·3	Decrease in large
Finland	1–19			8·4		7·7		7·8		8·6		9·1				General increase small after 1974
	500+			59·1		59·5		59·9		58·9		57·6				
France	1–19		6·5	6·8		7·0	7·6	7·7	6·6	7·5	7·6	8·0	8·7			General increase in small. 1977 is a blip
	500+		52·5	53·1		53·1	52·2	52·0	52·1	51·8	51·3	50·7	49·4			
Japan	1–29	26·5	26·1	26·5	26·9	26·4	27·1	27·9	29·0	29·4	29·3	28·8	28·3	28·2	27·8	Small peaks in 1978 and after for small. Declining for large
	500+	36·2	36·5	36·8	35·8	36·9	35·4	33·9	32·9	32·4	31·7	32·2	32·7	32·9	33·3	

Luxembourg	1–19		8·2				7·5	7·5	7·6	7·7			Little change in
	500+		62·4				60·9	58·8	56·4	55·0			small since 1977
													Decline in large
Netherlands	1–19						12·5	12·7	12·6	12·8	13·0		Increasing small
	500+						N.A.	N.A.	N.A.	N.A.	N.A.		
Sweden	1–19		9·8	9·9	9·8	10·0	9·7	9·9	9·8	9·5	9·8	9·8	10·2	No change in small
	500+		56·3	55·9	56·4	56·2	56·3	55·7	55·7	56·7	55·8	55·2	54·1	or large
United	1–19	N.A.	N.A.		N.A.	N.A.	N.A.	N.A.	N.A.	N.A.	N.A.			Continuous decline
Kingdom	500+	70·3	71·5		70·5	69·9	70·1	69·9	69·6	68·2	66·3			of large since 1973
United	1–19		4·8				4·9							Little change
States	500+		71·1				71·0							

Sources: OECD (1985); Storey and Johnson (1987)

than 20 employees), and the lower row provides data on the percentage of employment in manufacturing enterprises in the largest size of enterprise (generally more than 500 employees).

Whilst there are major problems in undertaking international comparisons of the contribution of different firm sizes to employment, it seems that this data is the best available. Analysis of Table 8.1 shows that in the majority of countries there is generally a *lower* proportion of employment in *large* enterprises at the end of the period than at the beginning. For *small* enterprises matters are reversed, with this size group generally having a *higher* proportion of employment at the end of the period than at the beginning.

These developments are shown in various countries. Del Monte (1987), for example, shows that in Italy between 1951 and 1961 establishments with less than five workers experienced a 2·7 per cent decline in employment, whilst those with more than 1,000 experienced a 4·2 per cent increase. Similar, but even clearer differences were apparent during the 1960s when the smallest sector experienced a 6·7 per cent decline and the large sector a 27·7 per cent rise. Matters were reversed in the 1970s when the large sector experienced a 13·1 per cent decline and the small sector a 23·1 per cent increase. Similar results were apparent from the Federal Republic of Germany, where Hull (1987) quotes the Bade (1985) results showing that within the manufacturing sector firms with 20–49 employees has increased their share of employment from 5·6 per cent in 1970 to 7·8 per cent in 1983. On the other hand firms with more than 1,000 employees experienced a decreased share of employment from 51·6 per cent to 48·9 per cent. The statistical material presented for the other EEC countries, which tends to cover only the late 1970s and early 1980s, appears to indicate that similar trends are taking place in these countries and that such developments, if anything, are currently accelerating.

WHY THE CHANGE?

Currently there is no wholly satisfactory explanation for this change, because in some countries the change is relatively recent, whilst in others such as Japan there has been little real change. The lack of a suitable explanation may also be that the matter has only now become the focus of attention since there was in some countries a reluctance to believe that the recent data indicated a genuine reversal of 30-year trends. This led to an unwillingness to search for explanations. Nevertheless, writing in the mid-1980s it is now clear that a change has taken place in the size structure of employment units within most developed economies, and that this change began in some countries more than a decade ago.

In this section we will review the six explanations which have been presented, not purely with a view to obtaining understanding for its own sake, but also to inform the policy debate. Presenting each of the explanations separately is designed to assist clarification of the arguments. It does not suggest that only one of them is 'correct' or that only a single explanation is relevant to a particular country, or region within a country.

Each of the following explanations will be considered in turn:

(a) technical change;

(b) growth of the service sector;

(c) growth of Third World competition and declining international competitiveness of large firms;

(d) rising energy prices and slow-down of world growth;

(e) political factors, promotion of enterprise culture, and anti-government bias; and

(f) fashion and changing tastes.

(a) *Technical change.* It is argued that the growth in, and applications of, new technology are of benefit to the growth of small firms rather than large firms. Small firms can benefit disproportionately from the availability of computer controlled lathes and machine tools, therefore enabling them to compete more effectively with large firms. Furthermore, many of the uses of and the writing of software, in particular, can be more satisfactorily undertaken in the types of creative environment which a small firm can provide.

Whilst these explanations seem plausible, and perhaps more likely to become of importance in future, it seems unlikely that it was the current technological revolution which stopped the tendency towards industrial concentration *during the 1970s*.

(b) *Growth of the service sector.* It has been argued that the increased interest in small firms is primarily a function of the relative growth of the service sector at the expense of manufacturing. Thus, for example, where demand for them is growing rapidly, many services are provided by small and often new firms. Illustrations of this include the provision of such business services as advertising, market research, public relations, together with more specialist services within conventional sectors such as retailing and wholesaling of goods. Since average firm size in the service sector is generally lower than that in the manufacturing sector, then growth in services will lead to an overall decline in average firm size.

Again, whilst there has clearly been a relative growth in services the increased relative importance of small firms has also occurred *within* the manufacturing sector (see Table 8.1), making it clear that the growth of small firms is not purely a reflection of sectoral shift.

(c) *Growth of Third World competition.* It is broadly true that large firms export a significantly higher proportion of their output than small firms, which are more likely to act as suppliers to the large firms. Hence, changes in export competitiveness are likely to have a disproportionate direct effect upon large firms. The growth of competition from Japan in the 1950s and 1960s during relatively buoyant times had a relatively modest effect upon displacing products from the existing developed countries — although their impact in the electrical and motor sectors was considerable. During the 1970s, however, Japan continued to increase its market share at a time when world trade was stagnant or declining. Furthermore, Japan was joined by other South East Asian countries — notably Taiwan, Hong Kong and South Korea. This led to the displacement of European and North American products which were provided by large firms. The impact upon the European shipping, motor and electrical sectors was considerable.

We believe this to be an important explanation for the relative growth of small firms, since large firms when faced with this competition either succumbed or responded by imposing additional requirements upon their (mainly small firm) suppliers. The classic example of this strategy is the response of the Fiat motor company in the early 1970s. Fiat reacted to the twin threat of union militancy and external competition by contracting out many activities which had previously been undertaken within their Turin plant. The new subcontracting firms were often former employees who had been encouraged by the promise of orders from Fiat to establish their own business. The response to Third World competition is therefore a major force in explaining the relative growth of small firms.

(d) *Rising energy prices and slow-down of world demand.* The increase in energy prices in the early 1970s had several effects. The first was the direct effect on price increase upon firms, particularly those heavily dependent upon oil. Storey (1982) argued that since large firms were more energy dependent than small firms, the effect was to raise the relative prices more for large than for small. However, Shutt and Whittington (1984) have pointed out that large firms may be more efficient users of energy and therefore not have experienced as rapid a rate of increase.

The increased energy prices, however, did have a major effect upon the growth rate experienced by the economies of the developed countries. The seventies and eighties have seen a progressive increase in levels of unemployment, partly in the face of depressed demand conditions, partly because of new competition referred to above, and partly because of technological change. The effect of this for most countries, however, has been at least one decade of rising unemployment and it is this which is presented as an important explanation for the increase and growth of very small enterprises. It is argued that an individual who is unemployed is significantly more likely to consider starting his own business than the same individual if he or she were in secure paid salaried employment. The growth of very small business is therefore, to some degree, a *response* to unemployment rather than a cure for it.

The evidence in support of these statements is somewhat mixed. In the UK the work of Binks and Jennings (1986) suggests that the statistical relationship between unemployment and business registrations, to their surprise, is negative — i.e. business registrations are *high* when unemployment is low. This contrasts with earlier analyses by Johnson and Darnell (1976) and with Binks' own interviews with entrepreneurs, nearly half of whom suggested they had begun their business as a direct alternative to unemployment. The important role of unemployment in inducing the formation of businesses in Belgium is discussed by Donckles and Bert (1987). They find that unemployment or the threat of unemployment is the third most powerful factor — after a desire for independence and a need to move out of a large company — influencing Belgian entrepreneurs. Hull (1987) also reviews the German evidence that most formations are related to recessionary conditions and suggests that this is an important factor explaining the increased importance of small new firms in that country.

(e) *Political factors, promotion of enterprise culture and anti-government bias*. During the late 1970s and early 1980s a number of governments of the political 'right' were elected in both Europe and North America. Such governments were committed to a programme of reducing the role of the state in the economy, enabling market forces to operate in a less restricted fashion and thus facilitating growth in output and ultimately employment. Under such a scenario it is not surprising that the small business became the focus of two forms of policy. The first was that of reducing government involvement in the operation of the economy and the second was that of providing assistance to enable businesses to compete 'fairly' with other, but larger, firms.

Clearly, the flurry of initiatives designed to assist small businesses which were introduced in Europe have led to a stronger and more numerous small-business sector than would otherwise have been the case. It is also true that the full effect of these initiatives has still to be felt and so assessment will have to be left for some years. Nevertheless, it is equally clear that since these are measures taken primarily in the 1980s they do not explain why it was that in the 1970s the relative importance of the large firm began to decline.

(f) *Fashion and changing tastes*. It remains broadly true that a sizeable proportion of small firms are direct suppliers to large firms, whilst a small proportion sell their product directly on the open market. In many respects the latter group has particularly benefited from the growth in incomes which occurred during the 1960s and, to a lesser extent, in the 1970s. Those small firms which provided a specialist product or service which the large firm was unwilling to supply found that demand continued to be buoyant if the product satisfied a consumer who was prepared to pay a premium for quality in the form of design, presentation, reliability, and so on. For its part the small firm was expected to be sufficiently flexible to change the product when it became clear that market requirements had changed. The classic example of this type of development was found in the north-east central areas of Italy, where the term 'flexible specialisation' was coined to characterise the growth of small firms in industrial districts producing high quality textiles, clothing, footwear, toys, jewellery, musical instruments, etc. These craft-based industries, selling at the top end of the market, were able to prosper at a time when there was a sharp fall in demand for those standardised products generally produced in the large-firm sector.

A separate but associated development was the view that large firms provided an unacceptable work-place environment in which the work itself was boring, repetitive and lacking in variety. The lack of work-force motivation meant that workers had to be paid higher wages, they were more likely to be unionised and were less flexible in switching between tasks. This was contrasted with the small firm, in which job satisfaction was higher, motivation stronger and yet wages lower.

A recognition of these latter factors may have influenced firm size to some degree, but the evidence on the importance of the flexible specialisation model is more extensive. Even so, whilst it is clear that the model does explain developments in that particular region of Italy, it is less clear that it is of importance either elsewhere within Italy or elsewhere in Europe. Indeed, it is possible that the growth of the artisan class in these industrial districts more strongly reflects the unique agricultural traditions of the area and so has few applications elsewhere.

DIFFERENT INTERPRETATIONS

In the preceding section, several explanations as to why small firms become relatively more important, and why large firms become relatively less so, were presented. Some, such as the declining competitiveness and Third World competition, refer to the falling importance of large firms, whilst others such as changing tastes and fashion refer primarily to the increased importance of small firms. The remaining explanations refer *both* to declining large firms *and* to increasing small firms.

There is a need to clarify which explanations, if any, or in what combinations, are valid before public policy can be considered. Thus, for example, the SME sector, whilst it is anxious to conduct its activities free from government interference, regards the removal of the competitive advantages which large firms are supposed to possess as essential to free trade. The extent to which the SME sector should become the focus of economic policy is clearly related to its role in relation to large businesses.

Some examples will make the point more clearly. If it is shown that the major factors leading to the relative growth of small business are recession, high unemployment and the political complexions of certain governments, then this might not justify a policy to assist smaller firms. On the other hand if the growth of smaller firms were attributable to an increasing technological sophistication and international competitiveness within new industries, with this being hampered by the defensive competitive practices of large firms this might provide a stronger case for promoting the SME sector.

Perhaps at the most simple of all levels, however, public policy makers need to know in what types of businesses jobs are being created and in what types they are being lost. The relative increase in importance of small firms could occur either because large firms are *shedding* labour (and moving into the small-firms sector) or because small firms are *increasing* their labour by becoming larger. Unfortunately, an examination of employment change over a period of time in establishments or enterprises of a given size will *not* provide helpful insights into this question. To identify fully the contribution to employment change made by different sizes of firm/establishment, it is necessary to have time series employment data on individual units. The data base also has to have data on employment units which are formed over the time series and data on employment units which cease trading. It is then possible to undertake an analysis of employment change within a population of firms. This analysis is known as 'the job generation process'.

JOB GENERATION

The term 'job generation' was coined in 1979 in a seminal study by David Birch (1979) then of the Massachusetts Institute of Technology. Birch had acquired a computerised data set from the US credit-rating firm of Dun and Bradstreet. The data set covered employment in 5.6 million establishments in the United States private sector economy between 1969 and 1976.

Although initially designed to be a study of urban employment change in the United States, when the Birch study was published, interest centred upon the statistic that 66 per cent of the *increase* in employment in the United States between 1969 and 1976 was found to have occurred in firms with less than 20 workers. In Birch's terms these small firms were the job generators.

However, to examine fully the contribution of different-sized

Figure 8.1: The job generation process

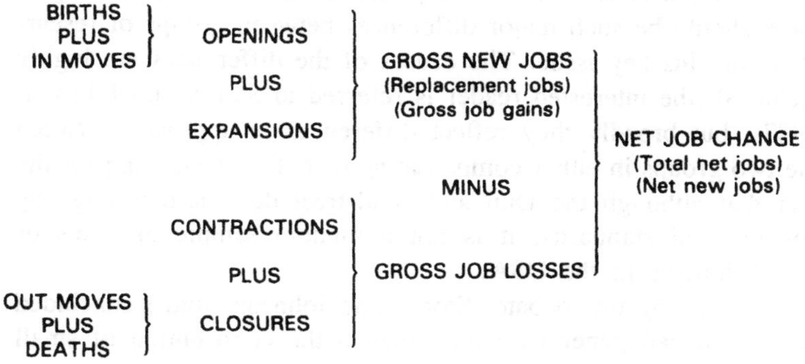

```
BIRTHS  ⎫
  PLUS  ⎬  OPENINGS    ⎫
IN MOVES⎭              ⎪
             PLUS      ⎬  GROSS NEW JOBS  ⎫
                       ⎪  (Replacement jobs)⎪
          EXPANSIONS   ⎭  (Gross job gains) ⎪
                                            ⎬  NET JOB CHANGE
                                            ⎪  (Total net jobs)
                          MINUS             ⎪  (Net new jobs)
                                            ⎪
          CONTRACTIONS ⎫                    ⎪
                       ⎪                    ⎪
             PLUS      ⎬  GROSS JOB LOSSES ⎭
OUT MOVES ⎫            ⎪
  PLUS    ⎬  CLOSURES  ⎭
 DEATHS   ⎭
```

Source: Centre for Environmental Studies paper, Policy Series 11

establishments to employment change, it is necessary to subdivide employment change into its major components and these are shown in Figure 8.1.

Reading from the right the figure shows that net job change comprises new jobs and job losses. It shows that job losses are subdivided between openings and expansions of existing firms and that job losses can be subdivided between contractions and closures. In principle, therefore, it should be possible to determine the extent to which employment in a given size grouping of firms is attributable to decline or growth.

The effect of the publication of the Birch results for the United States was two-fold. The first was that public policy-makers in several countries, who had been looking for some justification for promoting small firms, eagerly seized upon the results. The second reaction was that because of its importance, Birch's analysis was carefully examined and many questions were asked of it. In particular, a study by Armington and Odle (1982), also using Dun and Bradstreet data, for the 1978–80 period found that small firms were only creating jobs in proportion to their importance in the economy: that is, firms with less than 100 workers were creating about 39 per cent of new jobs whilst providing 38 per cent of the labour force. These results were then challenged by Birch and McCracken (1983) who *took the same data tapes* from Dun and Bradstreet that Armington and Odle had used, and analysed them. They concluded that firms with less than 100 workers created 70 per cent of the new jobs.

Clearly, it is unfortunate that, even using the same data tapes, there should be such major differences between groups of researchers on this key issue. The causes of the differences are highly technical (the interested reader is referred to Storey and Johnson, 1987), but broadly they reflect differences in approach between the two groups in either compensating or not compensating for the fact that although the Dun and Bradstreet data base is huge by conventional standards, it is not a random sample of firms or establishments in the USA.

In analysing this debate, Storey and Johnson (ibid.) concluded that Birch had generally overestimated the contribution of small firms to employment change, whilst Armington and Odle may have slightly underestimated that contribution. Hence, whilst Armington and Odle were probably closer to being 'correct', it remained the case that Birch had been the first to demonstrate that small firms were creating jobs somewhat faster than any other size group of firms.

The Birch results, and the debate with Armington and Odle, led to efforts to replicate the studies both in Europe, elsewhere in North America and in New Zealand (Bollard and Harper, 1986). Again, however, the problems arose that either the data base used was that of Dun and Bradstreet, which required substantial and subjective judgement, or that the alternative data bases were incomplete in the sense that they covered only a single region, or were restricted to manufacturing and so ignored the service sector.

Within Europe, the four countries in which job generation studies have developed furthest are the UK, West Germany, Ireland and Italy. The main studies are summarised in Storey and Johnson (1987). In the UK a Dun and Bradstreet-based study has been conducted by Gallagher and Stewart (1984) and by Doyle and Gallagher (1986). Both studies have indicated a substantially higher contribution to new employment being made by small firms than any of the local or regional studies which have primarily focused upon the manufacturing sector. The Gallagher studies, however, have also been criticised on similar grounds to the criticisms levelled at Birch. Nevertheless, it is also broadly true that in the UK, within the majority of studies, the large-firms sector *is* shedding labour and that the small-firms sector is generating new jobs.

152

There have also been a number of job generation studies undertaken in the Federal Republic of Germany, these being extensively reviewed by Hull (1987). He states that, whilst the aggregate data on changes in firm size suggest a decline in the importance of very large firms and a rise in the importance of very small firms, the job generation studies evidence is more ambiguous. Hull argues that studies which have confined themselves to *in situ* firms have generally indicated expansions amongst the small and contractions amongst the large. The introduction of births and deaths, however, makes the overall picture less clear because job loss rates from firm closure are particularly high for small firms. Indeed, Hull questions whether the results currently being obtained from job generation studies in Germany might not have been obtained if such studies had been undertaken 20 years ago.

In Italy there has only been the single job-generation study conducted by Contini *et al.* (1984), which is reported by Del Monte (1987). The prime focus of the Contini study was on regional differences and he showed that the southern regions of Italy generally had higher firm birth rates than the northern regions.

Job generation studies were also reported for Ireland, and by Guesnier (1987) for France. In both cases, small firms are the main contributors to new jobs, but an analysis of the Poition-Charentes region of France indicates that large firms also make an important contribution to job growth.

PUBLIC POLICY

This review has indicated that over the past 20 years there has been a notable shift in the relative importance of small and large firms. In some countries, such as the UK, these developments have been taking place for most of the last 20 years, whereas in other countries these changes are much more recent.

Whilst the evidence on whether these trends are likely to continue is mixed, and whilst it is also unclear whether it is possible to introduce public policies to promote the small-business sector, there appears to be increasing pressure for such initiatives. In this section we therefore speculate, on the basis of analysis and policy observation, on the most appropriate forms of public policy for promoting small firms.

This speculation must be undertaken in the face of two key uncertainties which are inherent within the contributions from each country. These uncertainties are:

(a) uncertainties over the *response* by the individual small firm to the provision of assistance — i.e. how many new jobs will be created as a result of the provision of assistance? and

(b) uncertainties over the effect of these 'additional' jobs upon the labour market — i.e. what is the net effect upon *unemployment* rates?

Only when it is possible to quantify the extent of these factors will it be possible to estimate fully the effectiveness of various policy options. It is, however, a characteristic of small-firms policy that politicians are not prepared to wait for the results of careful research studies before introducing new policies. Indeed, the absence of evidence sometimes appears to be viewed as a positive advantage when promoting policy initiatives in this sector, since it reflects the willingness of politicians and bureaucrats to act with the same type of entrepreneurial flair that is supposed to characterise the small firm sector which they are attempting to assist.

The remainder of this section is based on the assumption that whilst thorough and comprehensive research results are not available, it is possible to indicate in broad terms the directions of new policy options which may be considered.

The impact upon the individual firm

From the viewpoint of the small firm itself it is clear that the form of preferred public policy initiatives is that which reduces government involvement in the operation of the business. These initiatives include the reduction of the payment of corporate and personal tax rates, reduced restrictions on employment of labour, reduced planning controls and reduced compliance with regulations, government paper-work, and so on. From the viewpoint of society as a whole, these changes may not be judged to be necessarily desirable, although there may be opportunities for streamlining procedures which will benefit both small firms and society as a whole.

154

A second area is for public policy to rectify those cases in which small firms are currently at a disadvantage compared with large firms. Here, the provision of reduced interest or state-guarantee loans to small firms have been introduced in several European countries such as Ireland, The Netherlands, Italy and the UK. In most countries the schemes are relatively recent and it is not possible to determine their success, but where they have been well publicised and administered with a minimum of bureaucratic involvement, they appear to be popular with the firms. Their impact upon the economy has yet to be proven.

In many countries new initiatives designed to increase the rate at which new businesses are formed have been introduced. This sometimes involves specific encouragement directed towards unemployed individuals (for instance, in the UK, Ireland and France), but more often it reflects a belief that it is possible to encourage entrepreneurial spirit within an area. Whilst there has been considerable emphasis placed upon such initiatives, there is relatively little evidence that increases in new firm formation rates are attributable to public policy. Where increases have been experienced, they are equally likely to reflect increases in unemployment.

Our research on the small manufacturing firm in the United Kingdom indicated that policies which provide public subsidies to the small-firms sector are likely to be effective in increasing employment in relatively few firms. The UK subsidies are designed primarily to reduce the operating costs of small firms which, *ceteris paribus*, would be expected to lead to increased trading profits. Our research results suggested, however, that increases in *trading* profits were only weakly linked to increased employment within the firm. The latter was more strongly linked to increased *retained* profits, suggesting that whilst all small firms would benefit from a subsidy in the sense of having their profitability raised, relatively few would respond to this by increasing employment. In short, whilst the subsidy clearly benefits the owners of small companies, it may have significantly less effect upon employment (Storey *et al.*, 1987).

The impact on the labour market

Even if policies to promote small firms do result in an increase in labour employed in firm X the impact which this has upon the economy as a whole is less clear. Thus, for example if as a result of the assistance, firm X increases its share of the market at the expense of firm Y and the latter has to reduce employment, then total employment in the economy may not change, although it could be argued that this process is beneficial in the long term through the creation of a more competitive economy. Secondly, it has been shown that even if the jobs created in firm X do not result in any reduction in firm Y, they may not be filled by individuals who are unemployed. There is a real risk of labour market mismatch, with workers in small firms tending to be lower paid, female, part-time and not of prime age. The jobs being created are not therefore likely to be filled by workers from the larger-firms sector which is shedding labour. The clear need is for labour market intervention in the form of training, employment subsidies, and so on.

A NEW APPROACH

Our critique of public policy in EEC countries towards smaller businesses suggests the need for a major new direction. An analysis of employment trends in several European countries suggests that significant employment creation takes place in *relatively few small but fast-growing firms*. It also suggests that these fast-growing firms are most likely to export and be internationally competitive and that such firms could benefit from a targeting of public assistance towards them in order to overcome some of the barriers to growth which they experience.

The essential nub of the argument is that, out of every 100 new businesses which start, less than 50 will be in operation in ten years time. At that time the fastest-growing four will provide more than half the jobs in the cohort of firms. If we have a fixed sum of money available, £X, to spend on promoting the development of the group it can either be spent

(1) on attempting to help all 100 start-up businesses;

(2) on attempting to induce even more new businesses to start; or

(3) on helping only a few businesses.

There is no way that the fastest-growing four businesses (which will ultimately create half of the employment) can be identified at start-up. Equally it is almost impossible to identify at start-up the characteristics of firms which will fail early in life. Hence, there is a real risk that perhaps half of the public money will have, at best, a marginal effect since the businesses which it is used to support will fail within a short period of time. Since the £X is, by definition, a fixed sum, it means that if assistance is provided to all firms, then the firms which fail will receive assistance which might otherwise have been provided to firms which created jobs, and which might have grown more rapidly, had more assistance been available.

Strategy (2) (see above) suggests that assistance is provided to all those individuals wishing to start businesses because if there are more businesses started there will be more 'winners'. This will lead to the creation of an enterprise culture, exemplified by a willingness to work hard, take risks and reap the rewards of success. Here again the fallacy of this argument can be demonstrated by reference to the characteristics of the small-firm population. In the majority of markets which are entered by new firms there are already a number of firms which are trading, and in most cases the entry of one new firm will merely lead to the displacement of an existing firm. Furthermore, increasing the number of start-up business is normally achieved by lowering the entry barriers, but this can have undesirable consequences. If, for example, it is decided that the number of electrical businesses should be increased, this might be achieved by allowing 'untrained' workers to enter the industry. This, in turn, could lead to a reduction of the standards of the service or product supplied — a development which is presumably contrary to the other policy objectives.

The third and final strategy is to assist only a few businesses but the problem here is to identify which businesses to help and which ones not to help. As we noted earlier there is a strong *a priori* case for assisting those small businesses which grow rapidly — particularly in their early years. It is these businesses which alone create significant numbers of jobs and they have minimal displacement because they are more likely to be competing on international markets. There are, however, four arguments which are generally advanced against the selective policy:

(1) The 'winners' will succeed even without public policy.

(2) The 'winners' will be identified by the private sector and so the public sector does not need to provide assistance.

(3) Policy should promote small business start-ups since more 'start-ups' lead to more winners.

(4) It is inequitable and administratively clumsy to implement a selective policy.

Each of these arguments is analysed in detail in Storey and Johnson (1987) and so we will only here discuss them briefly. Firstly, since it is the fast-growth firms that experience major problems in locations where public assistance is available (premises, finance, information, etc.), it is clear that the 'winners' could be enabled to grow even faster if they were the major recipients of public policy.

The second argument, that assistance should be left exclusively to the private sector (banks, accountants, venture capitalists), fails to recognise that the private sector is interested in the financial performance of the firm (asset growth, profitability growth, etc.). The firms growing rapidly in these terms are not necessarily the same as those growing rapidly in terms of employment — which is presumably the focus of interest of the public sector. There is therefore no guarantee that in terms of employment, fast-growth firms would be the focus of attention of private sector financial institutions and might therefore benefit from public assistance.

The third argument, that resources would best be devoted to the promotion of 'start-ups', has been discussed above, but it is the fourth argument which is the most difficult to counter. Clearly, industrial policies in most countries frequently involve an element of discretion on the part of civil servants, with some firms being assisted and others excluded. Such policies are, however, not popular with firms since they generally involve considerable form-filling with no certainty that finance will be forthcoming. Civil servants also do not generally like such policies since they require the exercise of judgement on their part which can either be overridden by political masters or be proven to be incorrect over time.

Despite these reservations it is clear that the economic benefits of a selective policy are considerable and generally outweigh the lack of equity inherent in the strategy and the administrative problems which they pose. It is clear from this report that the small-firms policies which have been implemented in many member states have been aimed at assisting *all* small firms through a reduction in administrative burdens, provision of free advice, grants and subsidies, and so on. A second major strand of small-firms policies has been the encouragement of new firm formation, particularly amongst the unemployed. The evidence presented here suggests that such policies are likely to have high dead-weight and displacement effects, removing few people from the unemployment register. A selective approach to industrial and small-firms policy has recently been introduced in the Republic of Ireland. This involves the subsidisation of those firms which are likely to export a substantial proportion of their output, to displace imports, or to supply exporting firms. This is an increasing attempt to overcome the dead weight and displacement problems discussed above, and deserves to be closely examined.

REFERENCES

Armington, C. and M. Odle (1982) Small business — how many jobs? *Brookings Review*. Winter, pp. 14–17.

Bade, F. J. (1985) The economic importance of small and medium sized firms in the Federal Republic of Germany. In D. Keeble and E. Wever (eds), *New firms and regional economic development in Europe*. Croom Helm, London, pp. 256–74.

Binks, M. and A. Jennings (1986) Small firms as a source of economic rejuvenation. In J. Curran, J. Stanworth and D. Watkins (eds), *The survival of the small firm*, vol. 1, Gower, Aldershot, pp. 19–38.

Birch, D. L. (1979) *The job generation process*. MIT Program on Neighborhood and Regional Change, Cambridge, Mass.

———— and S. McCracken (1983) *The small business share of job creation: lessons learned from a longitudinal file*. MIT Program on Neighborhood and Regional Change, Cambridge, Mass.

Bollard, A. and D. Harper (1986) Employment generation and establishment size in New Zealand manufacturing. *International Small Business Journal*, *4*, 10–28.

Contini *et al.* (1984) *The determinants of productivity and employment in Italy's SME in manufacturing: a cross-section analysis 1973–1981*. Directorate General for Employment and Social Affairs (DGV), Commission of the European Communities.

De Jong, M. (1987) Netherlands. In D. J. Storey and S. Johnson (eds), *Employment creation in small and medium-sized enterprises in Europe*. EEC, DGV/1/A, Brussels.

Del Monte, A. (1987) Italy. In D. J. Storey and S. Johnson (eds), *Employment creation in small and medium-sized enterprises in Europe*. EEC, DGV/1/A, Brussels.

Donckles, R. and C. Bert (1987) Belgium and Luxembourg. In D. J.

Storey and S. Johnson (eds), *Employment creation in small and medium-sized enterprises in Europe*. EEC, DGV/1/A, Brussels.

Doyle, J. and C. C. Gallagher (1986) The size distribution, potential for growth and contribution to job generation of firms in the UK, 1982–84. *University of Newcastle upon Tyne, Department of Industrial Management, Research Report, 7.*

Gallagher, C. C. and J. Doyle (1986) Job generation research: a reply to Storey and Johnson. *International Small Business Journal, 4*(4), 47–54.

Gallagher, C. C. and H. Stewart (1984) Jobs and business life cycle in the UK. *Research Report, Department of Industrial Management, University of Newcastle upon Tyne, 2.*

Van Ginneken, C. C. P. M. (1985) *Who are working in SMEs? A comparison between the characteristics of the labour force in SMEs and in large enterprises.* Zoetermeer, EIM.

Guesnier, B. (1987) France. In D. J. Storey and S. Johnson (eds) *Employment creation in small and medium sized firms in Europe.* EEC, DGV/1/A, Brussels.

Hull, C. (1987) Federal Republic of Germany. In D. J. Storey and S. Johnson (eds) *Employment creation in small and medium sized firms in Europe.* EEC, DGV/1/A, Brussels.

Johnson, P. and A. Darnell (1976) New firm formation in Great Britain. *Working Paper, Department of Economics, University of Durham, 5.*

OECD (1985) Employment in small and large firms: where have the jobs come from? *OECD Employment Outlook,* 64–82.

Shutt, J. and R. Whittington (1984) Large firms and the rise of small units. Paper presented to Small Firm Conference, Nottingham.

Stockman *et al.* (1983) Konzentration und Reorganisation von Unternenneb und Betrieben. In M. Haller and W. Muller (eds) *Beschaftigungssystem im Gesellschaftlichen.* Wandel, Campus, Frankfurt/New York, pp. 97–177.

Storey, D. J. (1982) *Entrepreneurship and the new firm.* Croom Helm, London.

—— and S. Johnson (1987) *Job generation and labour market change.* MacMillan, London.

—— K. Keasey, R. Watson and P. Wynarczyk (1987) *The performance of small firms.* Croom Helm, London.

Part Two

Case Studies

9

The Role of Small and Medium-sized Enterprises in Regional Development: Conclusions Drawn from Recent Surveys

†Philippe Aydalot

INTRODUCTION

Research in the 1970s demonstrated the dominant role which large enterprises and multinational conglomerates played in the economies of industrialised countries. This form of economy was characterised by the Fordian organisation of work, polarisation of employment, the emergence of a two-fold market and the spatial division of labour distinguishing central from peripheral regions (Aydalot, 1976; Massey and Meegan, 1979). Since the end of the 1970s, social scientists have begun to emphasise rather different processes: the large increase in the number of small firms has been stressed, along with their apparent independence from large enterprises and their considerable contribution to employment. This was assumed to be linked to the development of services (the majority of which are provided by small and medium-sized enterprises), but these trends are just as apparent in manufacturing. The importance of SMEs (small and medium-sized enterprises) at different stages of technological innovation (especially newly emerging SMEs) has become apparent (Castells, 1984; Saxenian, 1985).

These developments can be seen as either a fundamental reversal of previous trends, or as the initial stages of a new cycle, with the formation of new enterprises, but which will ultimately lead to more classic methods of mass production (Markusen, 1985). In terms of space, the processes of concentration/polarisation mark the launching of initial stages in which the spatial dispersion processes clearly reveal the increasing role of large enterprises at the last stage of the cycle (Aydalot, 1986a).

This coincides with a sense of disillusion in the recent

literature on the role of small firms. Writers such as Castells (1984), Pottier (1986) and Swyngedouw (1986) have emphasised the importance of large corporations in the organisation of industry. Silicon Valley, for example, was once thought to reflect the growth of small firms, but nowadays is seen as an area dominated by large enterprises (Saxenian, 1985). This is partly the result of large enterprises undergoing recovery and partly the result of SMEs set up in the 1960s and 1970s which grew into large enterprises. Researchers have also emphasised the role of the state in promoting new sectors (through subsidies linked with the defence industry in particular — Markusen, 1984). Hence, there has been a reappraisal of the view which saw small firms as providing a new pattern of industrial development in which small enterprises flourished through ideas inherent in independent SMEs, human relations and local synergy. Instead, small enterprises are now viewed as unlikely to achieve a lasting independence and leave a strong mark on technological, economic and social development. This is not to deny the increase in the number of small enterprises or their growing contribution to employment, but instead it relates to their significance in comparison with that of large firms.

Since the early 1970s, a new division of functions between small and large enterprises has emerged. Increased unemployment imposes new responsibilities upon the firm in dealing with its workers, whilst market instability and rapid rates of technical change call for a greater flexibility in managing the labour force.

A key question is whether the employment growth in SMEs reflects the development of a new pattern of small-scale initiatives at a more local level, *or* whether it is merely a renewed form of large firm development whose activity will slow down through the ageing of the small firms. Furthermore, we also need to distinguish whether the latter falls into a different category from that of large enterprises, or if it is merely a product of it. In one sense SMEs closely belong to the local environment which gave birth to them and sustained their initial development, and yet in their relations with large firms and their dependence on them, the SMEs have to respond to external dynamics. The amount and the location of jobs created by small enterprises depend upon their relationships with large enterprises and on the degree of autonomy they can preserve in regard to large firms.

Before the second part of this chapter, which is devoted to the regional influence on the development of SMEs, it is important to

164

analyse in some detail the new linkages which are being formed between large and small enterprises. This analysis is difficult to conduct in statistical terms because of a shortage and ambiguity of data in France.

Information is often provided in terms of the establishment and not the firm (UNEDIC data); and moreover, statistics relating to enterprises do not, in general, describe their status — i.e. independent enterprises or subsidiaries of industrial conglomerates — thus making it difficult to draw satisfactory conclusions.

NEW TYPES OF RELATIONSHIPS BETWEEN LARGE AND SMALL ENTERPRISES

In the 1960s, there was a general feeling that the increased growth of large firms would push out small firms so as to eliminate them altogether. Instead, a new kind of relationship between small and large firms developed which reflected current demands. New waves of technical change had demanded greater flexibility from small firms as well as the need to develop new innovations. This means that large firms *make use* of small ones instead of *absorbing* them and disposing of them. The SME offers efficiency benefits which justify a new distribution of tasks between small and large firms. Large enterprises are willing to accept the redistribution of functions provided their dominance is now challenged. The following organisational changes have been introduced:

1. *Establishing subsidiary companies.* Here, the large enterprise still assumes financial and management risks, but benefits from a greater degree of flexibility in the management of social relations.

2. A posteriori *transformation into subsidiaries of small innovative enterprises.* When a dynamic highly innovative SME is constrained by its small size limiting its ability to undertake expensive R&D, a large enterprise can obtain a financial stake. This provides the large firm with an existing dynamic small firm in the chosen technology, so minimising initial technological risks.

It also makes optimum use of its innovation capital. These developments are commonplace in the southern suburbs of Paris, but sometimes mean that the large enterprise absorbs the research

165

activity of an SME, thereby reducing the latter's innovative potential. The SME is thus transformed into a specialised establishment (for example, la Sormel de Besançon, an innovatory enterprise in robotics which has become a subsidiary of Matra and which has lost part of its potential capacity in R&D).

This process is not unique to France. Whilst a poor-performing SME can continue for many years in the conventional sectors the same is not true for the high-tech sectors. Thus, from 36 enterprises set up producing semiconductors in the Silicon Valley between 1966 and 1979, only seven remained independent in 1979. If those enterprises have, as a whole, experienced high growth, they have not made high profits because of competitive pressures. This restricts the opportunities for undertaking new investment and so maintaining technological advantage. Thus, such firms are vulnerable to acquisition during periods of technological change when high levels of investment are called for. Generally speaking, this has resulted in a process of vertical integration in semiconductor production, so that users of electronic components acquired the producers of these components. Even enterprises which were very successful (which enabled them to expand) were taken over by industrial conglomerates belonging to another sector. Fairchild Camera was bought by Schlumberger, INTEL was to a large extent taken over by IBM, Siemens, Honeywell and Japanese enterprises took over the control of leading firms of the Silicon Valley. In contrast, in order to stay independent, producers of semiconductors have to become users of semiconductors themselves, through the production of items using semiconductors! This is illustrated in the case of Texas Instruments and National Semi Conductors, but it is a strategy which only large firms can exercise.

3. *Joint venture* is a similar solution to the previous one, but it is supposed to safeguard the independence of small firms more effectively.

4. *Subcontracting*. SMEs are becoming increasingly integrated into the production networks controlled by large enterprises. This is done either by classic subcontracting or by introducing a system in which exchanges of research and development knowledge are made. Thus, sometimes the SMEs acquire a new know-how which subsequently enables them to devise and produce original items while weakening or even avoiding any dependence in their

decisions on the large enterprise. However, the SMEs often maintain close links with the large enterprise so as not to lose the source of knowledge that the latter provides. In a large enterprise, subcontracting can take a variety of forms. Firstly, there is access to a source of new ideas (when the SME has a R&D laboratory). A second form is the ability to remove itself from a sector of business which it considers external to the main focus of the business. Thomson in Mayenne has, for about a dozen years, maintained the policy of a systematic development in subcontracting. The Thomson plant at Laval set up by LMT at the beginning of the 1960s has been gradually transformed into an 'electronic centre' with one-third of the workforce being engineers and technicians, whereas production has been transferred to SMEs located in small towns a few kilometres away (cf. Figure 9.1). In this way a spatial division of labour on a French department scale took place in Mayenne.

5. *Venture capital* is developing rapidly in France. Only two or three years ago, it was unusual, but now it is becoming increasingly common. There are two identifiable types of venture capital. Firstly, nationally available venture capital (mainly in Paris, but also in Lyon) is normally controlled by large enterprises, enabling them to monitor the development of SMEs to ensure that should the need arise, they can take financial control. Secondly, there is local venture capital, which has only developed on a very modest scale but provides support for the SME and which is designed to promote local economic development.

Sometimes, enterprises choose to take a minor role in innovatory SMEs such as Hewlett Packard in Grenoble, but more frequently they acquire partial ownership through the provision of venture capital. Examples of this in France are Elf Aquitaine and Olivetti. Large firms can become shareholders in venture capital companies, or create their own subsidiaries to act as venture capitalists. Even a limited participation enables the large firm to detect worthwhile enterprises.

The *conversion company* is a variant on the venture capital company. Since the beginning of the 1980s, large enterprises in France have set up so-called conversion companies, whose objective is to take part in enterprises or provide financial aid to new firms in an area where they are located or which they are about to leave. However, objectives can differ. In some cases establishing such a company is generally viewed as a social gesture, the intention of which is to minimise tension with the trade unions in an area in

Figure 9.1: The LMT/Thomson plant of Laval and its subcontractors

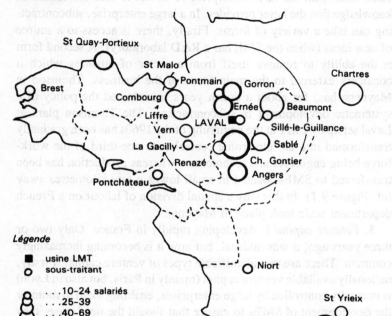

Légende

■ usine LMT
○ sous-traitant

○...10–24 salariés
○...25–39
○...40–69
○...70–94
○...100–129
○...130–169

100 km

0   50   100   150 km

Source: enquête LMT

which the company is closing a plant. Alternatively, the conversion company may be used to take a share in new enterprises as a purely commercial decision. Rhône-Poulenc, for example, has established a network of companies to reinforce the milieu of industrial enterprises of small and medium size which the conglomerate badly requires and Saint-Gobain Développement has entered into agreement with 350 enterprises. Sometimes several conglomerates are associated into one of those companies (Technova is a subsidiary which Rhône-Poulenc, Elf and Pechiney share).

6. *Co-ordination of research.* It is common practice among

industrial conglomerates to open their laboratories to SMEs or to collaborate in university research programmes. In Grenoble University laboratories, Bull provided a team of scientists; Saint-Gobain, Elf and Rhône-Poulenc have subsidiaries working on R&D with SMEs in various regions. The conglomerate's objective is to monitor the new products developed by SMEs. Bosch has established a research centre in Saint Etienne to be better informed of the needs of small firms with regard to special machinery (numerically controlled) as well as to share the experience of local enterprises.

7. *Activities within local associations.* Large firms often play a very active role in local business groups. By so doing this can benefit smaller firms in providing them with access to technical knowledge and to financing. To this end, large firms sometimes make use of their conversion companies, thus enabling them to monitor local technological developments.

8. *Spin-off from large enterprises.* Enterprises established by engineers or scientists originating from a large enterprise are becoming increasingly common. Generally, these spin-offs are welcomed by the large enterprise which perceives opportunities for technical collaboration or even financial participation.

The above developments do not have a single objective. Some reflect the fact that large enterprises wish to be kept informed about the development of technology, products, markets and possibilities offered by small enterprises. However, once large enterprise realise the benefits of collaboration with a small enterprise, they are likely to want to have some measure of control over the operation of the SME. Intervention may therefore be in two stages, the first resulting from the need of the large firm to be informed, the second from a desire to intervene or control.

A spectrum can thus be established characterising SMEs according to the degree of their independence from large enterprises.

Independent SME ⎰ wholly independent
⎱ supervised
⎱ linked with a large
⎱ enterprise (subcontracting)

Originally independent SME

$\left\{\begin{array}{l}\text{partial (up to 20 per cent}\\ \text{of the capital held}\\ \text{by a large company)}\\ \text{integrated (majority control}\\ \text{to total control)}\end{array}\right.$

— Joint venture
— Subsidiary of a large enterprise

Using these varied strategies, the large enterprise is able to facilitate the development of SMEs leading to increased employment in the small-firms sector. In terms of employment, the synergy between small and large firms can be very complex: for example, a large firm may be established in an area only because the network of small firms has created a reservoir of qualified employment of which the large firm takes advantage. Thus, in this situation, job creation by large firms results from the dynamism of small ones. Yet in the long run, the large firm may, through its demand for SME products, stimulate additional employment in those in the SMEs, leading to a virtuous upward spiral.

On the other hand, the large firm may reduce work subcontracted to small local firms, particularly when demand falls and the large firm wants to maintain employment amongst its own staff. Even so there are contrasting examples in which a large firm, in an effort to reduce expenses, transfers activities previously undertaken 'in-house', as in the case of Thomson in Laval. Hence, the way in which employment develops in SMEs cannot be clearly identified in advance.

All this suggests that the role of large enterprises has not so much diminished in size but rather that the nature of these activities is being redefined. New methods are being employed to restore some measure of the technological hegemony that large firms lost during the 1970s. SMEs are also following new patterns and these correspond with the primary stages in the development of new technologies. Ann Markusen notes the return to dominance by large enterprises in many new sectors after a period in which small firms made most of the running (Markusen, 1985). In robotics, for example, two independent firms which dominated the sector were linked together by five giant enterprises from other sectors (General Electric, IBM, Westinghouse, United Tech and Bendix); in photovoltaics, three of the five

170

largest enterprises are subsidiaries of petroleum firms. It is often the case that pioneering enterprises are quickly acquired by large, often foreign, firms once the sector becomes established and profitable.

The variety of ways in which the SMEs and large enterprises interact have been subject to change over time. Over the past century industrial complexes have gradually been developed. At the same time, *inter-industry relationships* have also been created so that an industrial milieu has been generated by combining inter-enterprise relationships, the most typical example of which is subcontracting. Since new, science-based firms began to appear in the last decade or so, another kind of relationship has been established, namely one in which technical exchanges opened up a new collection of *personal relationships*; exchanges now take place between firms, universities and large public research centres. Contracts with joint technical research centres, technical co-operation between enterprises and, above all, direct relations between engineers and scientists through informal contacts are all commonplace. Some of the most effective networks are often established between scientists and engineers who leave one firm and are subsequently employed in a different one.

Another type of local economic relationship should be mentioned. Here the concern amongst local interest groups about the future of an area has often led to the formation of loose organisations and groupings to facilitate economic progress. Networks have been built, associations created, and training conducted by local agencies which are branches of national institutions whose aim is the promotion of new technology. Even universities have improved their links with local industry. Interestingly, whereas personal contacts seem to play an increasing role in spreading innovations, industrial links, and classic subcontracting in particular, seem to be of declining importance. A detailed analysis of the innovation process in the Paris region (Decoster and Tabaries, 1986) has revealed that the formation of high-tech firms in the southern suburb constituted less of a technopolis than an industrial complex geared towards scientific and technical knowledge, even though the internal organisation of firms is often of a conventional hierarchical nature.

This suggests that there is a development in the nature of relations between enterprises according to the steps in the technological cycle. Relations between people are dominant in the initial stage, when knowledge is an essential factor, for these relations can be better adapted as a means of exchange and expansion of knowledge, whereas inter-industry relations dominate in the mature stage of development when the role of the small enterprise is based on its ability to provide low-cost production. This can be summarised as follows:

Movement between:	Stage of the cycle:	Function of SMEs:
predominant human relations	initial stage	technological capacity, differentiation of products
predominant inter-industry relations	maturity stage	capacity for low-cost production

This pattern is admittedly oversimplified, and empirical studies would have to be conducted in order to assess its validity fully. Nevertheless, it does appear to be a valid model. Changes in inter-enterprise relations are also linked to the character of the surrounding environment and with the different challenges it has to face. Individualistic forms of relationship appear to be preferred in new industrial areas, whereas collective action appears more common in areas which had experienced severe decline in their staple industries. The process by which the enterprise is redefining its inter-industry relations can be seen most clearly in areas where enterprises have survived a decline in demand for their product and are readapting.

Whilst some areas have been able to innovate by promoting mechanisms of knowledge conveyance, i.e. based on exchanges of information or on exchanges of technical processes, the traditional way of exchanging knowledge linked to inter-industry exchanges also remains important. The industrial complex probably remains the most common form of organising an industrial milieu, but here it is useful to distinguish between those formed by a single branch of high technology where direct exchanges are favoured, and zones in which innovation occurs as a direct result of inter-industrial exchanges (the southern suburb of Paris).

It is not enough to compile a list of the reasons for the interdependence of small firms upon large enterprises. Instead, the relationships have to be seen as part of the dynamics of new sector development. In every sector, the development of SMEs depends on a variety of factors, which vary in importance over a period of time. These include:

(a) The rhythm of *technical progress*.
(b) The level of *entry barriers* to a sector (if the cost is low, small enterprises will dominate the sector; if high, a monopoly is given to large enterprises).
(c) The *niches* available to small enterprises. If potential markets exist and can be developed simply by adapting existing products or by making innovations, small enterprises may be set up. If, however, the market is for a homogeneous product which can be mass-produced, big firms are likely to dominate.
(d) *State intervention* is always important in new sectors. In the USA, for example, the enormous market supported by national defence expenditure ensures the viability of many specialised enterprises. In France, the role of the state has been crucial to the development of the telecommunications industry as well as in defence-associated sectors (aviation, computing, missiles, new equipment). State procurement policies in France, however, seem to have favoured large enterprises. Swyngedouw (1986), for instance, shows that in France over 75 per cent of research aid public funds were given to giant enterprises, whereas small firms receive 5 per cent or less of public allowances.

Whilst levels of industrial concentration do vary from country to country, variations in the relative importance of small firms may occur not because of the characteristics of the country concerned but because the countries are at a different stage in the long-term cycle of innovation. If, for example, a new sector is developed in the USA and progressed in Europe, then it is likely that small firms will only be important at the start-up stage. Hence, it is not surprising that the semiconductor industry was initially developed by small firms in the USA, but when it ultimately began in Europe, many of these small firms had become large.

Finally, the definition of concentration depends to a large extent, on the level of sectoral disaggregation. A large number of enterprises in a given sector does not necessarily mean that small

Table 9.1: The size of firms in the French high-technology sector

	(1)	(2)	(3)	(4)	(5)	(6)	(7)
Firms, number 1976	4,531	156	32	730	147	37	891
Firms, number 1984	6,978	512	34	1,402	158	56	1,284
Increase	2,447	356	2	672	11	19	393
Employment 1984 (000)	484	52·9	17·5	83·25	53·4	14·9	65·5
Increase 1976-84 (000)	27·3	15·9	5·2	12·2	-6·9	6·1	-19·85
Average size firm 1976	100·8	237	384	97	410	237	96
Average size firm 1984	69·4	103	514	59·4	338	267	51

Key:

(1) All 25 advanced-technology sectors (NAP 600)
(2) Computers
(3) Missiles
(4) Electronic office equipment
(5) Aviation
(6) Semiconductors
(7) Telecommunication equipment

Source: Swyngedouw (1986), from INSEE

firms are predominant, nor is it equivalent to the theoretical notion of perfect competition since a greater degree of disaggregation may make some 'industries' appear more concentrated.

Data on employment and size changes in the advanced-technology sectors in France illustrate the point. Swyngedouw (ibid.) shows that in the majority of new-technology sectors (i.e. computing, semiconductors, aviation, electronic office equipment) the proportion of sales in the four largest enterprises often exceeds 90 per cent. Table 9.1 shows a tendency for the average size of enterprise to decline in five out of the seven sectors shown. Even so these sectors still have a size well above the average in the manufacturing industry.

We can then reinterpret the history of the capitalist mode of production through the changes in functions undertaken by small and large enterprises. Small firms decline in relative importance in maturity periods but increase during transition periods; and in terms of their function, there are parallel changes: subcontracting by large firms would seem to be dominant during stages of maturity whereas specialised subcontracting and technological niches would seem to characterise small firms in transition periods.

Following these developments there is also a changing pattern of the division of labour between SMEs and large enterprises. During maturity periods, there is a clear hierarchy of specialisation between the productive operations of SMEs and rather more strategic activities of large enterprises (even if the latter maintains a considerable level of routine activities). In transition periods, the division of tasks follows a much less hierarchical pattern in so far as functions and qualifications are concerned (although the managing role of large enterprises still continues).

Clearly, not all SMEs at all times correspond to the roles described. Nevertheless, it is clear that their role does vary markedly from one market to another and from one time period to another. Sometimes, it is their capacity for low-cost production which is the basis of their development; sometimes it is their capacity for radical, technological innovation, or their ability to find new technological niches, to invent products or services. Sometimes their flexibility proves to be indispensable, and on other occasions their role is based on an ability to survive in declining low-profit sectors. Some of these functions correspond to the beginning of the technology cycle, others to stages of maturity or decline. Over time new functions are evolved to reflect the needs of the large firm.

These changes in the role played by small firms have clear spatial impacts because of the different locations of small and large enterprises, and we propose to investigate these implications in the next section.

REGIONAL CAPACITY TO PROMOTE JOB CREATION BY SMEs

Industrial milieu is a function of location, and related to the industrial structure of an area. Nowadays, the ability of SMEs to create jobs depends on their *role in relation to larger firms* as well as on *their belonging to a region*. Hence, although the number of SMEs depends on local features (on the industrial milieu and the aptitude to produce industrial inventions), by contrast the development of forms of firm development, once the firms are established, depends upon large firms which are most frequently owned outside the local industrial milieu.

At a regional level, the structure of the local milieu is seen as a function of firm size (and sometimes establishment size) and this is clearly related to the capacity of a region to increase employment and to create new enterprises. Clearly, areas relatively dominated by small enterprises experience faster development and have a high 'birth rate' of new enterprises. In contrast, regions whose industrial structure is based upon large enterprises are undergoing sluggish employment growth and a lower rate of new enterprise formation. This is true of all enterprises as well as when only single sectors are examined. It follows that, for example, the more an area has a high proportion of small enterprises, the more its enterprises, including the largest ones, develop in a favourable manner. This is demonstrated in the calculations below, which take the data of UNEDIC for industry in 22 French regions for the period between 1 January 1979 and 1 January 1982.

For each region the rate of change in the labour force (L_r) between 1979 and 1982 was calculated. A measure of relative importance of small enterprises (S_r) was calculated as the percentage of total employment in firms with less than 50 employees divided by the percentage of employment in firms with more than 500 employees for each region. The correlation coefficient of L_r and S_r was estimated to be + 0·6.

It appears that a low average size of establishments in a region is associated with a better performance of the entire industrial labour force of that region. Table 9.2 *amplifies* this relationship

Table 9.2: Relations between the part of one category of establishment size in terms of regional employment, and the increase in regional employment, 1977–81

% of regional employment in establishments	Tertiary sector	Business services	Household services
1–9	0·49	0·61	0·39
10–19	0·52	0·38	0·71
1–19	0·50	0·60	0·55
1–49	0·51	0·61	0·56
50–99	−0·21	−0·40	−0·37
100–499	−0·65	−0·37	−0·31
500+	−0·32	−0·71	−0·33

The results should be read in the following manner: the linear correlation coefficient between the regional file (22 regions) percentage of tertiary employment in establishments employing 1 to 9 salaried employees and the rates of increase in the total tertiary sector employment (1977–81) in the regions is 0·49

showing that in regions with a relatively large number of small establishments, the growth of the latter is faster than the national average.

Analysts seem to agree that development occurs as if the sons of industrialists created new enterprises. O'Farrell (1986) showed that in Ireland the son of a freelance worker has a three-fold greater likelihood of establishing a firm than the son of a salaried employee. This tendency is even stronger in Denmark (Illeris, 1986). In France, it has been shown that the establishment of enterprises was closely related to the number of existing enterprises (Aydalot, 1986b). This means that regions with most small enterprises are dynamic in this respect, whereas regions with large enterprises, even if they are highly industrial in character, are much less dynamic. Thus, in the north of France, the rate of firm creation in the secondary sector is 2.5 times lower than the rate in Languedoc-Roussillon. This is because enterprises in the north employ relatively more workers than those in Languedoc: they are, on average, four times larger. The more enterprises that there are, the greater will be the number of newly established ones. The presence of existing enterprises engenders a climate which is favourable for enterprise creation. Every enterprise carries with it a certain potential for initiative, and constitutes a form of 'nursery' for new enterprises.

177

However, the industrial sector is a necessary but not a sufficient condition for the establishment of firms. In order that this potential leads to real creations, the environment has to provide favourable conditions which will lead to both high formation rates and to successful firms once they are formed. An area may be effective in stimulating the reaction of many innovatory SMEs but may not be capable of facilitating their development and growth. Thus, for example, the new industrialising area of Aix-en-Provence lacks industrial tradition and experience. Consequently, many enterprises, even ones which are extremely innovative, are managed by inexperienced entrepreneurs and have to face difficult problems with only limited support. As a result, these enterprises are isolated, and they experience particular difficulties in developing external markets and in developing links with industrial conglomerates. On the other hand regions of older industrialisation, even if they are less likely to produce new enterprises, are able to ensure a smoother development of the firms which are established.

CONCLUSION

This chapter has shown that there has been an indirect strengthening of the role of large enterprises hidden behind an apparent development of small ones. We have also observed the relationship between employment creation and the increasing number of enterprises at the regional level.

To understand these developments it is necessary to recall the strategy of large enterprises. For some decades after the war, there was a development of the Fordian system of production based upon a tendency to make labour homogeneous, which led to a differentiation of national territory according to the area's capacity to supply non-qualified labour. The result was a clear-cut division between the headquarters, where the management and economic buoyancy were found, and an outlying zone undertaking routine production. Nowadays, we are faced with a more complex division of space. Large enterprises need to obtain dynamism, markets, a great variety of technological know-how, and so for them the local environment is no longer just a reservoir of cheap unskilled manpower. Instead, it becomes once again an industrial milieu, supplying elements which cannot be obtained elsewhere and as a result, becomes a reservoir of enterprise. Thus, industrial conglomerates have an interest in preserving local industrial networks because they are increasingly dependent upon them.

The status of new enterprises is at stake. They are moulded by their environment, even if they often become subsidiaries of large multispatial industrial conglomerates. The latter accept that to maximise the potential contribution of the subsidiary it is necessary to maintain contact with the local milieu. Hence, an ambiguous process develops, one in which elements of *differentiation of space* and elements of *spatial homogenisation can be seen*.

The spatial division of labour has often been seen as the result of the specialisation of functions and activities within the large enterprises. This division might be expected to be reduced at a time when large enterprises were declining compared with small ones. Matters become more complex, however, when the location of new SMEs is considered, together with their links with the conglomerates. A pattern therefore appears giving a new focus to the spatial division of labour as well as reflecting the changes over time according to the development of respective roles of small and large enterprises.

It is difficult to supply clear answers to the questions of the regional job potential of SMEs in industry and services. Nevertheless, if the structure of regions determines the nature and sectoral distribution of employment, the number of jobs which will be created and their location depend on links between the local environment and national and international factors. In this relationship between local dynamics and external dynamics, large enterprises always play a decisive role, even if it is greatly transformed from that of the 1960s.

REFERENCES

Aydalot, P. (1976) *Dynamique spatiale et développement inégal.* Economica, Paris.
——— (1984) The reversal of spatial trends in French industry since 1974. In J. Lambooy (ed.) *New spatial dynamics and economic crisis.* Finnpublishers, Helsinki, pp. 41–62.
——— (1986a) Les technologies nouvelles at les formes actuelles de la division spatiale du travail. *Dossiers du CSE, 47.* Paris.
——— (1986b) The location of new firm creation, the French case. In D. Keeble and E. Wever (eds), *New firms and regional development in Europe.* Croom Helm, London, pp. 105–23.

Castells, M. (1984) Toward the informational city? High technology, economic change and spatial structure. *Working Paper, IRUD, Berkeley.*

Decoster, E. and M. Tabaries (1986) L'innovation dans un pole scientifique et technologique, le cas de la Cité Scientifique de Paris Sud. In P. Aydalot (ed.), *Milieux innovateurs en Europe.* GREMI, Paris, pp. 79–100.

Gordon, R. and L. Kimball (1986) Industrial structure and the changing global dynamics of location in high technology industry. *Silicon Valley Research Group, Santa Cruz, Working Paper 3.*

Illeris, S. (1986) New firm creation in Denmark, the importance of the cultural background. In D. Keeble and E. Wever (eds) *New firms and regional development in Europe.* Croom Helm, London, pp. 141–50.

Markusen, A. (1984) Defence spending and the geography of high tech industries. *Working Paper, IRUD, Berkeley.*

—— (1985) *Profits cycles, oligopoly and regional development.* MIT Press, Cambridge.

Massey, D. and R. Meegan, (1979) The geography of industrial reorganisation. *Progress in Planning, 10.* Pergamon.

O'Farrell, P. (1986) The nature of new firms in Ireland, empirical evidence and policy implications. In D. Keeble and E. Wever (eds) *New firms and regional development in Europe.* Croom Helm, London, pp. 151–83.

Perrat, J. (1986) Firmes multinationales et nouveau rapport a l'environnement spatio-économique. *Colloque 'L'insertion des PME innovatrices dans leur environement local'* (Aix en Provence), July.

Pottier, C. (1986) Innovation locale et strategies des groupes. In ASRDLF and CSE, *Technologies nouvelles et développement régional.* GREMI, Paris, pp. 323–3.

Saxenian, A. (1985) Silicon Valley and Route 128, regional prototypes or historical exceptions? In M. Castells (ed.), *High technology, space and society.* Sage, pp. 81–105.

Swyngedouw, E. (1986) The regional pattern and dynamics of high technology production in France. In ASRDLF and CSE, *Technologies nouvelles et développement régional.* GREMI, Paris, pp. 441–59.

10

The Role of Small and Medium-sized Manufacturing Plants in Regional Employment — A Swedish Perspective

Charlie Karlsson

INTRODUCTION

Many regions in the industrialised West with old industrial traditions are today the victims of structural changes in the world economy. These regions, often specialising in iron and steel, shipbuilding, textiles, etc. today face high unemployment rates. In earlier periods some of the unemployment problems in the peripheral regions resulting from structural change could be relieved by expanding industrial sectors in more prosperous regions, by locating new manufacturing plants in these regions and by labour moving to the more central expanding regions. For a number of years these mechanisms do not seem to have worked as efficiently as earlier during the 1950s and 1960s. In this situation politicians and planners on both the central and the regional level have turned to the small and medium-sized firms as the new 'life-preservers' for depressed regions.

These hopes for a new panacea have been supported by the remarkable conclusions reported by Birch (1979). In a study covering manufacturing and other sectors including services, he found that no less than two-thirds of all new jobs in the US were generated by small firms (i.e. those with 20 or fewer employees). Very young independent enterprises formed the lion's share of these small firms. His policy recommendations are equally dramatic. Do not count on, or address major resources towards, large corporations, he argues. Instead, seek out the small dynamic firm, which is the major replacer of lost jobs, and back it. Not surprisingly, many politicians and planners have seen Birch's findings as evidence of the correctness of their new approach.

Birch's results have, however, been questioned. With an

approach similar to Birch, Fothergill and Gudgin (1979) have drawn conclusions which are very different. They find that in Britain small and new firms are important, but they are not the overwhelming source of new jobs which Birch suggests.

The aim of this chapter is to give some indication of the role of small and medium-sized firms for regional employment in Sweden. Due to lack of data we limit ourselves to manufacturing plants as the basic unit of observation. Only official statistical data are used in the analysis. National data and data from one Swedish region — Värmland — are used in the analysis. The county of Värmland has for many years been the region with the second highest unemployment rate in Sweden. Pulp and paper, wood, iron and steel, and engineering industries have been and still are important sources of employment within manufacturing in Värmland.

The chapter is organised in the following way: the next section gives an overview of changes in the employment structure at a sectoral level in Sweden and Värmland. We then look more closely at total employment in the manufacturing sector in Sweden and Värmland, while in the fourth section we give a cross-sectional view of how the size structure of the manufacturing sector varies between different regions in Sweden. The next section is then devoted to an analysis of changes in the employment structure of the manufacturing sector over time in Sweden and in Värmland. Changes in total employment in different size categories are then described, while the penultimate section illustrates the growth potential of plants in different size categories in Värmland. The chapter closes with conclusions and policy recommendations.

THE CHANGING EMPLOYMENT STRUCTURE

In this section we will look at the changes in the employment structure in Sweden and in Värmland to provide a background for our later discussion about the role of small and medium-sized manufacturing plants in regional employment. In Table 10.1 we illustrate changes in the employment structure in Sweden (Table 10.1A) and in Värmland (Table 10.1B) for the four industrial sectors during the period 1950–80 according to population census. The four industrial sectors are:

Table 10.1: Relative employment shares (f) for different sectors during the period 1950–80 (%)

Sector	1950	1960	1965	1970	1975	1980
			Year			
A. Sweden						
(1) Primary	20·8	14·5	12·3	8·7	7·0	5·9
(2) Manufacturing	31·1	32·4	30·3	29·2	28·6	25·0
(3) Utilities, construction, transport, etc	16·8	17·4	17·5	17·8	15·9	15·3
(4) Commerce, public and private services	31·3	35·7	39·8	44·4	48·6	53·8
Total	100·0	100·0	100·0	100·0	100·0	100·0
B. Värmland						
(1) Primary	30·7	21·8	18·2	11·9	9·1	7·6
(2) Manufacturing	29·3	35·4	34·0	33·9	33·9	29·7
(3) Utilities, construction, transport, etc	16·2	17·5	16·5	17·1	15·7	14·5
(4) Commerce, public and private services	23·9	25·3	31·3	37·1	41·4	48·1
Total	100·0	100·0	100·0	100·0	100·0	100·0

Source: Census data, Swedish Yearbook of Statistics 1955, 1960, 1965, 1970, 1975, 1980 and 1985.
Note: Components may not sum to 100.0 due to rounding errors.

(1) the primary sector (agriculture, forestry, mining, quarrying, etc.);
(2) the manufacturing sector;
(3) the electricity, gas and water services, construction, transport, storage, communication, etc.; and
(4) commerce, and private and public services.

To analyse the structural changes that have taken place during the actual period we have constructed a special diagram (see Figure 10.1). On the y-axis we measure $f/(1-f)$, i.e. the relative employment share (f) divided by its complement ($1-f$). Studying the diagram we observe:

(a) that commerce, and private and public services have increased their employment shares rapidly;
(b) that utilities, construction and transportation show remarkably constant employment shares;

Figure 10.1: Changes in the employment structure in Sweden and Värmland, 1950–80

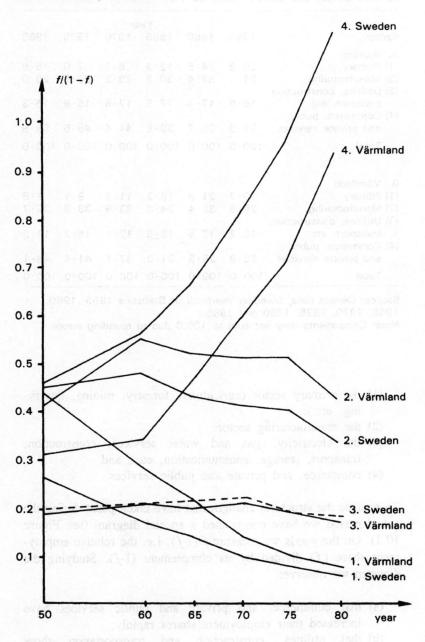

Source: See Table 10.1

Table 10.2: Total employment in manufacturing (in thousands)

	1950	1960	1965	1970	1975	1980
The whole country	967	1,050	1,046	995	1,013	937
Index	100	109	108	103	105	97
Värmland	36	42	41	39	39	36
Index	100	117	114	108	108	100

Source: See Table 10.1

(c) that the primary sector has constantly been losing employment shares; and

(d) that the manufacturing sector increased its employment share up to 1960 but shows a decreasing trend thereafter.

It may also be observed that the employment structure in Värmland follows the national structure but that there is a lag of at least five years, except for sector 3.

As a complement to the structural picture we also present data for total employment in manufacturing in Sweden and in Värmland during the period 1950–80 (see Table 10.2). The index number indicates that manufacturing employment has fluctuated more in Värmland than in the country as a whole during the period. We note further that manufacturing employment in Värmland in 1980 was the same as in 1950, while for the country as a whole there was a small decrease of 3 per cent.

THE MANUFACTURING SECTOR

It is now time to look more closely at the manufacturing sector. We leave the census data and turn to the official manufacturing statistics. In these statistics data for all plants with more than four employees are published. This means that these data can be expected to differ somewhat from the census data.

In Table 10.3 we present data for manufacturing employment in Sweden and Värmland for the period 1967–84. Data are also given for the total number of manufacturing plants and average plant size. It should be noted how employment fluctuates during the business cycles and that the period ends with a level of manufacturing employment both in Sweden and in Värmland that

Table 10.3: Total employment in manufacturing (in thousands), total number of plants and average plant size in Sweden and Värmland, 1967–84

	1967	1968	1969	1970	1971	1972	1973	1974	1975	1976	1977	1978	1979	1980	1981	1982	1983	1984
1. Total employment in manufacturing (in thousands)																		
Sweden	882	867	887	907	891	877	892	915	925	924	891	861	859	853	825	788	762	786
Index	100	98	101	103	101	99	101	104	105	105	101	98	97	97	94	89	86	87
Värmland	33	32	34	34	34	34	35	36	36	37	36	34	34	33	32	30	29	29
Index	100	98	101	104	103	102	104	108	110	111	107	103	100	100	96	90	87	87
2. Total number of plants																		
Sweden	13,965	13,864	13,583	13,352	13,038	12,709	12,419	12,261	12,216	11,879	11,383	10,794	10,393	10,152	9,281	9,423	9,220	9,223
Index	100	99	97	96	93	91	89	88	87	85	82	77	74	73	70	67	66	66
Värmland	405	397	388	391	389	381	383	379	376	374	365	352	335	321	307	290	283	284
Index	100	98	96	97	96	94	95	94	93	92	90	87	83	79	76	72	70	70
3. Average plant size																		
Sweden	63	63	65	68	68	69	72	75	76	78	78	80	83	84	84	84	83	83
Index	100	100	103	108	108	110	114	119	121	124	124	127	132	133	133	133	132	132
Värmland	82	82	87	88	88	89	90	94	96	98	97	97	102	103	103	103	102	101
Index	100	100	106	107	107	109	110	115	117	120	118	118	124	126	126	126	124	123

Source: Official manufacturing statistics

Figure 10.2: Total employment in manufacturing (index)

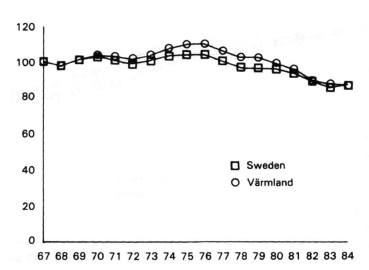

is 13 per cent lower than in the first year — the lowest figures during the whole period! In fact, Figure 10.2 shows that manufacturing employment both in the whole of Sweden and in Värmland reaches its peak in 1975–6 and then decreases continuously until 1984, with the minor exception being that for Sweden as a whole, there is a small increase in manufacturing employment between 1983 and 1984.

It can also be seen that the number of manufacturing plants declines more or less constantly during the period (see Figure 10.3). In Sweden as a whole the number of manufacturing plants in 1984 is 34 per cent lower than in 1967, and for Värmland the figure is 30 per cent. This has resulted, as is illustrated in Figure 10.4, in an increase in the average plant size in both Sweden as a whole and Värmland. For the country as a whole the average plant size has increased from 63 to 83 employees, while in Värmland it has increased from 82 to 101. It is to be observed, however, that the increase in average plant size stopped in 1980 and that after 1982 there has been a slight decrease in average plant size in both Sweden as a whole and in Värmland.

The increase in average plant size indicates that it might be instructive to look further at what has happened with plants in different size categories.

Figure 10.3: Total number of manufacturing plants (index)

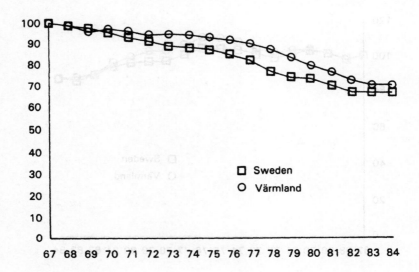

Figure 10.4: Average plant size in employment terms (index)

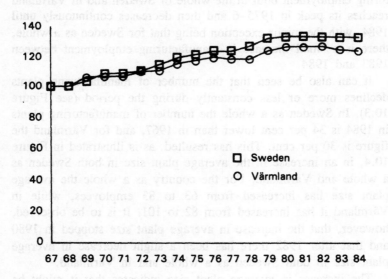

is 15 per cent lower than in the first year — the lowest figure during employment both in the whole of Sweden and in Värmland reaches its peak in 1975-6 and then decreases continuously until 1984, with the exception being that for Sweden as a whole, there is a slight increase in manufacturing employment between 1982 and 1984.

It can also be seen that the number of manufacturing plants declines more or less continually during the period (see figure 10.3). In Sweden as a whole the number of manufacturing units in 1984 is 34 per cent lower than in 1967, and for Värmland the figure is 30 per cent. This has resulted, as is illustrated in figure 10.4, in an increase in the average plant size in both Sweden as a whole and Värmland. For the country as a whole, the average plant size has increased from 63 to 83 employees, while in Värmland it has increased from 82 to 101. It is to be noted, however, that the increase in average plant size stopped in 1980 and that there have since been a slight decrease in average plant size in Värmland, and a levelling off in Sweden.

The increase in average plant size indicate that it might be instructive to look further at what has happened with plants in different size categories.

THE SIZE STRUCTURE OF THE MANUFACTURING SECTOR

The size structure of the manufacturing sector varies between different counties in Sweden. Table 10.4 shows the share of plants with up to 19 employees in 1981, the share of the total manufacturing employment in these plants and the average plant size measured in number of employees in different counties in Sweden.

The share of plants with up to 19 employees varies between 66 and 79 per cent, with a national share of 73 per cent. The county of Värmland has a share of 67 per cent. Only one country has a lower share, while three other counties have the same share.

Table 10.4: The size structure of the manufacturing section in 1981 (including mining and quarrying)

Country	A	B	C
Stockholm	79	16	82
Uppsala	69	13	92
Södermanland	66	13	97
Östergötland	67	11	109
Jönköping	78	28	51
Kronoberg	73	24	57
Kalmar	71	18	76
Gotland	71	22	60
Blekinge	74	10	128
Kristianstad	75	23	61
Malmöhus	73	17	82
Halland	74	22	62
Göteborg o Bohus	77	13	109
Älvsborg	75	20	69
Skaraborg	72	19	71
Värmland	67	13	101
Örebro	67	11	99
Västmanland	80	9	137
Kopparberg	77	18	86
Gävleborg	67	11	116
Västernorrland	69	13	95
Jämtland	75	30	46
Västerbotten	69	19	72
Norrbotten	72	13	102
Sweden as a whole	73	16	83

Notes: A. Share of total number of plants with up to 19 employees (per cent).
B. Share of total number of employees employed in plans with up to 19 employees (per cent).
C. Average plant size measured in number of employees.
Source: SOU, 1984:74, p. 128

The share of total manufacturing employment in these small plants varies between 9 and 28 per cent, with a national share of 16 per cent. For the county of Värmland this share is 13 per cent. Only five counties have a lower share, while four other counties have the same share.

The column for average plant size shows a picture that fits well with the pattern presented above. The average plant size varies between 51 and 137 employees, with a national average of 83 employees. For the country of Värmland the average plant size is 101 employees and only in six counties is the average plant size greater.

The data given in Table 10.4 clearly indicate that the importance of small plants for regional employment in manufacturing varies a great deal between different regions in Sweden. We now leave this cross-sectional view for an analysis of how the size structure in the manufacturing sector has changed over time. This will be the subject of the next section.

CHANGES IN THE EMPLOYMENT SIZE STRUCTURE OF THE MANUFACTURING SECTOR OVER TIME

In this section we look at how the distribution of employment in manufacturing between plants in different size categories has changed over time. We will look at the total manufacturing sector in Sweden and in Värmland. Three categories will be used:

(1) small plants = plants with 5–19 employees;
(2) medium-sized plants = plants with 20–499 employees;
(3) large plants = plants with 500 or more employees.

In Figure 10.5 we can see how the employment distribution in the total manufacturing sector in Sweden has changed between 1974 and 1984. The picture is very clear. The tendency is for medium-sized plants to increase their share and for small and large plants to lose ground. The trends have been the same in Värmland, as is indicated in Figure 10.6.

The significance of these changes has been tested with the following simple regression equation:

$$\ln [f/(1-f)] = a + bt + \varepsilon$$

190

Figure 10.5: Employment distribution in manufacturing industry in Sweden $(f/(1-f))$

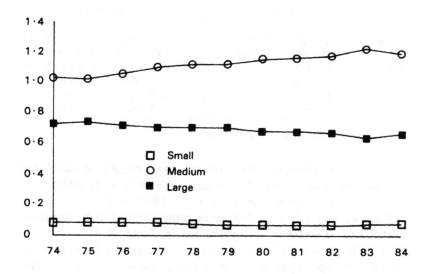

Figure 10.6: Employment distribution in manufacturing industry in Värmland $(f/(1-f))$

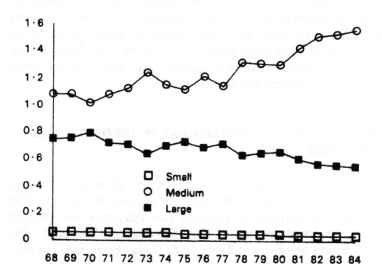

Table 10.5: Changes in employment shares in manufacturing industry (SNI 3)

Size	Sweden			Värmland		
category	a	b	R^2	a	b	R^2
Small	−2·490	−0·021	0·74	−2·737	−0·027	0·80
	(90·892)	(−5·097)		(−78·177)	(−7·824)	
Medium	0·002	0·017	0·93	−0·11	0·025	0·86
	(0·154)	(11·307)		(−0·404)	(9·527)	
Large	−0·306	−0·013	0·91	−0·231	−0·020	0·78
	(−32·842)	(−9·317)		(−8·107)	(−7·266)	

Note: t-values are given in parenthesis.

where f = employment share for the size category, a and b are parameters to be estimated, t = time with 1974 = 1, 1975 = 2, . . . etc. for Sweden, and 1968 = 1, 1969 = 2, . . . etc. for Värmland, and ε is a random error term assumed to be normally distributed. The results are presented in Table 10.5.

It will be observed that the explanatory power is quite good and that the speed parameter, b, is significant in all six cases. The value for the speed parameter is higher for Värmland than for Sweden as a whole, which indicates that the employment structure has been restructured at a faster rate in Värmland than in the country as a whole.

To summarise, then, the results indicate that small plants are losing employment shares both nationally and in the Värmland region and thus that their employment potential seems to be decreasing. Medium-sized plants have, on the other hand, gained employment shares and consequently, we may say that their employment potential has increased.

CHANGES IN TOTAL EMPLOYMENT IN DIFFERENT SIZE CATEGORIES

Having looked at changes in the employment distribution between different size categories in the previous section, we now consider how total employment in different size categories has changed during the actual periods in both Sweden and Värmland. The actual figures are given in Table 10.6. It may be pointed out that:

(a) total employment has decreased between 1974 and 1984 in all three size categories in both Sweden and Värmland;

Table 10.6: Employment in different size categories in manufacturing industry

Year	Sweden Total	Index	Värmland Total	Index
		Small		
1968	N.A.	—	1,771	95
1974	70,199	100	1,868	100
1984	50,263	72	1,198	64
		Medium		
1968	N.A.	—	16,695	88
1974	463,341	100	19,018	100
1984	416,340	90	17,249	91
		Large		
1968	N.A.	—	13,706	94
1974	383,003	100	14,652	100
1984	301,562	79	9,907	68

   (b) the largest relative employment decrease in both Sweden and Värmland is to be found in small plants, with a somewhat lower relative decrease of employment in large plants and the lowest relative decrease of employment in medium-sized plants; and

   (c) for both small and large plants, the relative employment decrease has been larger in Värmland than in the country as a whole.

The figures indicate that the employment potential of small plants has been quite low during the actual period and that this tendency has been even more marked in the Värmland region.

THE GROWTH POTENTIAL OF PLANTS IN DIFFERENT SIZE CATEGORIES IN VÄRMLAND

The changes in employment shares and total employment in different size categories are the net result of a number of processes of change involving the closure of plants, contractions or expansions in surviving plants, and the establishment and growth of new plants. The formulation of a relevant job creation policy is heavily dependent on the correct evaluation of the

193

relative importance of the different processes that give the net results observed in published statistical tables.

Table 10.7 presents a probability matrix for closures, openings and movement between size bands for the total 1977 stock of plants in Värmland. This table shows that the likelihood of a plant employing 5–9 employees in 1977 moving up to a higher size category up to 1984 is only 0.141; almost 55 per cent of them are closed and a further 31 per cent remained in their original size group. The probability of achieving upward mobility above nine employees (0.141) is almost identical to that reported by Storey (1981) — 0.13 — for plants of 1–9 employees in Cleveland between 1965 and 1976, and to that reported by O'Farrell (1985) — 0.14 — for plants of 0–10 employees in Ireland outside Dublin between 1973–81, however in both cases for slightly longer periods. We can see that the highest growth rates are to be found among plants in the size bands 5–9, 10–19 and 100–199. The highest contraction probabilities are found in the size bands 50–99 and 500 plus, while the highest death rates are found in size bands 5–9, 10–19 and 200–499. The greatest chance of remaining in the original size band is found in the three size bands containing the largest plants, i.e. 100–199, 200–499 and 500 plus. This can be compared with the results of O'Farrell (ibid.), who found the highest employment stability in the size band 0–10.

Turning to plant openings we can see that more than a quarter of the plants established during the period were closed during the period, but also that more than a quarter of the openings during the period had 50 or more employees in 1984.

From Table 10.7 we have estimated the total employment effects of closures, contractions, expansions and openings, in different size bands. The results are given in Table 10.8. The table shows that over 12,000 jobs have been lost during the period. More than 70 per cent of the losses have been the result of closures. The highest number of job losses through closures is in the size band 200–499. The highest number of job losses due to contractions is found in the size band 500 plus. We can also see that more than 6,400 new jobs have been created and that of these, more than 70 per cent have been created through openings. The largest number of new jobs is found in the size band 200–499. The largest number of new jobs through expansions is to be found in the size band 100–199. The estimated net job loss is 5,754 jobs, which is somewhat lower than the actual job loss of

Table 10.7: Closures, openings and movements between size bands of all 1977 plant stock in Värmland: probability matrix

Employment size band in 1977	Employment size band in 1984								Number of plants in 1977	Number of new plants 1978–84
	Closures	5–9	10–19	20–49	50–99	100–199	200–499	500–		
Openings	0·286	0·091	0·182	0·208	0·078	0·104	0·078			79
5–9	0·547	0·312	0·109	0·016	0·016				64	
10–19	0·473	0·140	0·258	0·108	0·022				93	
20–49	0·374	0·011	0·143	0·385	0·088				91	
50–99	0·282		0·051	0·256	0·359	0·051			39	
100–199	0·310				0·103	0·448	0·138		29	
200–499	0·407					0·111	0·481		27	
500–	0·062						0·250	0·688	16	
Total									359	

Table 10.8: Estimated total employment effects of closures, contractions, expansions and openings in different size bands in Värmland, 1977–84

	Closures		Contraction		Expansions		Openings	
	Number	%	Number	%	Number	%	Number	%
5–9	245	2·77	–	–	154	8·82	50	1·07
10–19	659	7·44	104	3·12	324	18·55	216	4·60
20–49	1,191	13·44	288	8·64	320	18·32	575	12·25
50–99	825	9·31	519	15·57	149	8·53	462	9·85
100–199	1,349	15·23	224	6·72	800	45·79	1,232	26·26
200–499	3,846	43·41	599	17·97	0	0	2,157	45·97
500–	744	8·40	1,600	47·99	–	–	0	0
Total	8,859	100	3,334	100	1,747	100	4,692	100

12,193

6,439

7,175 jobs. The difference is due, among other things, to employment changes within size bands. The difference does not change our main results, however, which are that closures are more responsible for job losses than contractions and that openings are more important than expansions for job gains.

CONCLUSIONS AND POLICY RECOMMENDATIONS

In this chapter we have seen how the manufacturing sector reached its highest employment share in both Sweden and Värmland around 1960. This was also the case for total employment in manufacturing. Employment in manufacturing has fluctuated, however, and a new but lower peak was reached in the mid-1970s. Since the late 1960s the number of manufacturing plants has been decreasing and this has resulted in an increased average plant size in both Sweden as a whole and Värmland. Among other things this means that the total number of manufacturing units to be located has decreased. The role of small and medium-sized plants in regional employment varies a great deal between different regions in Sweden. The importance of small plants for employment is lower in Värmland than the national average.

The employment size structure of the manufacturing sector has changed over time in a very interesting manner. For both Sweden and Värmland it can generally be said that small and large plants have lost employment shares, while the medium-sized plants have gained employment shares.

Looking at total employment in the three different size categories we observed job losses in all three categories both in Sweden and Värmland, with the largest losses for the smallest size category. We also saw that Värmland lost relatively more jobs in small and large plants than Sweden as a whole.

Behind the observed net job losses there are processes of closures, contractions, expansions and openings. The number of employees hit by these changes is much larger than is indicated by the net figure. In Värmland during the period 1977–84, closures have been responsible for more than 70 per cent of all job losses, while openings have been the source of more than 70 per cent of the job gains. Thus, new openings are more significant than expansions as a source of new jobs within manufacturing. All the new jobs created through expansion were created in plants with less than 200 employees.

197

What policy recommendations can therefore be made? Given the results of the study presented here, the following recommendations are offered:

(1) Policy-makers anxious to use the small and medium-sized plants as a means of employment growth in depressed regions ought to make sure that existing data on small and medium-sized firms are fully analysed to give as good a description as possible of the actual situation and the historical development. These analyses must, of course, also include the service sector.

(2) Given the rapid decrease in both employment shares and total employment for small manufacturing plants, it seems important in a long perspective to analyse the driving forces behind these processes. Might it be the case, for example, that the situation for the small-scale entrepreneur in manufacturing has become worse due to new laws and increased administrative regulation, concentration on different markets, changes in the links and networks in the industrial sector, and so on? It seems important, for example, to increase our knowledge about the extent and nature of the survival of small plants through their adaptation to altered conditions resulting from changes further along the line of either backward or forward industrial and service linkages. It might be expected that the 'death' of plants frequently expresses their inability to adapt. Personal contact in facilitating adaptation by small enterprises to rapid alterations in market taste and fashion in the design of final products might play a key role in this connection.

(3) Given that the role of medium-sized manufacturing plants in regional employment has increased in importance, analyses ought to be made of the relevant policy measures needed to support and increase employment in these plants. One reason for this is that, in the short term, the formation of new firms will not really have any noticeable impact on total employment. Another reason is that medium-sized and large plants provide markets for ancillary or auxiliary industrial products and services for small plants through subcontracting. A process of growth for medium-sized and large plants might 'spawn' relatively high birth and survival rates of small plants.

(4) Lastly, and most importantly, perhaps, it seems natural to

stress the importance of stimulating the opening of new plants, since historically they have been the major source of new jobs. Policy-makers, however, need to have more knowledge about entrepreneurship in a region. Some of this knowledge exists today but there are still many unexplored areas awaiting meaningful research. Thus, policies aimed at stimulating the establishment of new plants must also contain a reasonable share of research to increase the available knowledge.

REFERENCES

Birch, D. L. (1979) *The job generation process*. MIT Program on Neighbourhood and Regional Change, Cambridge, Mass.

Fothergill, S. and G. Gudgin (1979) The job generation process in Britain. *Centre for Environmental Studies, Research Series, 32*.

O'Farrell, P. N. (1985) Employment change in manufacturing: the case of surviving plants. *Urban Studies, 22*, 57–68.

SOU (1984) *Regional utveckling och mellanregional utjämning*. (*Regional development and interregional equalisation*) (in Swedish). Liber, Stockholm, p. 74.

Storey, D. (1981) New firm formation, employment change and the small firm: the case of Cleveland County. *Urban Studies, 18*, 335–45.

11

Regional Economic Potential in The Netherlands: Approaches in Empirical Research, with Special Reference to Small and Medium-sized Firms

Piet H. Pellenbarg

INTRODUCTION

Regional differences in economic development have been a subject of continuing interest for geographers and economists in most European countries during the last three or four decades. The situation in The Netherlands fits this general rule, illustrated by the numerous publications on the subject throughout this period. When measured by European standards, the regional disparities in a small country like The Netherlands are of course not impressive. They are certainly not comparable to the grave contrasts that exist between the northern and southern parts of Italy, or between central and southern France, between south-east England and Northern Ireland, and so on. On a smaller scale, they nevertheless constitute a matter for serious national concern.

This concern is based on two rather different problems. On the one hand, there is a certain fear of severe overconcentrations of population and economic activity in the western part of the country, where the four big cities of The Netherlands are located (Amsterdam, Rotterdam, The Hague and Utrecht; see Figure 11.1). It must be said that in recent years this fear has lessened because of the slower pace of national economic growth and the slowing down of the rate of population growth. On the other hand, there is the much more persistent problem of some regions in the periphery of the country, where incomes and unemployment remain substantially below the national average. This situation is in fact the hard core of the regional development problem in all European countries, although differing in severity, persistence and background. In The Netherlands, the problem is most clearly found in the northern provinces of Groningen,

Figure 11.1: Centre and periphery in The Netherlands

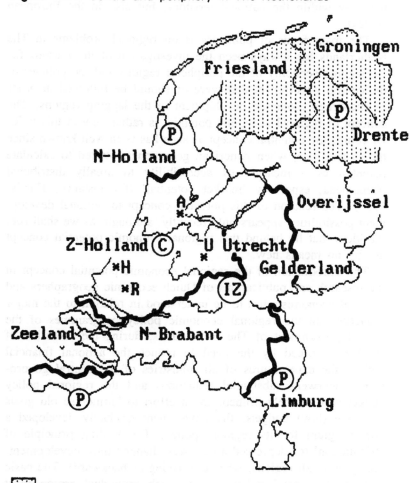

Northern Netherlands

Urban agglomerations:

A = Amsterdam
H = The Hague
R = Rotterdam
U = Utrecht

C = Central Area
IZ = Intermediate Zone
P = Periphery

Source: Wever (1985)

Friesland and Drente (Figure 11.1) which happen to be peripheral not only within the national territory, but also in the European context.

The main focus of publications on regional problems in The Netherlands has always been the investigation of the reasons for the lagging economy of the peripheral regions and the policies of the central government that were or should be followed in order to encourage economic development in the lagging regions. The concept of regional economic potential is rather new in this field. Of course the potential concept as such has been well-known since the early fifties, when American geographers started to calculate potential as a measure of accessibility to areally distributed phenomena, especially 'market potential' (for instance, Harris, 1954). The relation of this potential concept to regional development possibilities appears only recently, although, as we shall see, the ideas that lie behind this regional economic potential concept are by no means new.

The introduction of the regional economic potential concept in the research and publications of Dutch economic geographers and regional economists has to be understood in relation to the major reductions in the regional economic policy programmes of the central government of The Netherlands, during the recession of 1980–84. Forced by the need to reduce the national financial deficit, the expenditures of all ministries of the central government underwent substantial reductions and the regional policy budget was severely pruned. In an effort to harmonise old goals and new (low) budgets, the government gradually developed a new adagium for its regional policy. The leading principle of 'stimulation' (of depressed areas) was changed into 'development' (applying to all regions, whether thriving or backward). The basic idea in this 'new' policy is that each individual region must develop and exploit its own intrinsic economic possibilities, for which the word 'potential' was introduced. The introduction of the new philosophy was accompanied by some decentralisation of industrialisation incentives from the central to the regional (provincial) government.

The development of the potential-based regional policy in The Netherlands after 1980 coincided with a growing international interest in the subject of small firms, as a result of which both issues became more or less interrelated. The growing importance of small and medium-sized establishments (SMEs) in the employment structure of many European countries led many regional authorities, especially in depressed areas, to place greater emphasis upon new and small firms of regional origin, rather than on importing large branch plants from outside the region. Stimulating SMEs of regional origin thus became a focal point of interest within the global goal of developing regional economic potential.

Naturally, the economic potential of a region cannot be developed without a clear knowledge about the nature of such potential. The adoption of the potential approach in regional policy thus aroused new research activities from geographers and economists, at a national as well as a regional level. These investigations follow divergent analytical lines, because they are based on different theoretical foundations. As a consequence, the impression they offer of development possibilities in the various parts of The Netherlands is not always the same.

The purpose of this chapter is to present the most interesting results of the regional potential studies in The Netherlands of the last few years, when possible with special reference to SMEs, and to draw some conclusions from them. This is preceded by a short discussion of the various research strategies that can be used for such studies.

THEORETICAL AND RESEARCH APPROACHES TO THE ECONOMIC POTENTIAL CONCEPT

A necessary starting point for a survey of theoretical or research approaches to any concept is the formulation of a clear-cut definition. We will adopt the definition that was suggested in a recent literature survey on the subject by Roelofs and Wever (1985), which identifies the economic potential of a region as 'the particular aspects of region and/or firm characteristics that give a region an advantage over other regions concerning the possibility of one particular kind of economic development'. This definition immediately suggests two different and opposing theoretical approaches: either the development possibilities are associated with characteristics of the region itself, or they are thought of as being a consequence of certain characteristics of firms located in that region.

A number of well-known economic-geographical theories are associated with each of these two viewpoints. The first viewpoint, regarding potential as a matter of regional qualities or — an alternative name for the same phenomena — location conditions, can also be found in the export base theory, the theory of cumulative causation, growth pole theory, and the product life cycle theory. Alternatively, the viewpoint that local firm characteristics are a measure for the development potential of their area is incorporated into the classical as well as the behavioural location theory, industrial complex theory, impact theory, and in theories which associate economic development with the presence of new firms, innovating firms, high growth firms, and so on.

It may be noted that most of these theories are by no means new. Regional economic potential may therefore be new in terms of regional development policy; it certainly is not new or revolutionary in terms of its scientific background. Roelofs and Wever (ibid.), from whom the above enumeration of theories was taken, conclude that theory gives no concerted explanation for the development possibilities of regions. One theory stresses the importance of one particular factor, a second theory stresses another, and especially the empirically orientated representatives of the firm characteristics approach seem in particular to deal more with the effects of regional economic potential than with its causes.

Recent empirical investigations into regional economic potential in The Netherlands broadly correspond to the above theories. Roelofs and Wever divide empirical research into two broad categories: direct approaches, which are explicitly meant to discover regional economic potentials and indirect approaches, where this is only a secondary motive. Components-of-change analysis, input–output analysis, and matrix-analysis of production environments may serve as examples of this indirect approach. The direct approach is followed where investigators consciously try to map firm or place characteristics that may be thought to reflect economic potential. This is done in feasibility studies, studies of regional attraction or innovation profiles, studies of high-tech or high-growth firms, and so on. We will also consider studies of regional economic 'health' and investigations into the generation of new and small firms as direct approaches, contrary to Roelofs and Wever, who call them indirect.

The next two sections concentrate only on the results of the direct empirical approaches to the regional economic potential concept. The selection of figures is divided into two categories, following our earlier distinction in theoretical backgrounds between the regional approach and the firm or sector approach.

DIRECT APPROACHES TO REGIONAL ECONOMIC
POTENTIAL: CHARACTERISTICS OF REGIONS

Two recent Dutch studies of characteristics of regions have served as an input for a detailed analysis of economic potential. The aim of the two studies was rather different, The first, by van der Knaap and Struyk (1984) focused upon the general economic 'health' of regions, while the purpose of the NEI (1984) study was to discover one particular aspect of that 'health', namely the potential for generating and supporting industrial innovations. The methods that were used were not identical (a partial least squares method by van der Knaap and Struyk, and a multi-criteria method by the NEI study) but they are nevertheless more or less comparable, being both multivariate research techniques. Both studies use COROP-regions (40 statistical regions, smaller than the eleven provinces depicted in Figure 11.1) as the regional basis for calculations.

The economic health as calculated by van der Knaap and Struyk has two important aspects: regional income and regional potential. Regional income was measured as mean income *per capita* and the mean total income per income drawer. Regional potential was estimated through a variety of individual indicators, such as the region's work-force, road infrastructure, industrial sites, investment activity, and so on. In the resulting map of economic health (Figure 11.2), all these characteristics are brought together, but the income and potential aspects are still separately identifiable. Figure 11.3 shows the results for the potential aspect alone.

The second study using a regional approach, from NEI (1984), also adopted a two-sided approach, combining regional data about the production system (big/small firms, new/old firms, R&D activities, government incentives) and the production environment (industrial sites, accessibility, agglomeration factors, quality of labour force, presence of R&D centres, living conditions). As a result of multi-criteria analysis on these data a map of 'regional innovation profiles' was produced (see Figure 11.4).

Figures 11.3 and 11.4 show a remarkable resemblance. Both maps depict the Central Area of The Netherlands (Figure 11.1), where the four big urban agglomerations are located, as the part

Figure 11.2: COROP-regions in The Netherlands by economic health

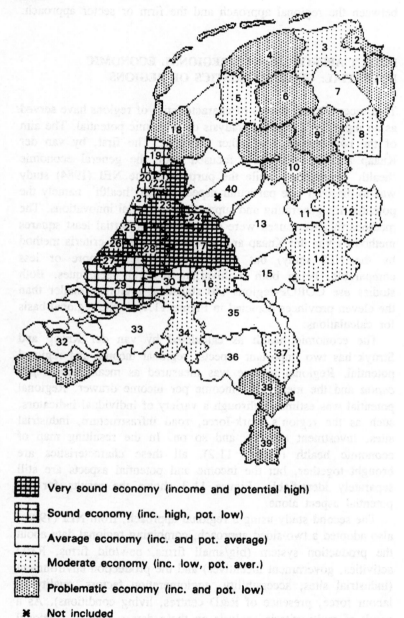

■ Very sound economy (income and potential high)

⊞ Sound economy (inc. high, pot. low)

□ Average economy (inc. and pot. average)

▦ Moderate economy (inc. low, pot. aver.)

▨ Problematic economy (inc. and pot. low)

✖ Not included

Source: Van der Knaap and Struyk (1984)

Figure 11.3: Scores of COROP-regions on the potential aspect (partial profile of economic health — see Figure 11.2)

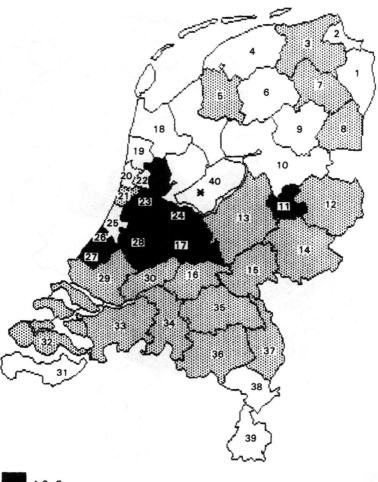

■ >0·5

▨ −0·5−0·5

☐ <0·5

✖ not included

Source: Van der Knaap and Struyk (1984)

Figure 11.4: Innovation profile of COROP-regions in The Netherlands

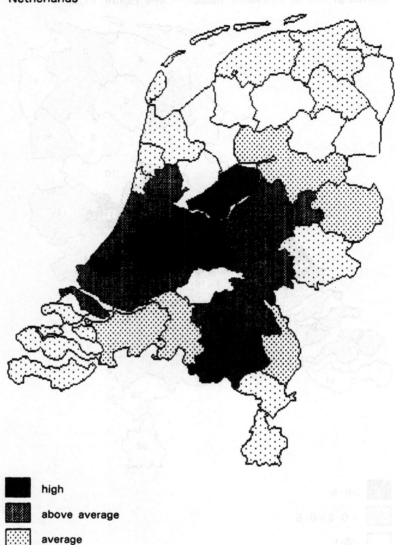

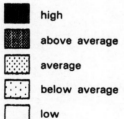

- ■ high
- ▨ above average
- ▧ average
- ⬚ below average
- ☐ low

Source: NEI (1984)

of the country with the highest economic potential. The calculations confirm the classic image of this central, highly urbanised area as a prosperous, dynamic region, where new activities originate and develop, supported by favourable location conditions. The Intermediate Zone, taking advantage of its adjacent location to the Central Area and acting as a recipient of spread effects, also has a moderate or high potential. According to the NEI study (Figure 11.4) this especially holds true for a north–south corridor connecting the attractive landscape of northern and central Gelderland with the eastern part of the province of Noord-Brabant, where the headquarters of the international Philips concern is located in the city of Eindhoven. The counterpart of these regions with high potential is found in the Dutch northern and southern Periphery region (white areas in Figure 11.3, white and lightly shaded areas in Figure 11.4). The northern part of The Netherlands especially shows a low profile, confirming its role as a long-standing problem region, on which regional policy programmes of the central government have focused since World War II.

The stigma of a low economic potential for the Dutch Periphery region is most clearly shown in Figure 11.4, where the potential is associated with innovation possibilities for manufacturing or service firms. However, Figures 11.2 and 11.3 show that at least a few regions within the Periphery (COROP-regions 3, 5, 7 and 8 in the North, and 11, 12, 14 and 37 in the East and South) have 'average' potential. At the same time a few regions in the Central Area (notably COROP nos. 20, 21, 22 and 25) have low potential (Figure 11.3). Their 'sound' economy (Figure 11.2) is attributable only to the relatively high incomes of their inhabitants. Of course, these are only minor exceptions to the general rule of a potential Centre and a non-potential Periphery. However, as we shall see, more of these exceptions become apparent when an approach to the economic potential concept using firm characteristics instead of regional characteristics is used.

DIRECT APPROACHES TO REGIONAL ECONOMIC POTENTIALS: CHARACTERISTICS OF FIRMS

Many features of firms can be used to characterise the economic potential they confer upon their areas of location. In recent studies of The Netherlands the investigators have mostly chosen firm characteristics relating to the 'dynamic capacity' of regional economic systems, i.e. the ability of the regional production systems to produce new firms, new types of firms and new products and services, especially in the category of SMEs. Criteria that were used are the opening up of new firms, the presence of small and medium-sized firms, high-growth firms, firms in high-tech sectors, frequency of innovations, and business performance in terms of exports and profitability.

New firms

Figure 11.5 shows that the rate at which new firms are established differs greatly between individual regions within The Netherlands. Medium and high rates are found in the Central Area as well as in the Intermediate Zone, notably in Noord-Brabant (see Figure 11.1). In the new-firm creation process, the Periphery again lags behind, although it has become clear from a study by de Jong (1984) that the high firm-creation rates in the Central Area are not to be exclusively attributed to the quality of the big urban agglomerations as incubation milieux. On the contrary, the highest rates when measured by relative standards are found in smaller cities and rural areas that surround the big agglomerations (Table 11.1). The Intermediate

Table 11.1: Firms established after 1975 as a percentage of all firms, in different location types, in the Central Area, the Intermediate Zone and the Periphery of The Netherlands[a]

Location types	Regions[b]		
	Central Area	Intermediate Z.	Periphery
Rural municipalities	43·0	35·2	31·0
Urbanised rural municipalities	41·9	41·3	35·5
Small cities	42·1	35·9	36·0
Medium-sized cities	36·6	38·0	35·5
Large cities	37·6	36·9	38·5
Total	39·4	38·6	35·1

Notes: a. Selected industrial sectors.
   b. De Jong's delimitation of the three zones is slightly different from Figure 11.1.
Source: de Jong (1984)

Figure 11.5: Establishment of new firms by Chambers of Commerce districts, 1970–9

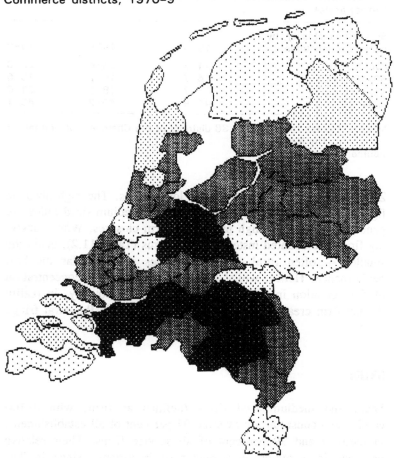

Number of new firms, compared with the number of existing firms:

▫ Relatively very few new establishments

▨ Relatively few new establishments

▦ Even share of new establishments

■ Relatively great number of new establishments

Source: NMB (1984)

Table 11.2: Surviving firms as a percentage of the total number of new firms established in 1970, 1975 and 1980 in The Netherlands[a]

Size of municipality, by number of inhabitants:	1970	1975	1980
over 100,00	24·7	25·4	23·3
50–100,000	14·7	16·2	15·6
25– 500,000	18·7	18·2	21·0
under 25,000	41·9	40·2	40·1

Note: a. Figures for 17 of the 38 districts of the Chambers of Commerce in The Netherlands.
Source: Wever (1984)

Zone and Periphery seem to have lower rates. The high absolute figures for firm creation in the large and medium-sized cities are generally offset by a high number of firm closures. When surviving firms are counted instead of new firms (Table 11.2), again the smaller — often rural — municipalities show by far the best performance. Hence, whilst Figure 11.5 suggests a concentration of firm creation in the urbanised parts of the country, in reality the net firm creation rates are actually highest in the rural fringe zones.

SMEs

Small and medium-sized firms (defined as firms with 0–100 employees) constitute on average 97 per cent of all establishments in industry and 99 per cent of all service firms. Their relative presence in a region is a matter of importance since in The Netherlands small firms (up to ten employees) are disproportionately represented in expanding sectors (see Table 11.3).

In industry and services the SMEs provide 37 and 60 per cent respectively of the total employment. There is some regional variance around these average figures, but this is not clearly related to regional differences in the growth rates of new firms. Thus, for example, the percentage of the total work-force in SMEs is relatively high in several regions that had a low number of new firms, for example, the Open Heart of the Central Area, the northern part of North Holland, some parts of the northern Netherlands, and — for service firms — southern Limburg (Pellenbarg et al., 1987).

212

Table 11.3: Percentage of work-force in firms in manufactⁿⁱring
industry, by size category and life cycle stages, 1981

Life cycle stage	Small firms %	Medium-sized firms %	Large firms %	Total %
Expanding	21·2	28·9	50·0	100·0
Some stagnation	2·6	12·3	85·1	100·0
Stagnation	12·8	29·0	58·2	100·0
Saturation	14·3	43·2	42·4	100·0
Some recession	14·3	44·3	41·4	100·0
Strong recession	9·0	32·3	58·7	100·0
Total	10·4	26·6	62·9	100·0

Note: Elements may not sum to 100.0 due to rounding errors.
Source: Webbink (1985)

High-growth firms

The concept of 'high-growth firms' can be interpreted in different
ways, but unfortunately there is no official data on the annual
growth of individual firms. The growth of firms can only be
measured and mapped at a more aggregate level, as is done in
Figure 11.6. Of course this is not very satisfactory as a measure
of economic potential, because fluctuations in real development
are eliminated in the ten-year index figures. Nevertheless, it is
striking to see that the urban agglomerations of Amsterdam and
Rotterdam are in the next-to-lowest category. High growth (black
areas in Figure 11.6) is concentrated in the COROP regions
between these two agglomerations and to the north and south of
them. This is no doubt a reflection of the industrial suburbanisa-
tion process that takes place in this part of the country. The
satisfactory growth in parts of the Periphery (dark shaded areas)
is also noteworthy.

A more sophisticated approach to high growth, which is also
more directly related to the potential concept as a measure for
future development possibilities, is followed by Alders and de
Ruyter (1984). They conducted an investigation based on a list of
'opportunity sectors' which had been made up by a government
commission chaired by Gerry Wagner, former president director
of Royal Dutch Shell. This list of promising activities was
compiled using criteria like market prospects, productivity and
competitiveness. No special interest was paid to the size aspects
of the firms in the chosen sectors. Originally the list only

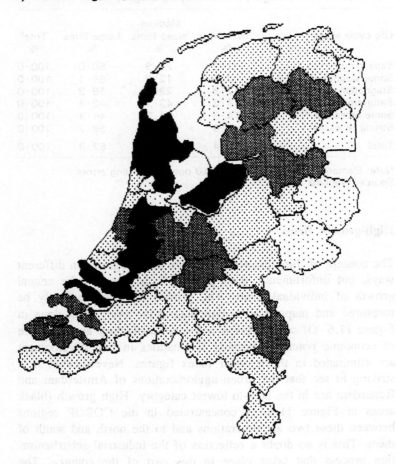

Figure 11.6: Growth of the work-force in industry and services by COROP-regions, 1973–82 (1973 = 100)

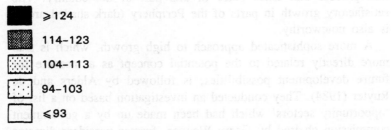

≥124

114–123

104–113

94–103

≤93

Source: Wever (1985)

contained industrial activities, but later it was extended, by another commission, to the service sector.

The commission's list of opportunity sectors was translated to the three-digit industrial classification of the data bank operated by the Dutch Chambers of Commerce. Figure 11.7 shows the location quotients for all sectors, and then for the industrial, service and wholesale sectors. Figure 11.7 is somewhat complex, but it is clear that most regions within The Netherlands have a fair share of these promising activities. Regions where they are relatively overrepresented (location quotients above 1) occur in the Central Area as well as outside it (Figure 11.7a). A separate mapping shows that promising industrial sectors concentrate in the northern and southern Periphery (Figure 11.7b), whereas promising service and wholesale sectors concentrate in the Central Area and parts of the Intermediate Zone (Figures 11.7c and d). It is also interesting to note that within the promising sectors there is a clear distinction in the location pattern of small and big firms. The latter ones dominate the Periphery, whereas small firms show a more dispersed pattern between Centre and Periphery (Figures 11.7e and f).

High-tech firms

Bouman *et al.* (1985) made a further selection of ten branches of manufacturing industry (partly also featuring on the Wagner list of 'opportunity sectors') which they designed as the 'high-tech sector'. The branches are all part of the metal and engineering industries, and comprise the ISIC sectors 35.81, 35.93, 36.93–95, 37.71, 38.11, 38.21, 38.31 and 38.41 (codes from the data bank of the Dutch Chambers of Commerce).

Table 11.4 shows the spatial distribution of the ten high-tech sectors. A substantial number of the 1,287 firms that are listed as high-tech are located in the Central Area. However, when we compare the distribution of these high-tech firms with the distribution of all industrial and service firms in The Netherlands, the dominance of the Central Area is less clear-cut. Instead, the Periphery has its fair share of high-tech firms. Figures 11.8a and b provide similar results at the level of COROP regions, showing that a relatively high percentage of high-tech firms is found in the Central Area and the Periphery.

Figure 11.7: High-growth firms (selection of 'opportunity sectors') – location quotients by COROP-regions

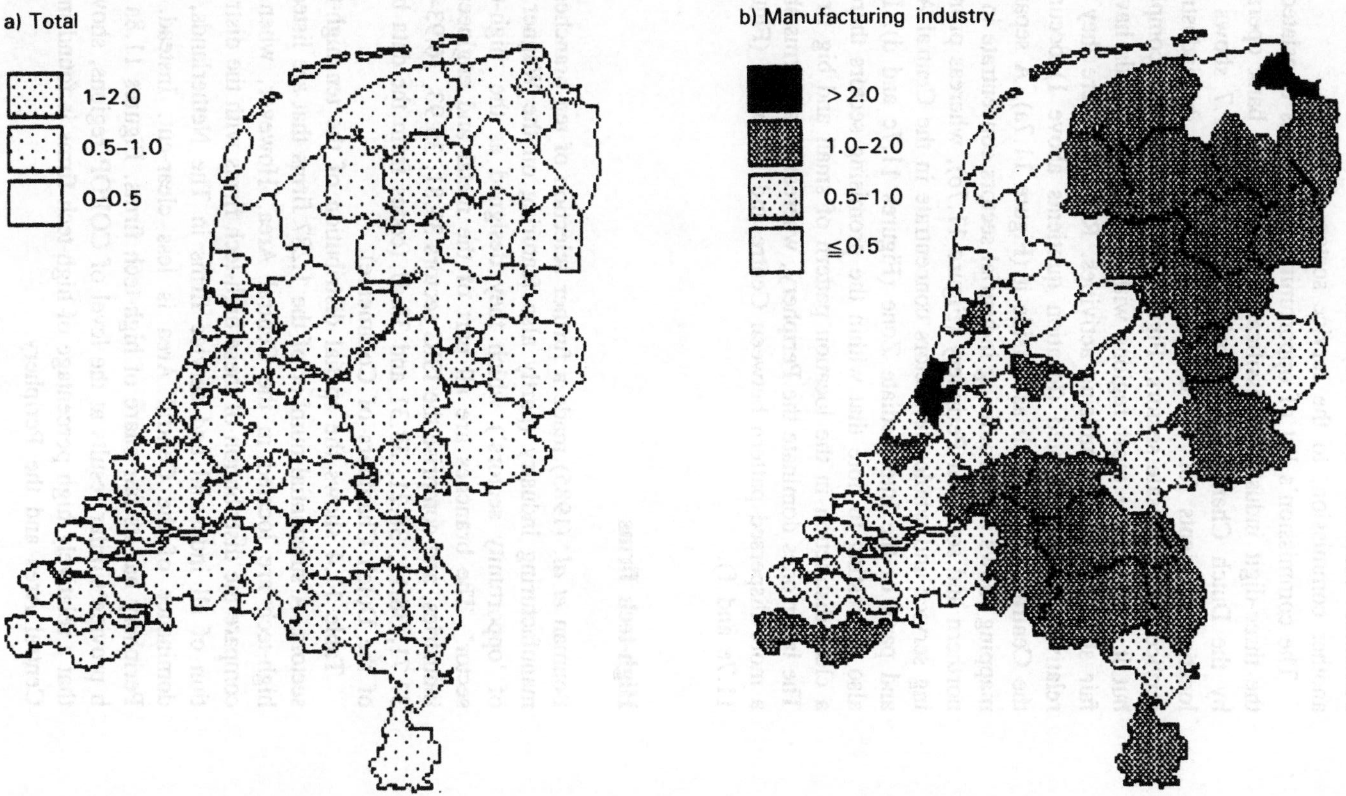

b) Manufacturing industry

- ■ >2.0
- ▨ 1.0–2.0
- ⊡ 0.5–1.0
- □ ≤0.5

a) Total

- ⊡ 1–2.0
- ⊡ 0.5–1.0
- □ 0–0.5

Figure 11.7: contd

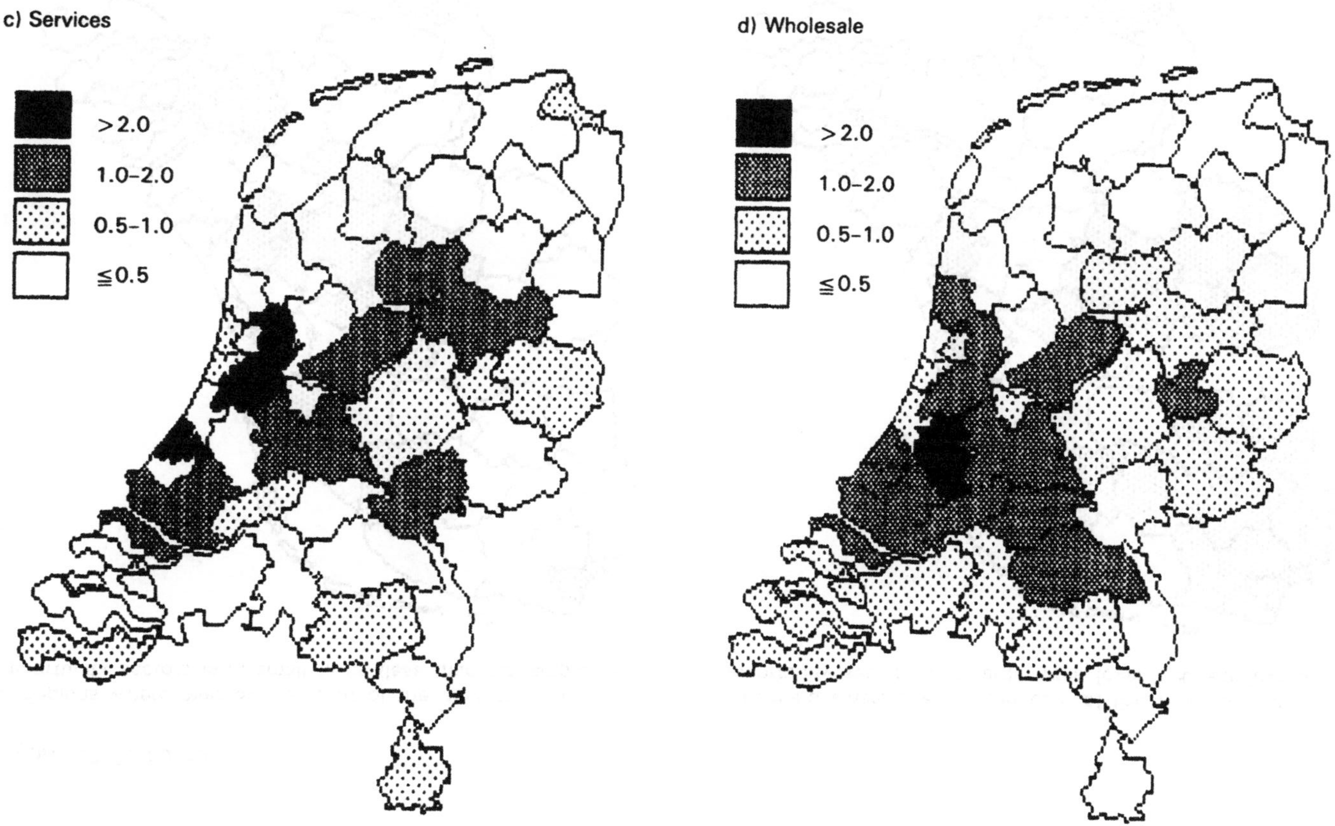

c) Services

	> 2.0
	1.0–2.0
	0.5–1.0
	≦ 0.5

d) Wholesale

	> 2.0
	1.0–2.0
	0.5–1.0
	≦ 0.5

Figure 11.7: contd

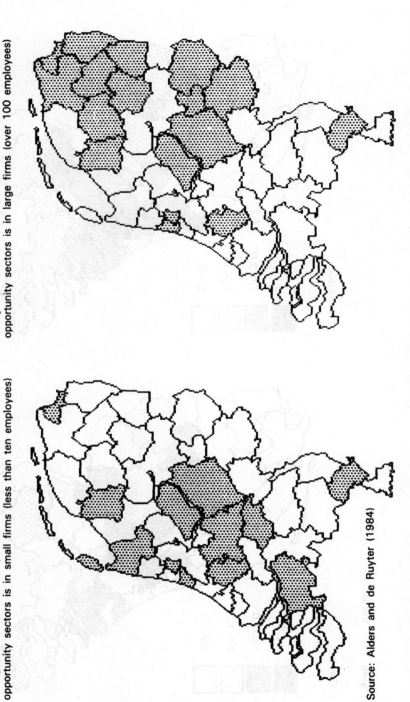

e) Regions where over 30 per cent of the work-force in opportunity sectors is in small firms (less than ten employees)

f) Regions where over 50 per cent of the work-force in opportunity sectors is in large firms (over 100 employees)

Source: Alders and de Ruyter (1984)

Table 11.4: Spatial distribution of high-tech sectors, compared with the distribution of all industrial and service sectors, by number of firms

	High-tech sectors		Industrial sectors		All service and industrial sectors	
	No.	%	No.	%	No.	%
Central Area	545	42·3	17·953	38·7	223,942	43·0
Intermediate Zone	374	29·1	16,813	36·2	175,033	29·7
Periphery	368	28·6	11,641	25·1	121·659	27·3
Total	1,287	100·0	46,407	100·0	520·634	100·0

Source: Bouman *et al.* (1985)

Figure 11.8: High-tech firms (workers) as a percentage of all firms (workers) (in industry and services) by COROP-regions, 1984

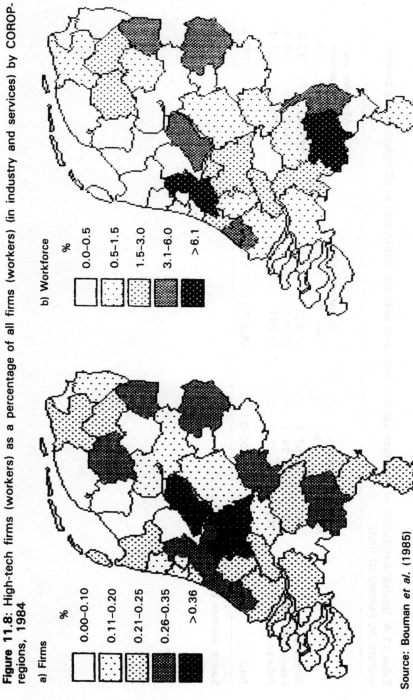

a) Firms

%

0.00–0.10

0.11–0.20

0.21–0.25

0.26–0.35

>0.36

b) Workforce

%

0.0–0.5

0.5–1.5

1.5–3.0

3.1–6.0

>6.1

Source: Bouman *et al.* (1985)

Innovating firms

Many recent discussions about revitalising national economies stress the importance of industrial innovations: fundamental renewals of a firm's production, its organisation, or its marketing strategy, leading to new development cycles in the industrial system. Whilst innovation is a good indicator of economic potential it is difficult to grasp because there is no statistical registration of it.

Figures 11.9 and 11.10 offer two attempts to visualise the regional distribution of innovating firms in The Netherlands. In Figure 11.9 the number of patents that were officially registered in the period 1982–3 is taken as an indicator of innovativeness (only industrial patents, no privately owned ones). Figure 11.10 was compiled on the basis of a telephone inquiry among a 1 per cent sample of all SMEs in the industrial, wholesale, transport and business services sectors. Using a specific operational definition of innovation, one-third of these SMEs were identified as 'innovators' (for further explanation of the method used, see Kok *et al.*, 1984). The first impression of the two maps is the dispersed character of the spatial distribution that is portrayed. There is a concentration (large circles) in the Central Area, but many innovative firms are also present in the Intermediate Zone and they are certainly not absent in the Periphery. This impression is reinforced by the figures in Table 11.5, where the number of firms with patents and

Table 11.5: Survey of innovation indices: location quotients by province

Firm size ISIC sectors Province	Published patents all firms 2,3 only industrial patents	Random sample SMEs (0–100 employees) 2, 3, 61, 62, 76, 84	
		All innovations	Only primary and secondary innovations
Groningen	72	113	79
Friesland	131	83	95
Drente	89	91	–
Overijssel	104	140	244
Gelderland	114	127	125
Utrecht	125	80	51
Noord Holland	68	85	52
Zuid Holland	108	106	139
Zeeland	73	50	68
Noord Brabant	128	78	78
Limburg	62	126	60

Source: Kok *et al.* (1984)

Figure 11.9: Dutch innovating firms: published firm patents

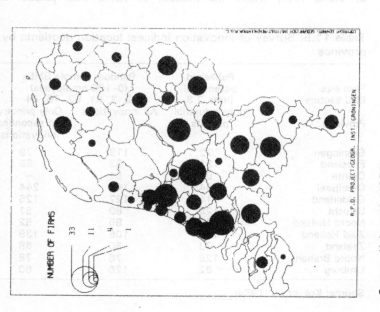

Source: Kok *et al.* (1984)

Figure 11.10: Dutch innovating firms: results from a telephone inquiry

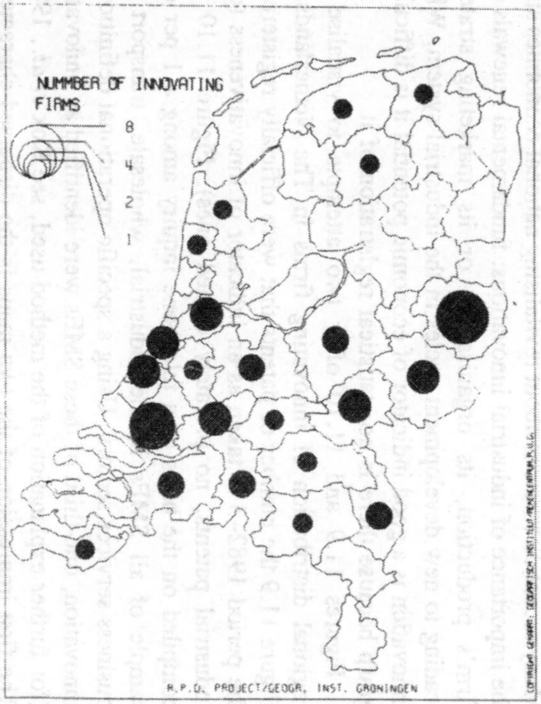

Source: Kok *et al.* (1984)

innovations is related to the total number of firms by province. High location quotients are apparent in the Intermediate provinces of Gelderland and Overijssel in the eastern part of the country. The Central Area offers some surprisingly low quotients, especially for Noord-Holland. Groningen, Friesland and Drente in the Periphery are slightly below unity for some indicators. Overall there is little support for the hypothesis of an innovative centre and a non-innovative periphery.

Exports and profits

As final examples of a direct approach to regional economic potential using firm characteristics, two maps are presented in which the 'business performance' of firms is taken as a measure for their potential. Profits are of course the ultimate standard, but export performance, also frequently emphasised as an important stimulus for the economic system, is taken as a second one.

Figures 11.11 and 11.12 provide us with some information about the regional distribution of firms with relatively high exports and profits, based on the annual inquiry of the Dutch Chambers of Commerce. The percentages are given for all firms and all large firms (over 50 employees) separately. Exports are high in parts of the Central Area, and the southern parts of the Intermediate Zone (Figure 11.11a). For large firms, however, the accent shifts entirely to the Intermediate Zone (b). Satisfactory profits are also frequent in the Intermediate Zone, but some peripheral regions are also above the national average. Several parts of the Central Area have a rather bad score for all firms with profits (Figure 11.12a). Profits for large firms (Figure 12.b) show a very dispersed pattern.

RÉSUMÉ: MAIN FEATURES OF THE DISTRIBUTION OF REGIONAL ECONOMIC POTENTIALS IN THE NETHERLANDS

The different approaches to the economic potential concept produce a kaleidoscope of regional patterns, in which a general pattern is not easily discernible. Some main features can nevertheless be identified:

Figure 11.11: Firms with exports as a percentage of all firms by Chambers of Commerce districts

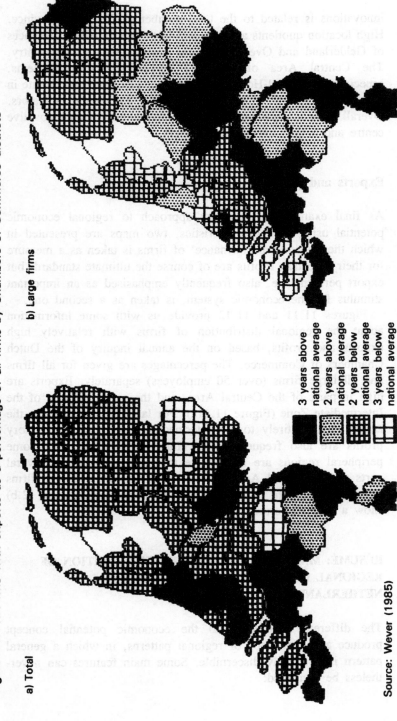

a) Total

b) Large firms

3 years above
national average

2 years above
national average

2 years below
national average

3 years below
national average

Source: Wever (1985)

Figure 11.12: Firms with sufficient profits as a percentage of all firms by Chambers of Commerce districts

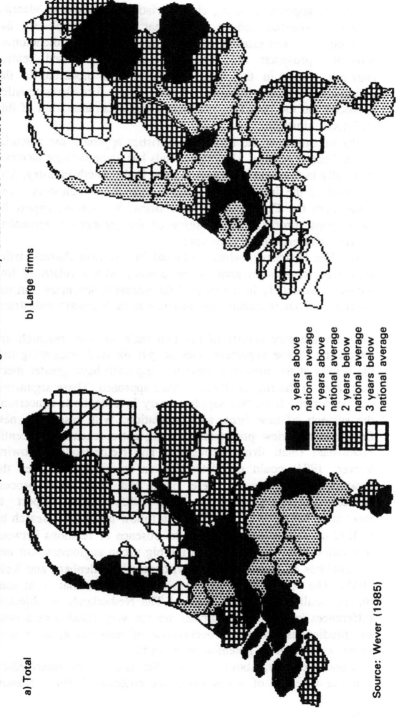

a) Total

b) Large firms

3 years above
national average

2 years above
national average

2 years below
national average

3 years below
national average

Source: Wever (1985)

(a) The approaches using characteristics of regions to identify economic potential deliver results that seem to emphasise the traditional, well-established centre–periphery dichotomy: economic prospects are favourable in the urbanised central provinces, poor in the rural periphery, and moderate in the intermediate zone between them. The firm-characteristics approach, on the contrary, produces signs of an alteration of this traditional situation.

(b) According to the firm-characteristics approach the potential of the Central Area of The Netherlands has some definite lacunae, especially in the field of new firms and high-growth industry. The potential of the Intermediate Zone is, for some indicators, even better than the Central Area (new firms, innovation, export by large firms, profits). The position of the southern Intermediate provinces is especially favourable.

(c) The Periphery, when measured by the firm-characteristics approach, remains an area of the country with a relatively low potential, especially in the case of the northern provinces, but not entirely without prospects, for instance in high-growth industries.

The contradictory results of the two main lines of research are interesting. Some arguments can be put forward suggesting that the results of the firm-characteristics approach have greater merit than those of the region-characteristics approach. These arguments can be derived from two supplementary investigations concerning the subjects of new firms and innovation. With respect to new firms, an interview programme among entrepreneurs of recently established small firms throughout The Netherlands (following Wever, 1984) could not determine an association between the locational conditions of these firms and their 'start process characteristics' (Bleumink et al., 1985). With respect to innovating firms, especially SMEs, a follow-up of the research by Kok et al. (1984) demonstrated the absence of relations between innovation activities of firms in the big urban agglomerations and the qualities of these location environments (Pellenbarg and Kok, 1985). The conclusion from these results can be that — at least on the small geographical scale of The Netherlands — objective differences in location conditions are not very reliable as a basis for predictions about the occurrence of new firms, innovating firms, or economic potential in general.

Conclusion (b), above, stresses the rise of the Intermediate Zone as a region of strong economic potential. Various reasons for this can be proposed. Firstly, the region's adjacent position to the Central Area makes it the main recipient of spread effects, for example, in the form of migrant firms from the Central Area. The Intermediate Zone also contains some of the country's most attractive landscapes, making it a desirable residential area. A third factor might be its closer location to the other countries of the Common Market, especially the main trade partners of The Netherlands: Germany, Belgium and France. The outstanding position of the southern province of Noord Brabant in several of the maps we presented is significant in this respect.

New-firm creations are few in the Periphery but in rural areas the survival ratio is high. Innovation rations are modest. High-tech and high-growth firms are adequately represented in several parts of the Periphery. Distances to the Central Area of The Netherlands never exceed 200 kms, which is certainly not prohibitive when supplies and markets are located in the Central Area. In a small country, however, small distances may be regarded by entrepreneurs as major barriers. This brings us to some final remarks on the subject of spatial cognition.

CONCLUSION: THE NEGLECT OF SPATIAL COGNITION ASPECTS

Whether regional economic potential is thought to be related to region or firm characteristics, in both cases their calculation uses objective, statistical data. Yet the entrepreneurs do not operate with this calculated, objective reality, but with their own subjective perception of it. The actual objective economic potential of a region is meaningless when entrepreneurs are not aware of its existence. Even more serious than possible lack of knowledge is incorrect knowledge. A negative image of a region among entrepreneurs, even when it is undeserved, may be a major negative factor.

In the situation of The Netherlands, this can easily be demonstrated by the contours of the mental map of entrepreneurs (Figure 11.13). It is quite obvious that the northern Netherlands constitutes the low-lying plain in this landscape of preferences, which greatly hampers the possibility of developing the economic potential of this region, limited as it may be. Physical distance may be no problem for the development of high-growth industry in this part of the Periphery, but mental distance certainly is!

Figure 11.13: Locational preference of Dutch entrepreneurs: average rating of 70 locations (three-dimensional representation)

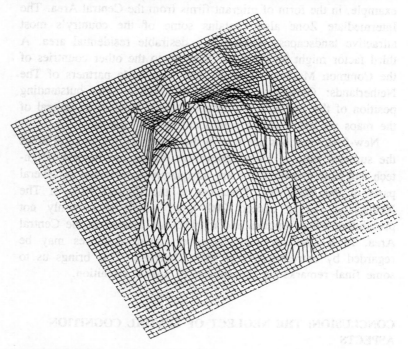

Source: Pellenbarg and Meester (1984)

It is not the purpose of this final section to enter into a detailed discussion of the images of regions in The Netherlands. Nevertheless, it demonstrates that the study of regional economic potential should not be restricted to a pure economic approach. Behavioural aspects of business decisions should also be taken into account. Mental maps and spatial images of entrepreneurs are a neglected, but still necessary complement of data on labour qualities, industrial sites, R&D centres, high-tech firms' presence, and so on. Regional scientists have to develop a systematic viewpoint to the coherence of these apparently divergent domains of policy.

REFERENCES

Alders, B. C. M. and P. A. de Ruyter (1984) *De ruimtelijke spreiding van kansrijke activiteiten in Nederland*. STC/PSC-TNO, Apeldoorn/Delft.

Bleumink, P. H. M., G. B. de Groot, J. Bilderbeek and E. Wever (1985) *Nieuwe ondernemingen en regio.* Vakgroep Economische Geografie, K. U. Nijmegen.

Bouman, H., T. Thuis and B. Verhoef (1985) *High tech in Nederland, vestigingsplaatsfactoren en ruimtelijke spreiding.* R. U. Utrecht/V. U. Amsterdam.

Harris, C. D. (1954) The market as a factor in the localization of industry in the U.S. *Annals of the Association of American Geographers,* **44**, 315–48.

Jong, M. de (1984) *Ruimtelijke dynamiek van het midden- en kleinbedrijf.* Economisch Geografisch Instituut, Universiteit van Amsterdam.

Knaap, G. A. van der and E. Struyk (1984) *Regionaal-economisch Analyse-Systeem.* Coördinatie-orgaan Regionaal Economisch overleg voor Noorden Midden Limburg.

Kok, J. A. A. M., G. J. D. Offerman and P. H. Pellenbarg (1984) The regional distribution of innovative firms in The Netherlands. In M. de Smidt and E. Wever (eds) *A profile of Dutch economic geography.* Assen, Van Gorcum, pp. 129–49.

NEI (1984) *Technologische vernieuwing en regionale ontwikkeling in Nederland.* (TRANSFER), Rotterdam.

NMB (1984) *Jaarverslag* (Annual Report).

Pellenbarg, P. H. and J. A. A. M. Kok (1985) Small and medium-sized innovative firms in The Netherlands' urban and rural regions. *Tijdschrift voor Economische en Sociale Geografie,* **76**(4), 242–52.

Pellenbarg, P. H. and W. Meester (1984) Location decisions and spatial cognition. In M. de Smidt and E. Wever (eds) *A profile of Dutch economic geography.* Assen, Van Gorcum, pp. 105–28.

Pellenbarg, P. H., S. Grit and N. J. Kemper (1987) *Atlas van Nederland deel 9 Bedrijven.* Staatsuitgeverij, 's Gravenhage.

Roelofs, B. and E. Wever (1985) Regio en economische potentie: een literatuurverkenning. *Rijksplanologische Dienst, 's Gravenhage, Studierapport,* **28**.

Webbink, A. H. (1985) *Groot en klein in de industrie.* Economisch Instituut voor het Midden- en Kleinbedrijf, Zoetermeer.

Wever, E. (1984) *Nieuwe bedrijven in Nederland.* Van Gorcum, Assen.

—— (1985) *Regionaal-economisch perspectief.* Geografisch en Planologisch Instituut/Van Dien & Co., Nijmegen.

229

12

Innovative Behaviour, Location and Firm Size: The Case of the Dutch Manufacturing Industry

Han Dieperink, Alfred Kleinknecht and Peter Nijkamp

INTRODUCTION

The economic stagnation which has affected Western countries in recent years has stimulated economic research into the determinants and effects of technological innovation (see, for example, Freeman, 1982; Coombs *et al.*, 1987; Kleinknecht, 1987a). It has also been increasingly realised that innovative behaviour is not spread uniformly over all regions and sectors of a national economic system (cf. Nijkamp, 1986). Industrial restructuring calls for favourable geographical conditions (for instance, accessibility, availability of urban amenities, a skilled labour pool, and so on), and there are presently clear indications that the configuration of regional dynamics in most industrialised countries is drastically changing. It is also at present often taken for granted that the driving force for growth in lagging areas lies in the development of a more competitive production system, frequently based on high-technology industries. It is then also assumed that such developments have a favourable impact on the service sector, especially on the advanced business service sector (cf. Gershuny and Miles, 1983), and as a consequence the role of business services in regional development strategies receives more and more attention (cf. Pedersen, 1986).

Another observation which has been made besides the spatial dimension of innovative behaviour is that industrial innovations do not only differ across different sectors, but also across different firm sizes. The latter phenomenon has called for a thorough attention for the functioning of small- and medium-scale local economies and for the pervasiveness of innovations at the firm level (cf. Gillespie, 1983). In this context also, ownership conditions at a local level (for example, branch plants versus locally owned firms) are increasingly being investigated. The same holds true for the (often unknown) innovative stimuli provided by informal economic activities (cf. Gershuny, 1979).

Firm size and location may thus have a significant and specific impact on innovative behaviour. The conventional assumption made in the geography of innovation is that large agglomerations induce innovations, but this assumption has recently been questioned (see Malecki, 1983): medium-sized agglomerations sometimes appear to possess an even higher innovation potential. A similar observation can be made regarding the impact of firm size. Though it is frequently taken for granted that large companies have a relatively high innovation rate, this is not always supported by empirical information. In addition, the degree to which a firm used R&D (either internal or external) is co-determined by its geographical location and its size. There is therefore a need for a more thorough empirical analysis of the triangular relationship between innovative behaviour, location and firm size. This will be done in this chapter on the basis of data from a large-scale postal survey on innovation in Dutch manufacturing industry.

REGIONAL DISTRIBUTION OF INNOVATION

General remarks

Various data used in the present study are derived from an investigation of technological innovation, recently carried out by Kleinknecht (1987b) among Dutch entrepreneurs. A postal questionnaire among some 2,917 industrial firms in five different classes of firm size (in terms of number of employees) resulted in a 63.1 per cent response rate (i.e., $n = 1,842$). The postal questionnaire contained several questions concerning standard innovation indicators, such as patenting, licensing and R&D. Moreover, a new 'output' indicator, consisting of numbers of innovation projects with radical natures of varying degrees, was included. Since it turned out that (at least in the specific Dutch circumstances) patenting and licensing do not appear to be adequate innovation indicators (see Kleinknecht, 1987b), we decided to concentrate on both the innovation output indicators (product and process innovations) and the innovation input

231

Figure 12.1: The agglomeration index

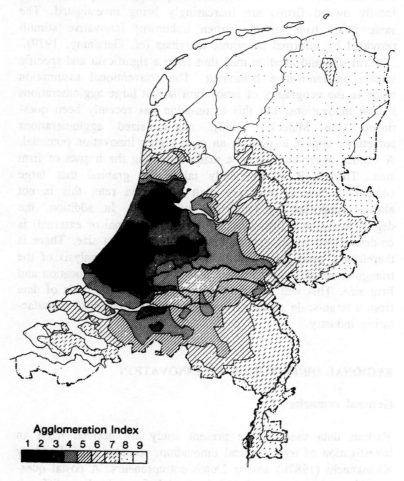

Agglomeration Index
1 2 3 4 5 6 7 8 9

indicators (i.e. R&D). The innovation output and input indicators are discussed for different firm size classes in the next two subsections.

The five firm size classes were defined as follows:

A: firms with less than 51 employees — $n(A)$ = 765;
B: firms with 51–99 employees — $n(B)$ = 419;
C: firms with 100–249 employees — $n(C)$ = 403;
D: firms with 250–500 employees — $n(D)$ = 139;
E: firms with more than 500 employees — $n(E)$ = 116.

232

It is noteworthy that the number of large firms is relatively small, but since the questionnaire was sent to 75 per cent of all Dutch large firms (with a response rate of 71.2 per cent), the resulting pattern may be assumed to be fairly reliable.

In order to analyse the spatial dimensions of innovation, a new spatial subdivision of The Netherlands has been created (see Dieperink and Nijkamp, 1986a). This regional classification used to establish the empirical connection between location and degree of innovation is called the agglomeration index. It is based on the approximation of agglomeration economies, that are thought to depend on city size, distance to the nearest agglomeration, and inter-urban effects (for further details see ibid.). By using this general classification, the danger that the methodology would be too much restricted to the specific Dutch situation of highly concentrate densities of agglomerations was avoided. The classification that results from the agglomeration index in the case of The Netherlands is illustrated in Figure 12.1. Note that the index ranges from 1 (strong agglomeration economies) to 9 (very low agglomeration economies). The distribution of firms over the nine agglomeration indices and the five firm size classes is included in Table 12.1.

Table 12.1: Distribution of firms over agglomeration index and firm size

Firm size	Agglomeration index								
	1	2	3	4	5	6	7	8	9
A	55	93	80	122	65	95	91	141	23
B	39	46	49	45	28	46	55	96	15
C	32	51	45	52	24	53	50	86	10
D	12	16	14	21	9	22	14	20	11
E	15	24	9	17	10	11	17	11	2

Innovation output indicators

Product innovation

A whole variety of indicators is used in various innovation studies to measure product innovation (Dieperink and Nijkamp, 1986b; Kleinknecht, 1987a). Many of those indicators, like the mean number of realised product innovations, are very sensitive to outliers, sometimes caused by a limited number of larger firms. Because comparison of the innovation indicator between different

233

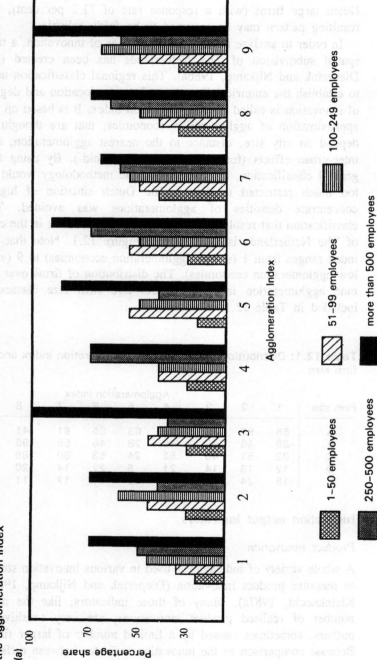

Figure 12.2a, b: The percentage share of firms that realised one or more product innovations during 1983, categorised by the agglomeration index

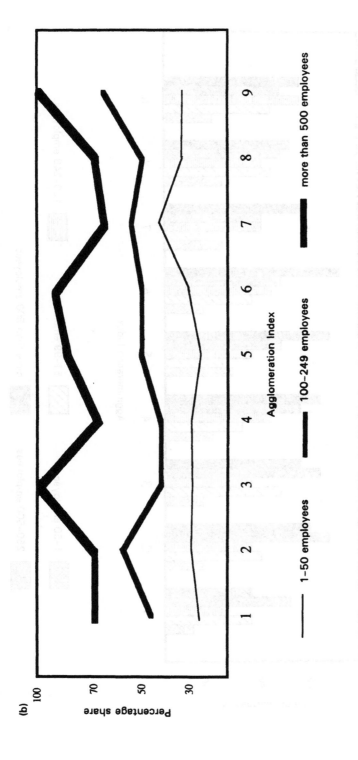

(b)

Percentage share

100
70
50
30

1-50 employees   100-249 employees   more than 500 employees

Agglomeration Index

1   2   3   4   5   6   7   8   9

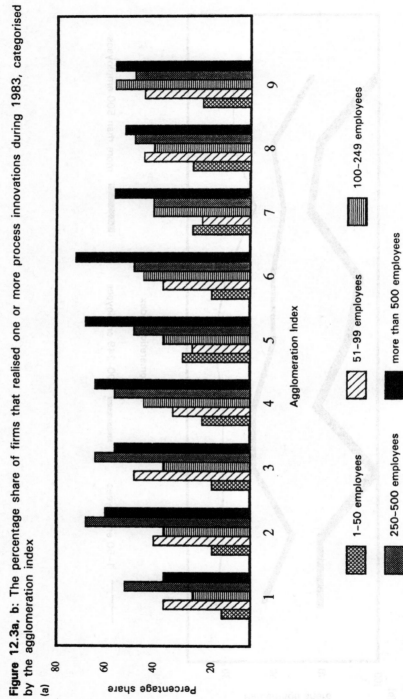

Figure 12.3a, b: The percentage share of firms that realised one or more process innovations during 1983, categorised by the agglomeration index

(a)

Percentage share

Agglomeration Index

1–50 employees

51–99 employees

100–249 employees

250–500 employees

more than 500 employees

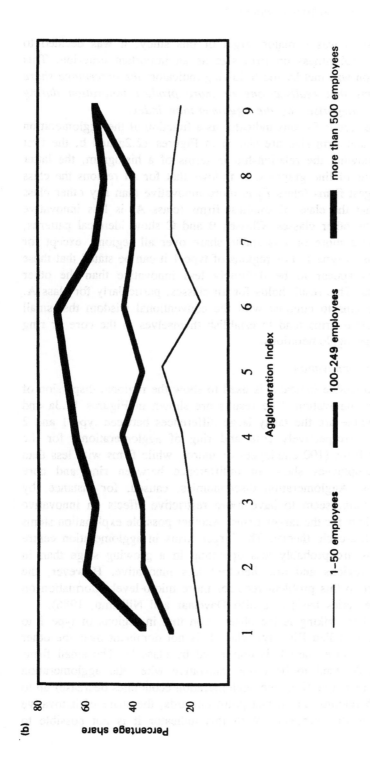

(b)

Percentage share

80
60
40
20

1   2   3   4   5   6   7   8   9

Agglomeration Index

— 1-50 employees   — 100-249 employees   — more than 500 employees

firm sizes was a major target of this study, it was decided to impose robustness on firm size as an important criterion. This criterion was met by the following indicator: *the percentage share of firms that realised one or more product innovation during 1983, categorised by the agglomeration index.*

The results for this indicator as a function of the agglomeration index and firm size are shown in Figures 12.2a and b, the first one showing the relationship in terms of a histogram, the latter in terms of line graphics. It follows that for all regions the class of largest firms (class E) is more innovative than any other class and that the class of smallest firms (class A) is less innovative than the other classes. Classes B and C show identical patterns, namely a more or less stable share over all regions, except for regions of type 1. For regions of type 1 it can be stated that these regions appear to be definitely less innovative than the other regions. This result holds for all classes, particularly for class A. This seems to contrast with the conventional wisdom that small innovative firms tend to establish themselves in the core or ring of large agglomerations.

Process innovation

A comparable indicator is used to show the regional dispersion of process innovation. The results are shown in Figures 12.3a and b. Notable are the fairly large differences between type 1 and 2 regions (respectively core and ring of agglomerations) for the larger firms (100 employees or more), while firms with less than 100 employees show an indifference between ring and core regions. Agglomeration diseconomies, caused, for instance, by congestion, seem to have more restrictive effects on innovative behaviour for the larger firms. Another possible explanation stems from life-cycle theory. The larger firms in agglomeration centre regions are probably less operating in a growing stage than in other regions and are therefore less innovative. However, the answer to this problem requires more micro-level information on a time series basis (see also Davelaar and Nijkamp, 1986).

Rather striking is the observation that in regions of type 1 to 3 (the so-called Rimcity), class E is not dominant over the other classes, since class E is dominated by class D. The small firms (class A) tend to be more innovative when the agglomeration index increases (i.e., the agglomeration economies decrease) up to type 5 regions. From that point onwards, the share of innovative firms again decreases. With this indicator it is not possible to

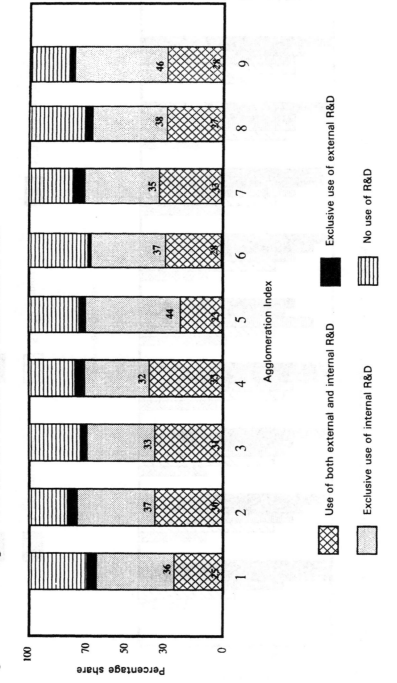

Figure 12.4: Percentage of firms that used external and/or internal R&D in 1983

Agglomeration Index

Percentage share

Use of both external and internal R&D

Exclusive use of internal R&D

Exclusive use of external R&D

No use of R&D

Figure 12.5a, b: The percentage share of firms that spent money on R&D within the firm itself

(a)

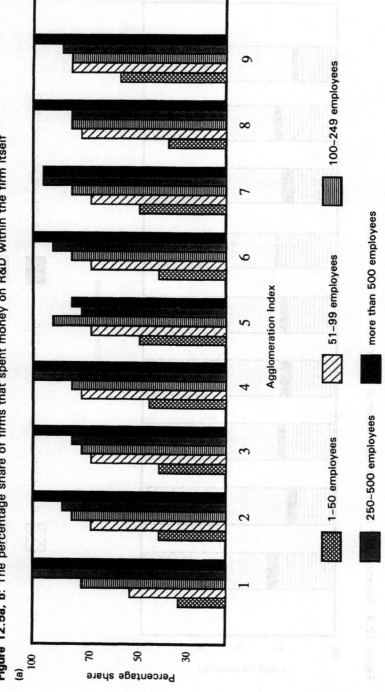

Percentage share

Agglomeration Index

1–50 employees

250–500 employees

51–99 employees

more than 500 employees

100–249 employees

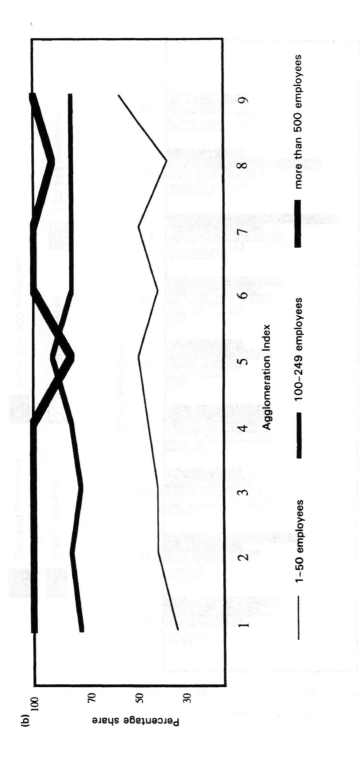

(b)

Percentage share

100
70
50
30

1   2   3   4   5   6   7   8   9

Agglomeration Index

——— 1–50 employees   ▬▬ 100–249 employees   ▬▬ more than 500 employees

Figure 12.6a, b: The percentage share of firms that performed R&D through others

(a)

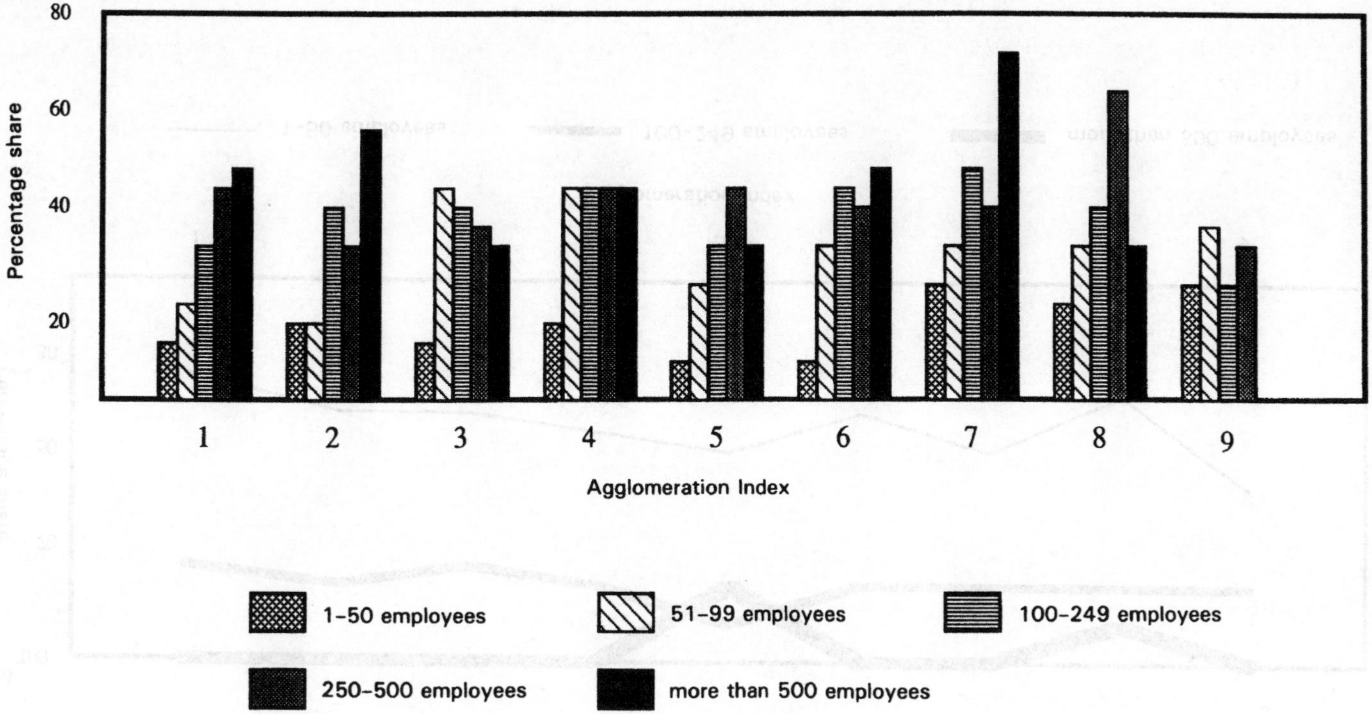

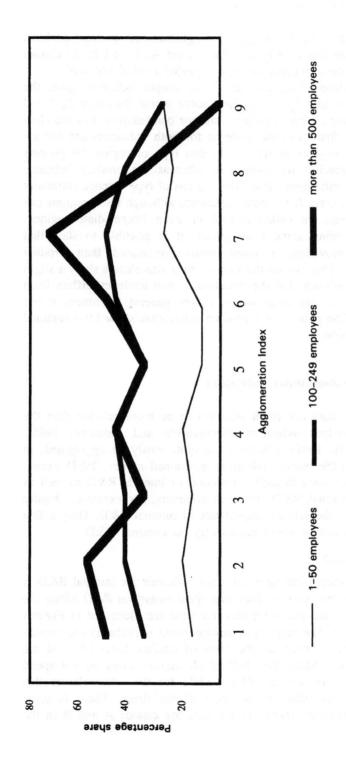

Percentage share

80
60
40
20

1   2   3   4   5   6   7   8   9

Agglomeration Index

—— 1–50 employees   —— 100–249 employees   ■■■ more than 500 employees

conclude that regions of type 1 (agglomeration centres) perform worst, since this is only true for classes A, C and E. In classes B and D these regions of type 1 perform relatively well.

Comparison of the two innovation output indicators gives the following result. Type 1 regions score worse than type 2, 3 and 4 regions for all but one class/indicator combination. For the class of smaller firms (A) the patterns for both indicators are similar except for regions of type 5. In that type of region the process indicator reaches its maximum, whereas the product indicator reaches its minimum value. The regions of type 7 score extremely well within class A for both indicators, although these regions can by no means be called central or even intermediate regions. Notwithstanding some reservations, it is possible to state that process innovation is more location-orientated than product innovation. The data on the various firm size classes show a slight regional tendency, but the direction of that tendency differs from size class to size class which makes general inferences rather difficult. The patterns for product innovation show little regional discrimination.

The innovation input indicators

R&D indicators are often assumed to be more reliable than the previous output indicators (Kleinknecht and Mouwen, 1985). Furthermore, R&D indicators can quite easily be aggregated, in contrast to the output indicators mentioned earlier. R&D expenditures take place through intramural or internal R&D as well as through external R&D (research contracts, for example). Figure 12.4 shows the relative importance of internal R&D. Only a few firms turn out to spend exclusively on external R&D.

Internal R&D

As in the output indicator case, the indicator for internal R&D is defined by *the share of firms that spent money on R&D within the firm itself*. The results for this indicator are illustrated in Figures 12.5a and b. The most eye-catching result is probably the significant difference between the class of smaller firms (A) and the other classes. More than half of all smaller firms do not spend any money on internal R&D, while for the other classes this amount is less than 30 per cent of the firms. There is some regional tendency shown in the data for classes A and B in the sense that the share of firms that spent internal R&D increases (with a few exceptions) from index 1 to 9. For the other classes there is no proof of a relation between location and innovation.

External R&D

The results for external R&D are shown in Figures 12.6a and b for *the share of firms that performed R&D through others.* Regional tendencies for internal R&D were difficult to detect. For external R&D, however, there are distinct relations between location and the above-mentioned indicator. For all firm size classes, for instance, type 7 regions are more innovative (in terms of our indicator) than type 6 regions. Type 6 regions are more innovative than regions of type 5 for nearly all class sizes. Regions of type 5 are also uniformly dominated by type 4 regions, while those regions also dominate regions of type 3. Regions of type 4 and 7 can be described as local maxima for each firm size class and regions of type 5 as local minima.

Another noteworthy observation is the non-dominance of class E, probably caused by the fact that class E firms have their own R&D capacity and therefore are less dependent on external resources as far as R&D is concerned.

REFERENCES

Coombs, R., P. Saviotti and V. Walsh (1987) *Economics and technological change.* Macmillan, London.

Davelaar, E. J. and P. Nijkamp (1986) The incubator hypothesis: revitalization of metropolitan areas? *Research memorandum, Free University, Amsterdam, 1986-87.*

Dieperink, J. P. and P. Nijkamp (1986a) De Agglomeratie-Index. *Planning, 27,* 1–8.

―――― (1986b) Spatial dispersion of industrial innovation. *Research memorandum, Free University, Amsterdam, 1986-9.*

Freeman, C. (1982) *The economics of industrial innovation.* Frances Pinter, London.

Gershuny, J. I. (1979) The informal economy. *Futures, 11*(1), 3–15.

―――― and I. Miles (1983) *The new service economy.* Frances Pinter, London.

Gillespie, A. E. (ed.) (1983) *Technological change and regional development.* Pion, London.

Kleinknecht, A. (1987a) *Innovation patterns in crisis and prosperity. Schumpeter's long cycle reconsidered.* Macmillan, London; St Martin's Press, New York.

―――― (1987b) *Industriële innovatie in Nederland, Een enquête-*

onderzoek. Van Gorcum, Maastricht and Assen.

—— and A. Mouwen (1985) Regionale innovatie (R&D): Verschuiving naar de 'halfwegzone'? In W. T. M. Molle (ed.), *Innovatie en regio*. Government Publication House, pp. 125–42.

Malecki, E. J. (1983) Technology and regional development. *International Regional Science Review*, 8(2), 89–125.

Nijkamp, P. (ed.) (1986) *Technological change, employment and spatial dynamics*. Springer Verlag, Berlin.

Pedersen, P. O. (1986) The role of business services in regional development. *Scandinavian Housing and Planning Research*, 3, 167–82.

13

Small and Medium-sized Enterprises and the Regional Distribution of Industry in Spain: A New Stage

Juan R. Cuadrado Roura

INTRODUCTION

This chapter describes those factors characterising the geographical distribution of industry in Spain over recent decades. Broadly speaking there has been a process of marked concentration in a number of productive centres, although industry remains well spread throughout the country and a large number of centres have developed significant industrial activity.

There can be no simple explanation for the phenomenon, but emphasis will be placed on the fact that the leading role in this *geographical distribution* of industry has been played by the small and medium-sized enterprises, whose weight and driving force in the Spanish economy are of great significance.

Past regional policy has included measures aimed at promoting the development of small and medium-sized enterprises with rather inconsistent results. Some of these measures may be effective, but as a result of the changes that have taken place in the economy due to the crisis and the process of integration into international markets, there are many problems experienced by small and medium-sized firms. Hence, in the final section, we summarise current developments in Spain.

GEOGRAPHICAL DISTRIBUTION OF INDUSTRIAL ACTIVITY: A CHANGING PROCESS

When considering the Spanish economy over the long term, certain key facts stand out, one being the relationships between industrial activity and areas. They show a development that initially tended towards a marked concentration, but which later gave way to a certain dispersion. Starting from other analyses already carried out, we will attempt to set out the basic outlines of this process.

Dispersion versus concentration

Fifty years ago, Perpiñá Grau (1936) demonstrated empirically the marked economic, and especially industrial, concentration that existed in the Spanish economy. He also attempted to define the forces — demographic, economic and geographic — that had promoted and fomented this concentration, and he predicted that the process would tend to continue in the future. The map stemming from this analysis was composed of a small number of production centres or areas mainly located in the coastal strip, with a broad inland zone where a limited number of nuclei stood out that were termed as being somewhat more dynamic. Barcelona (Catalonia), Vizcaya (Basque country) and Madrid appeared in this layout as the most important centres of production in the country, followed by Valencia, Guipuzcoa (Basque country) and Asturias, and more distantly, by Alicante, Vigo, Santander and Malaga on the coast, and Zaragoza, Seville and Cordoba inland.

The regional economic data for 1960 still match this design of spatial concentration fairly well. By then most of these provinces occupied the leading positions amongst the 50 provinces of Spain, and the distances between the first five and the rest had widened, particularly from the industrial standpoint.

This picture began to change slowly from the middle of the 1960s, when Spain embarked on a process of swift growth, which gave rise to major modifications in the productive structure of the country and brought about extremely important migratory movements.[1] Indeed, the transformation of the Spanish economy between 1960 and 1975 is almost unique in Europe. The leading role was played by the industrial sector, but we should not overlook the contribution of some service activities — mainly those linked with tourism — and the process of technification and modernisation of part of the agricultural sector.

Data on regional industrial production for the period show that although industrial activity continued to be concentrated in the areas of already advanced industrialisation (in 1975 Barcelona,

Madrid and Vizcaya represented 39·5 per cent of industrial value added and 38·9 per cent of total employment in the sector, and the regions of Catalonia, Madrid and the Basque country concentrated 51 per cent of the gross value added and 48·01 per cent of employment), from the middle of the sixties a process of *greater spatial dispersion* of industry took place which has gained even more momentum in recent years.

In 1985, the latest financial year for which we have data on a regional level, the three regions we referred to above account for 46·1 per cent of the gross industrial value added, i.e. five points less than in 1975; and furthermore, a series of provinces, both in the coastal strip and inland, now make a very significant contribution to the industrial value added, both in absolute and relative terms. The variations in the volume of regional industrial employment have also been considerable, although a clear downward trend in overall industrial employment has been followed since 1975 as a result of the crisis and the process of de-industrialisation.

The resultant map is now noticeably different from that of half a century ago, even though it retains some points in common. Barcelona continues to be the leading industrial centre, but a considerable manufacturing expansion has taken place on its outskirts. Madrid is the second industrial centre, whilst Vizcaya has lost ground and Valencia, with a long tradition of fairly sectorally diversified small and medium-sized industries, has now taken its place. However, provinces such as Alicante, Tarragona, Gerona, Zaragoza, Seville, Valladolid, and Burgos, are also highly placed on the list.

Explanatory elements: superimposed pieces or processes

To explain these developments we need to discuss three processes which have occurred simultaneously, and which we may term *polarised growth, endogenous industrialisation*; and *de-industrialisation.*

The first of these processes basically evolved in the fifties and sixties and is undoubtedly the most significant one. In the stage prior to the opening up and liberalisation of the Spanish economy initiated in 1959–60, the actual prevailing autarkic system, enclosed and with very few markets, fomented industrial concentration. Moreover, this proved to be especially encouraged in the case of Madrid, whose industrial development sprang from and relied upon direct state initiatives on its predominant political position and on the actual structure of the national communications system.

The industrial expansion of the 1960s received the full support of the authorities who, by means of generous credit, tax and capital goods and raw materials import incentives, tried to achieve a set of *sectoral* industrial production aims, laid down as objectives in the first two four-year development plants. The concentration of public investments, the backing given to the basic industries and the actual establishment of minimum dimensions for new industries are good indicators of the *concentrated* focus for industrial activity. However, in the mid-sixties a process got under way that was to lead to the development of new industrial nuclei in cities not located in the Basque country, Madrid or the immediate surroundings of Barcelona. There are two main reasons for this occurrence. Firstly, the improvements in the communications system, together with the costs imposed by large agglomerations, the advantages offered by certain markets and the working conditions in more remote areas caused certain companies — amongst these, some multinationals or with foreign capital holdings — to consider alternative locations for their new factories or branches. Secondly, the authorities offered incentives for the location of such companies or plants (policy of 'poles', estates and areas of preferential location) at specific geographical points, in the belief that these poles would later attract other activities towards the less developed regions and that these, in turn, would spread the effects of development in their surrounding areas.

Although this did not occur on a wide scale, a few urban nuclei scattered throughout Spain did become more industrially developed. In a few cases this was because of the establishment of large companies, but it mainly occurred because of small and medium-sized enterprises, both of local origin and branches or investments of companies from outside the area.

Paralleling this process, a *dispersion* of industrial activity took place in the surroundings of the main metropolitan areas (chiefly Madrid, Barcelona and Bilbao). The surveys conducted[2] indicated that, after a period of marked productive concentration, a process of dispersion (or of relative de-concentration) of industrial activity was initiated from the centre of the metropolitan areas towards their outskirts and towards a number of axes of dispersion which relied on communication facilities. New medium-sized and small companies then sprang up or were developed in this environment, either linked to other existing ones with which they co-operated, or to take advantage of external economies and the important market available.

The origin of some industrial nuclei currently in existence and that of a certain number of manufacturing companies located in rural areas and nuclei cannot be attributed solely to the process of de-concentration of activities that we have just described. In many aspects, their establishment and development may be identified with what has been termed (Fuà, 1983; Vazquez, 1983, 1984) as a process of *endogenous industrialisation*.

It is not easy to characterise this type of industrial development as its features are relatively heterogeneous, although they coincide at various points (Vazquez, 1986). In general terms, it is a case of industrial activities that have been developed using resources belonging to the area where they are implanted — at times just human and financial ones, but at others, raw materials as well — and which are located in small nuclei, with hardly any direct aid from the authorities.

Some of the research carried out in recent years in Spain[3] has shown that the phenomenon of endogenous local industrialisation is widespread in Spain, although there is a relative concentration in the Mediterranean coastal strip, the Basque country and the Ebro valley, with other significant nuclei in the provinces of the Centre, Andalusia and Galicia. The companies are always medium/small-sized, with the figure of the entrepreneur being a key factor. They are highly integrated into their area and cultural environment, and yet this does not prevent many of them from operating competitively in international markets.

The final factor in explaining the great geographical dispersion of industry in Spain is the actual *process of de-industrialisation*, which started as a result of the economic crisis and stems from the adjustments that this imposed on the industrial sector, particularly on specific basic branches (iron and steel, basic metals, chemicals, shipbuilding, etc.), as well as of processing and consumption. The presence of companies engaged in these industries has imposed severe dislocation in some areas, whereas others, with a greater degree of diversification and a more flexible type of small or medium-sized company, have been able to prosper.

As in other countries, although perhaps with greater severity

251

owing to the delay in tackling the problem, Spanish industry has had to embark on an extensive programme of reconversion on a sectoral basis, mainly involving large companies, both private and public. However, the small and medium-sized enterprises have suffered as well; in some cases, as a consequence of what happened to the large ones which were their customers; in others, independently, as a result of the toughening of market conditions and the variations in production costs. All this has brought about heavy cut-backs in industrial employment and in the total number of industrial establishments.

Nevertheless, this has had a more marked effect on the more traditional regions or centres of industrial concentration and on some industrialised nuclei in less developed areas, whereas in many intermediate provinces and areas of dispersion the destruction of companies and jobs has been less. The consequence of this has been a relative improvement in the position of the industry in these latter areas or regions.

THE INCREASINGLY IMPORTANT ROLE PLAYED BY THE SMALL AND MEDIUM-SIZED ENTERPRISES

The process of intense industrialisation that has taken place in Spain since the start of the 1960s initially stemmed from the expansion of large basic industries already in existence as well as from the development and establishment of other new ones, also linked to basic sectors (iron and steel, chemicals, petrochemicals, motor vehicles and shipyards), which often had ties with foreign companies and groups.[4]

The large company[5] has therefore undoubtedly played an extremely important part in the industrial development of the country, and continues to do so. We only have to remember that a small number of large industries (0·4 per cent of the total of establishments) contribute 37 per cent of the value added of the manufacturing sector, employing around 23 per cent of the industrial labour in the country. However, the role played by the small and medium-sized enterprises (SMEs) in the process of industrial expansion which we have outlined was also quite decisive, not only for their growing weight in production and employment terms, but also for their contribution towards the spatial dispersion of industry. Their importance has grown further in recent years as a result of the changes imposed by the crisis

— mainly in the technological field and as regards the scale economies — as well as through the greater flexibility that this type of firm can display in more difficult economic circumstances.

The boundaries between the small, medium-sized and large enterprises may be defined according to differing criteria, with a validity that is always subject to discussion. Without going into this question here, we propose to consider that the volume of employment is, with all its limitations, the basic criterion, with the result that we shall rate as small industrial companies those that have up to 49 employees, as medium-sized those with between 50 and 499 employees, and as large those exceeding 500 employees in size.

The most recent data in Table 13.1 show us that the SMEs represent around 99.6 per cent of the total of Spanish industrial establishments (1982 figures) and 77.1 per cent of industrial employment. Their contribution to value added lies at slightly above 63 per cent of the total for the manufacturing sector.

There are no satisfactory data that will enable us to chart the development of the SME over the last 25 years. However, within its limitations, the information available does allow us to state that the weight of the SME sector has tended towards a slight increase, both in the number of establishments and in employment, even though its share in industrial value added has fallen by almost two points. The figures for the period 1969 to 1982 reveal an increase in relative terms as to the number of establishments and employees of the SME sector in respect of the industrial total (Table 13.1). At the same time (Table 13.2), we observe a decline in the average number of employees in the smallest companies (less than 49 workers) and a trend towards

Table 13.1: Relative participation (%) of the number of plants and employment of small and medium-sized enterprises 1969 and 1982 (total industrial sector = 100%)

| | No. of plants | | Employment | |
	1969	1982	1969	1982
Up to 49 people occupied	94·8	96·1	38·8	39·8
50 to 499 people occupied	4·5	3·5	38·1	37·3
	99·3	99·6	76·9	77·1

Source: Prepared with figures from the Ministry of Industry and National Institute of Statistics.

Table 13.2: Average size (number of employees) of the small and medium-sized enterprises in Spain, 1969 and 1982

	1969	1982
Up to 49 people occupied	7·3	6·6
50–99	69·7	70·1
100–199	138·7	139·8
200–499	298·5	303·0

Source: As Table 13.1.

increasing size at the other levels, i.e., in the medium-sized companies. We should also point out that, between these dates, total employment has dropped in absolute terms as a result of the economic crisis.

A further aspect to be borne in mind in relation to the current role played by SMEs in the national economy is that, according to a recent survey and other Ministry of Industry data, 97 per cent of the Spanish exporting companies are small and medium-sized and that their share in industrial exports is equivalent to approximately 42 per cent, a percentage that has followed an upward trend over the last ten years.

From the spatial standpoint, i.e., as regards the location of the SMEs and their participation in the industrial activity of each region, we can show that the proportions between large, medium-sized and small companies vary noticeably in the different provinces and regions, not only in terms of the number of establishments, but also in relation to employment and the respective industrial value added. Table 13.3 shows that[6] regions with a marked industrial specialisation usually coincide with a lower presence — in relative terms — of SMEs, as happens in the Basque country, Catalonia, Madrid, Asturias and Cantabria. At the same time, the SMEs have an equivalent, or more than proportional, weight in the regions with a lower share percentage in the national industrial product, as are the cases of Navarre, Rioja, Andalusia and Galicia.

Secondly, on a provincial scale, i.e., below the regional level, industrial dispersion has been of some importance in the provinces closest to the large metropolitan and industrial nuclei that existed at the start of the 1960s. The cases of the provinces of Alava, Burgos, Logrono and Navarre bordering on Vizcaya, Tarragona and Gerona bordering on Barcelona, and those of Toledo and Gudalajara, though to a lesser degree, bordering on Madrid, all

Table 13.3: Spatial distribution of industry and of SMEs

	Share in the added value of industry (%)	Index of specialisation in industry	Regional share in the SMEs (%)
Andalusia	10·3	78·8	11·9
Aragon	3·3	99·3	4·5
Asturias	4·2	*131·1*	2·6
Balearics	1·6	74·0	2·1
Basque country	9·4	*137·0*	5·0
Canary I·	2·2	64·5	1·8
Cantabria	1·6	*106·2*	1·2
Castile-La Mancha	3·2	91·0	6·9
Castile-Leon	6·0	96·9	9·1
Catalonia	22·2	*118·8*	19·2
Extremadura	1·1	63·3	3·2
Galicia	6·1	96·9	8·7
Madrid	12·2	81·4	6·8
Murcia	1·8	82·6	2·8
Navarre	1·8	*113·2*	1·9
Rioja	1·0	*122·8*	1·3
Valencian Com.	12·2	*115·7*	11·5
Total	100·0		100·0

Note: Elements may not sum to 100·0 due to rounding errors.
Source: Prepared by the author, based on figures from the Ministry of Industry and Ministry of Finance.

represent good examples of this process. The driving force behind this dispersion can clearly be put down to the SMEs sector.

Thirdly, taking the country as a whole, there are now certain industrial nuclei whose development was influenced through their being considered as 'poles' in the regional industrial development policy embarked upon in the mid-1960s, even though the efficacy of this instrument was very uneven. The cases of the poles of Valladolid, Burgos and Zaragoza are the clearest and the SMEs played a decisive part here. The case of Huelva in Andalusia is, however, very different, as the large companies — mainly chemical — were responsible for the industrial upsurge.

Finally, when we go down to a scale below the province, the national map also shows many small centres or areas scattered fairly widely throughout the country, where it only seems possible to explain the development of SMEs on the basis of endogenous industrialisation patterns, one of the features of which is the scant support that these firms received from the authorities.

255

THE CURRENT OUTLOOK: PROBLEMS AND INSTRUMENTS

In Spain, as in other countries, the economic crisis has meant that the aims of regional industrial development and the struggle to reduce regional disparities have given way to concerns which are much more focused on sectoral aspects (restructuring and matching of supply in the sectors in crisis), on the technological changes in progress, and on ensuring that industries, regardless of their location, achieve suitable levels of performance that enable them to be internationally competitive. Spain's entry into the EEC has served to reinforce these orientations.

This does not imply that the regional component has disappeared from the aims and guidelines of industrial policy. The new political structure of the country enables the regional governments to give even greater attention to the specific problems of their respective Autonomous Community, providing resources and incentives to attract new industries. Nevertheless, central government has retained some instruments designed to encourage the establishment of industries in the less developed regions[7] and, furthermore, has identified seven Zones of Urgent Industrialisation (ZUR) in those parts of the country especially affected by restructuring processes for iron and steel works, shipyards and certain metal industries. In spite of all this, attention has increasingly been focused on tackling the specific problems facing already-existing industries, regardless of their location, and on ensuring that the authorities (both national and regional) give backing to the development of the technological and organisational improvements required for international competitiveness. Hence, at this time, the policy relating to SMEs, whether existing or new, gives much greater attention to matters of economic efficiency than spatial location.

In this respect, the problems are similar to those of the other countries of the EEC. The main areas in which these problems exist for SMEs are: research and technological innovation; training, information and consultancy; financing; labour relations; taxation; subcontracting and public contracts; and exporting.

In the appended summary table, we have attempted to synthesise, for each of the different areas mentioned, the main problems, aims and instruments in Spain. In some cases measures were first introduced four or five years ago; in others, the initiatives are rather more recent; and lastly, there are actions in which both the central authorities and some of the regional governments co-operate or overlap.

256

Rather than discuss each measure individually, two general points have to be made. The first is the priority that is being given, as a rule, to the introduction and development of technological improvements in SMEs. The result of this development of new technologies was that, initially, it seemed best for attention and assistance to be given to companies directly linked with the so-called vanguard or advanced-technology sectors. Now, without these possibilities being given up entirely, what is considered as the prime objective is that of encouraging the introduction of new technologies in the whole industrial fabric in order to accelerate its modernisation and enhance competitiveness. This includes spreading knowledge of the new technologies, encouraging their adaptation and, in short, promoting technical change in all those branches where it is possible and necessary.

The second question concerns the importance that is being conferred on the role of the services supplied to companies, both from the public sector and on the part of the private sector. The demand for a series of services is undergoing considerable expansion (consultancies, design, market surveys, financial engineering, information and control, etc.), since they constitute genuine *inputs* into the production function of the companies, which are of equal or greater importance than other factors. However, supply is still inadequate, as is shown by some studies,[8] and this represents an obstacle to the modernisation of the industrial structure, particularly in the case of SMEs. This is the reason why both the central and regional authorities are paying closer attention to this type of restriction, even though the real possibilities of accelerating the provision of services on a regional scale are not high.

NOTES

1. For further details see Donges (1976) and Gonzalez (1979) for the general aspects, and Saenz de Buruaga (1975) and Cuadrado (1985) regarding regional changes.
2. See Alemany *et al.* (1985) and SETEC (1986).
3. See Vazquez (1983, 1984, 1986), CEAM (1986) and SETEC (1986).
4. See Donges (1976), Carballo *et al.* (1981), Lorca *et al.* (1981) and Cuadrado (1985).
5. We consider as a large company that which has 500 workers or more.

6. The analysis by sub-sectors is, of course, much clearer, since the productive specialisation of each zone appears linked, in a good number of cases, to the medium size of the companies located there.

7. Based on granting certain credit and tax incentives besides other advantages concerned with the land. The instruments are connected with: the Main Areas of Industrial Expansion; Zones of Preferential Location of Farming Industries; and industrial estates. A new Law of Regional Incentives has codified these types of measures, bringing them into line with EEC requirements.

8. See FIES Fundacion (1986).

REFERENCES

Alemany, J. *et al.* (1985) Tendencias económicas y políticas metropolitanas en el área de Barcelona. *Estudios Territoriales, 19,* 91–112.

Carballo, R. *et al.* (1981) *Crecimiento económico y crisis estructural en Espana 1959–1980.* Akal Edit., Madrid.

CEAM (1986) Areas rurales espanolas con capacidad de industrializacíon endógena. Mimeo, ITU, Madrid.

Cuadrado, J. R. (1982) Regional economic disparities. An approach and some reflections on the Spanish case. *Papers of the Regional Science Association, 49,* 113–30.

——— (1985) Economía y desequilibrios regionales en España. In F. Fernández *et al.*, *La España de las Autonomías.* IEAL, Madrid, pp. 149–218.

——— *et al.* (1982) *Presto Proyect. Case Study: Andalusia.* FAST, EEC.

Donges, J. B. (1976) *La industrializacíon en España. Políticas, logros, perspectivas.* Ed. Oikos-Tau, Barcelona.

FIES, Fundacíon (J. R. Cuadrado, Director) (1986) *Supply and demand of services and regional development.* FAST Series, No 93, EEC, Brussels.

Fuà, G. (1983) L'industrializzazione nel Nord Est e nel Centro. In Fuà y Zachia, *Industrializzazione senza Fratture.* Il Mulino, Bologna.

Gonzalez, M. J. (1979) *La economia política del franquismo (1940–1970).* Edit. Technos, Madrid.

Lorca, A., A. Martinez and L. Garcia (1981) Una evaluacíon de la política de polos de desarrollo. In Varios, *La España de la autonomías.* Ed. Espasa-Calpe, 2 Vols, Madrid.

Ministerio de Industria (1985) El impacto de la entrada de España en la CEE para las pequeñas y medianas empresas. Madrid.

Perpiñá Grau, R. (1936) De Economía Hispana; reprinted in *De Economía Hispana y otros ensayos.* Ed. Rialp., Madrid.

Rodriguez, V. (1985) Crecimiento regional y ajuste sectorial en los periodos — 1964–1973 y 1973–1981. *I. C. Española, 1986.* (April).

Saenz de Buruaga, G. (1975) Política regional y urbanística. In L. Gámir (ed.), *Política económica de España.* Ed. Gaudiana, Madrid.

SETEC (1986) Pausas de localizacíon territorial de empresas industriales. Mimeo, ITU, Madrid.

Vazquez, A. (1983) Industrialization in rural areas. The Spanish case. OECD Meeting, Senigallia (Italy), June.

—— (1984) Desarrollo con iniciativas locales en España. *I.C.E.*, *609*, 57–69.

—— (1986) El cambio del modelo de desarrollo regional y los nuevos procesos de difusión en España. In *Estudios Territoriales*, *20*, 87–110.

APPENDIX: SUMMARY TABLES

Problem areas of the SME in Spain and current developments (I)

Area	Problems	Measures	Effected through:
A. Research and technological innovation	— Introduction of new technologies — Lack of financial resources — Dispersed efforts — Lack of co-ordination between firms and research centres and universities	— Providing incentives for technological innovation (processes and products) — Promoting co-operation (between firms on a sectorial scale) — Agreements between sectors and research centres with financial support — Development of selective research programmes — Intensification of technical information and technological advisory services	— The State and Autonomous Communities: providing aid and credit — CDTI (Centro Nacional de Desarrollo Tecnológico) (National Centre for Technological Development) — CAYCIT (Comisión Asesora de Investigación Científica y Técnica) (Scientific and Technical Research Advisory Commission) — Specific bodies in certain regions
B. Business Training	— Low level of training — Difficult access to information	Diffusion of economic information: technical and concerning markets: Businessman's Information Service Technical assistance: in setting up businesses; sectoral; for subcontracting	— IMPI (Instituto Mediana y Pequeña Empresa Industrial)(Institute of the Small and Medium-sized Industrial Firm) — Several Autonomous Communities have created specialised Institutes — Chambers of Commerce

C. Financing

- Inadequate own funds
- Discrimination in the amount, term and cost of external resources
- Guarantees

— Special loans (interest and term)
— Selective state participation in firms
— Promotion of risk-capital companies
— Tax concessions
— Access to the Stock Exchange (second market)

— SODI (Industrial Development Companies)
— SGR (Sociedades de Garantía Recíproca)(Reciprocal Guarantee Companies)
— SSA (Sociedad de Segundo Aval)(Second Guarantee Company)
— State and private banks: special credit facilities
— Many Autonomous Communities have their own support programmes

Problem areas of the SME in Spain and current developments (II)

Area	Problems	Measures	Effected through:
A. Labour relations	— Rigid labour legislation — Labour institutions unsuitable for SME — High labour costs — Vocational training	— Increased flexibility in contracting regulations: trainee contracts, part time, etc. — Selective financial support for contracting young workers and those over 40 — Occupational retraining for sectors in recession	— Legislative reforms (initiated in 1986)

Area	Problems	Measures	Effected through:
B. Taxation	— Heavy tax burdens — Complex bureaucracy — National Insurance payable by the company	Favouring fiscal neutrality (according to sector and size of business) Simplification of Corporation Tax	— Reforms of current regulations (partially pending)
C. Subcontracting and public contracts	— Lack of information and transparency — Complex administrative procedures with public bodies and inequality of contracting	Creation of data bases and access Promoting contacts between firms	— National/Regional Subcontracting Commission (Ministry of Industry) — Chambers of Commerce and Industry

D. Exports

- Ignorance of potential markets and export procedures
- Limited supplies of the products offered
- Financing

- Incentives for exports; promotion and diffusion of information
- Producers' associations and export consortia
- Participation in trade fairs; subsidies and credit

- INFE (Instituto Nacional de Fomento a la Exportación)(National Institute for the Promotion of Exports)
- Banks and private bodies
- Reforms in the fiscal legislation

14

Regional Dimensions of Small and Medium-sized Enterprises in Greece

Maria Giaoutzi

INTRODUCTION

In the context of the recent patterns of structural changes and economic fluctuations tormenting the world's regions in recent years, some radical changes both in scientific and policy interest have emerged in the search for effective tools to cope with the new problems. Policy priorities in various countries are to a large extent dependent on the interpretations of the underlying causes of the current economic crisis.

The neoclassical explanations of economic growth mainly reflected in the economic policies of the United States can be contrasted with the technology-based explanations which are adopted by virtually all other countries. In the neoclassical explanation the importance of technological change in the process of economic development is not explicitly recognised except in so far that increasing unemployment better enables firms to seek improved productivities through the purchase of modern labour-saving equipment (Rothwell and Zegveld, 1982). In 'modern' explanation of growth, technological change is considered as the driving force of the process itself. Structural changes taking place within countries are considered as reflections of the structural changes in the world economies which call for policy choices centrally involving the exploitation of new technologies and the development of particular groups (ibid.). In this respect SMEs have become the realm of concern of both policy-makers and scientists since it has been widely accepted that they possess the necessary potential which will enable policy-making to deal more effectively with the current issues at hand in most of the world's regions (Storey, 1982). SMEs in this context are highly valued as both agents of socio-economic revitalisation promoting goals of equity and efficiency, as well as vehicles of technological changes.

A great deal has been written concerning the innovativeness of SMEs in comparison with larger firms. However, the role attributed to them varies from nation to nation and reflects in all respects the economic structure of the various regions, along with their value systems and cultural backgrounds. This inevitably implies that there is no SME contribution of general applicability since it can be both region-and firm-specific.

The focus of this chapter will be to study the role of SMEs in the Greek regional context along with the policy framework in support of the SMEs development.

THE SME SECTOR IN GREECE

SMEs in Greece play a very important role in the national economy since in the main they constitute the secondary sector. According to the 1981 Census, firms with less than ten employees accounted for 96·1 per cent of the total number of firms and 52 per cent of the total employment. Despite the significance of SMEs in Greece it is only recently that they have attracted the interest of policy-makers in respect of their role in the national economy, their problems and their developing prospects. This can be interpreted as the result of the strong sectoral orientation of the Greek policy framework reflecting, even until recently, the economic policies towards industrialisation dating from the 1950s. These were mainly orientated towards attracting foreign capital and fostering the creation of large firms which, according to the theories of the period, were considered to be the main agents of development.

Even until recently the SME sector was, to a large extent, a handicraft sector, although the transitional stage from a handicraft- to a manufacturing-orientated sector is far from being completed.

Table 14.1 shows the distribution of establishments by employ-ment size throughout the SME sector. It shows that 96.1 per cent of establishments have less than ten employees, which fact reflects part of the likely weaknesses involved in such a structure.

Table 14.1: Number of establishments in the SME sector in Greece

Size of firm	No. of firms	Percentage
1–2	101,772	68·1
3–9	41,760	28·0
10–49	4,481	3·0
50–99	747	0·5
100–499	508	0·3
500	90	0·1
Total	149,358	100·0

Source: Commercial and Industrial Chamber of Greece, 1984

Table 14.2: Employment in the SME sector in Greece.

Size of firm	No. of employees	Average no. of people employed per firm	Percentage
1–2	141,462	1·39	18·9
3–9	188,756	4·52	23·3
10–49	85,850	19·16	21·1
50–99	50,939	68·21	7·4
100–499	101,747	200·37	17·7
500	89,700	1000	11·6
Total	658,454	—	100·0

Source: Commercial and Industrial Chamber of Greece, 1984

Table 14.2 shows that whilst establishments with less than ten workers constitute 96 per cent of the population, they provide only 42 per cent of all jobs in 1984. It also shows the dominance of the very small (less than ten employees) firm within the SME sector.

The sectoral distribution of the SMEs is very clearly shown in Table 14.3 based on 1978 sources. In almost all cases with a few exceptions — namely, basic metals and tobacco — the highest concentration of establishments falls within the group of ten employees or less. In some sectors such as food, beverages, footwear, wood and cork, furs, printing and publishing, metal products, electrical machinery and transport equipment, the concentration in the under-ten size accounts for above 90 per cent of the total.

The spatial distribution of SMEs is shown in Figure 14.1 which shows the highly polarised pattern of the sector in the regions containing the two main urban centres of the country —

Table 14.3: Sectoral distribution of SMEs in Greece

Sectors	Size of establishment		
	0–9 (%)	10–49 (%)	50 and more (%)
20 Food except beverages	94·29	4·77	0·94
21 Beverages	93·25	5·52	1·23
22 Tobacco	38·51	37·27	24·22
23 Textiles	80·95	14·62	4·43
24 Footwear and sewing of fabrics	95·81	3·76	0·43
25 Wood and cork	97·21	2·55	0·24
26 Furniture and fixtures	96·42	3·34	0·24
27 Manufacture of paper	68·90	25·52	5·58
28 Printing and publishing	87·81	10·65	1·54
29 Leather and fur products	91·96	7·35	0·69
30 Rubber and plastic products	83·24	13·87	2·88
31 Chemical industries	71·84	21·06	7·10
32 Petroleum and coal refining	54·10	34·43	11·47
33 Non-metalic mineral products	88·39	10·19	1·42
34 Basic metal industries	25·80	32·28	41·94
35 Fabricated metal products except machinery	95·70	3·60	0·70
36 Machinery and appliances except electrical	87·81	11·00	1·19
37 Electrical machinery, apparatus appliances and supplies	91·00	6·90	2·10
38 Transport equipment	96·07	3·07	0·85
39 Miscellaneous manufacturing industry	95·67	4·00	0·33
	93·51	5·46	1·03

Source: Chamber of Commerce, 1978.

namely, Greater Athens and Thessaloniki. It is worth mentioning that, despite the strong efforts undertaken during the recent years by policy-makers to decentralise SMEs, the impact has been small (Iliopoulou, 1987). As is clearly shown in other studies, a number of barriers such as limited market range, lack of skilled labour, inefficient communication networks, limited access to information, are more important than capital availability or access to cheap labour in the peripheral areas, especially for innovative and growing firms (see Giaoutzi 1986a, b). This has resulted in many cases in a choice of location at the fringes of the core regions, where they share both the opportunity to enjoy the incentives supplied for peripheral areas and the incubation advantages of the core regions, namely Athens and Thessaloniki (Davelaar and

Figure 14.1: Spatial distribution of employment in the Greek SME sector

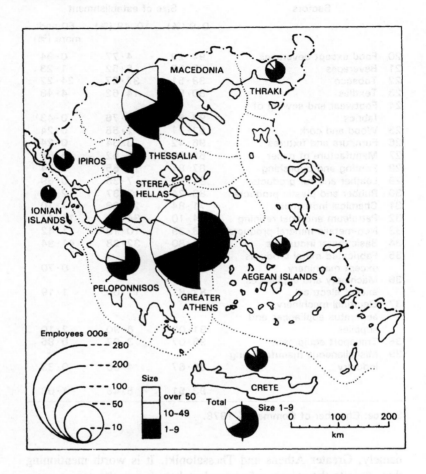

Nijkamp, 1986). There are also certain structural characteristics in the SME sector in Greece, such as a lack of traditional expertise in certain sectors and regions which magnify the inherent difficulties of SMEs to undertake risky ventures, despite their entrepreneurial inventiveness and flexibility. This very often leads to either very high death rates of firms or movements in search of more profitable market niches and investment opportunities.

SPATIAL ASPECTS OF THE SME SECTORAL STRUCTURE

To obtain a better insight into the structure of the SME sector at regional level, an evolutionary picture of their sectoral specialisation per nomos (nomos constitutes the smallest administrative division) will be presented. This highlights the structural strengths and weaknesses of the SMEs in Greece (see Table 14.4, in conjunction with Figure 14.2). These spatial patterns reflect the following inherent problems:

(1) Drastic shifts in specialisation from one sector to another within regions experiencing temporarily concentrated industrial development, largely reflect high birth and death rates of firms and, to a lesser extend, shifts of firms towards faster-growing sectors.

(2) The industrial structure in many regions is changing composition very rapidly, which means that linkages between firms in the same region are subject to considerable stress. The high birth and death rates of firms mean that customer and supplier patterns are constantly changing.

(3) The high death rates of SMEs are generally attributable to a concentration of firms in weak sectors, poor management, lack of external equity capital and an unwillingness to utilise modern technology and information.

PATTERNS OF TECHNOLOGICAL DEVELOPMENTS

The above patterns of SMEs reflect both the existing characteristics of Greek regions and the lack of success of policies to promote decentralisation and technical change. Given that SMEs in almost all countries in the world have enormous potential, and may decisively contribute to the process of technological change in the various regions, we now identify some of the problems of the technological environment of Greek SMEs. This is designed to highlight policies leading to a better integration of SMEs into their local production systems.

The problems and characteristics exhibited in 'the selection environment' of firms in the various regions, defined by Camagni and Cappellin (1983) as consisting of those local factors which are likely to contribute to its technological environment:

Table 14.4: Indices of specialisation of the SME sector

Nomoi[a]	Indices of specialisation					
	1963		1973		1983	
	high	low	high	low	high	low
Region of Attica						
1. Greater Athens area	food & tobacco	textile	chemicals, petroleums & coal-refining, basic metals, transport equipment	printing	chemicals, petroleums & coal-refining, basic metals, transport equipment, microelectronics	
2. Aitoloakarnania		wood & cork		food & tobacco		
3. Rest of Attica	beverages, chemicals, petroleums & coal-refining, basic metals, non-metallic minerals		textiles, rubber, plastic products, non-metallic minerals, electrical machinery		textiles, rubber, plastic products, non-metallic minerals, electrical machinery	
4. Viotia	clothes & footwear, wood & cork	fabricated metal products	wood & cork		wood & cork	
5. Euboea	non-metallic minerals				transport equipment	
6. Evritania	food, wood & cork		food, wood & cork		food, wood & cork	

7. Fthiotida	wood & cork	food, clothes & footwear	non-metallic, minerals	non-metallic, minerals
8. Fokida	food, wood & cork, furs & leather		food, wood & cork	food, wood & cork
Region of Peloponisos				
9. Argolida	food		food	food
10. Arkadia	food, wood & cork		food, wood & cork	food, wood & cork
11. Achaia	food, textiles, paper industry		beverages, textile industry, paper industry	beverages, textiles, paper industry
12. Ilia	food		food	food
13. Korinthia	food, beverages, paper industry		food, beverages, petroleum & coal-refining	food, beverages, petroleum & coal-refining
14. Lakonia	food, beverages, wood & cork	clothes & footwear	food, beverages, wood & cork	food, beverages, wood & cork
15. Messinia	food, tobacco		food, tobacco	food, tobacco
Ionian Islands				
16. Zakynthos	food		food	food
17. Kerkira	food		food, beverages, wood & cork	food, beverages, wood & cork

Table 14.4: *contd.*

	Indices of specialisation					
	1963		1973		1983	
Nomoi[a]	high	low	high	low	high	low
18. Kefallinia	food		food, beverages, wood & cork		food, beverages, wood & cork	
19. Lefcada	food, beverages	wood & cork, clothes & footwear	food, wood & cork		food, wood & cork	
Ipiros						
20. Arta	food, wood & cork		food		food	
21. Thesprotia	food		food, wood & cork		food, wood & cork	
22. Ioannina	wood & cork		beverages, tobacco, non-metallic minerals		beverages, non-metallic minerals	
23. Preveza	food		food, petroleum & coal-refining		food, petroleum & coal-refining	
Thessaly						
24. Karditsa		food, wood & cork		food, wood & cork	food, wood & cork	

Region				
25. Larissa	wood & cork, transport equipment		paper industry	paper industry, transport equipment
26. Magnisia	tobacco, electrical machinery		fabricated metal products	fabricated metal products, electrical machinery
27. Trikala	wood & cork		wood & cork	food	wood & cork
Macedonia				
28. Drama	non-metallic minerals, furniture, tobacco		wood & cork, non-metallic minerals	non-metallic minerals, food
29. Imathia	textiles, wood & cork	food processing	food, textiles, wood & cork	food, textiles
30. Thessaloniki	non-metallic minerals, tobacco, beverages	textiles, electrical appliances	basic metal, tobacco, clothes & footwear, wood & cork, elastic products & plastics	
31. Kavalla	tobacco		tobacco	food, clothes & footwear, tobacco, non-metallic minerals

Table 14.4: *contd.*

Nomoi[a]	Indices of specialisation					
	1963		1973		1983	
	high	low	high	low	high	low
32. Kastoria						
33. Kilkis	furs & leather	food, clothes & footwear	furs & leather	food, clothes & footwear	furs & leather	clothes & footwear, textiles, final metal products, electrical appliances & plastics
34. Kozani	fur & leather		fur & leather, chemicals		fur & leather, chemicals, food, non-metallic minerals	
35. Pella		non-metallic products, wood & cork, textiles	food		food, plastics, textiles	
36. Pierria	wood & cork, non-metallic minerals	clothes & footwear	wood & cork		food, clothes, non-metallic minerals	
37. Serres	food, wood & cork		food, wood & cork		food, wood & cork	non-metallic minerals, final metal products, clothes & plastics

38. Florina	beverages, food, non-metallic minerals	beverages, food, metallic minerals	food, non-metallic minerals	electrical machinery & appliances
39. Chalkidiki	electrical machinery & appliances, wood & cork, food, textiles	electrical machinery & appliances, food processing	final metal products	basic metals, food processing
Thrace				
40. Evros	wood & cork, non-metallic minerals, beverages	wood & cork, beverages	food processing	food, clothes & footwear, non-metallic minerals, textiles
41. Xanthi	tobacco	beverages, wood & cork, food		clothes & footwear, food, non-metallic minerals, final metal products, wood & cork
42. Rodopi	wood & cork, food, clothes & footwear	wood & cork		wood & cork, clothes & footwear, textiles

Table 14.4: *contd.*

		Indices of specialisation				
	1963		1973		1983	
Nomoi[a]	high	low	high	low	high	low
Aegean Islands						
43. Dodecanessos	beverages, clothes & footwear, miscellaneous		beverages, non-metallic minerals, miscellaneous		beverages, non-metallic minerals, miscellaneous	
44. Cyclades	textiles	foods	transport equipment		transport equipment	
45. Lesvos	food, furs & leather	wood & cork	food, beverages, furs & leather		food, beverages, furs & leather	
46. Samos	beverages, tobacco, wood & cork, furs & leather		beverages, food, fur & leather		beverages, food, fur & leather	
47. Chios	food, furs & leather, non-metallic minerals		food, beverages, furs & leather		food, beverages, furs & leather	

Crete

48. Iraklion	food, beverages		food, beverages	food, beverages
49. Lasithio	beverages, clothes & footwear, wood & cork	food	food, beverages, wood & cork	food, beverages
50. Rethimo	food, beverages furniture		food	food, beverages
51. Chania	food, beverages, transportation equipment		food, beverages, transportation equipment	food, beverages, transportation equipment

Notes: a. See Figure 14.2.
b. Indices for 1983 have not yet been completed.

Figure 14.2: Administrative division of Greece

(a) Almost all service activities directly related to R&D are in an infant stage.

(b) Links with the universities are very weak and sometimes where they do exist there is an atmosphere of distrust.

(c) Technological relationships which do exist are restricted to larger firms and often to a small number of foreign subsidiaries and their immediate associates (Giaoutzi, 1985a).

(d) In almost all non-core regions a number of impeding factors are present such as: a very limited number of highly skilled personnel, shortage of managerial skills, centralised public administration, low levels of education, and lack of tradition in certain social values such as consistency, co-operation and professionalism.

(e) The condition of networks can be unsatisfactory outside the core regions, especially in respect of road, sewage, telecommunication and new information technology networks.

(f) There is a limited access from the peripheral areas to the two main core regions of the country (inefficient railway and airline services) which in many cases leads to separate office-plant location of firms.

(g) Inter-firm relationships are very limited outside the core regions which in many cases is the result of the vertical structuring of firms.

(h) The degree of social consensus in peripheral areas is under strain. In the peripheral areas firms owned by non-local people have responded to the recent incentives for decentralisation. This has led to clashes with the traditional value systems in local communities attempting to create a state of regional identity.

(i) The evidence suggests that innovation adoption is strongly conditioned by the combination of the above factors involved in each particular environment (Giaoutzi, 1985b).

A POLICY PERSPECTIVE

SME policies in Greece cover assistance of firms and more recently the promotion of innovation in these firms.

The support provided to SMEs under the umbrella of the law 1262/82 mainly consists of a collection of incentives concerning the provision of grants which may cover up to 50 per cent of the firm's investment costs, accelerated depreciation rates, interest rate subsidies and tax reliefs. The above incentives vary between areas whilst larger incentives are also provided for firms employing advanced technology or carrying out applied research.

In an effort to promote innovation in SMEs the following policies have been employed, some of which have only just been implemented.

(1) Evaluation of inventions and innovations throughout the country from an economic commercial and technical point of view.

(2) Subsidising of innovation projects to facilitate the production of prototypes.

(3) Granting of loans on favourable terms for the creation of those enterprises exploiting Greek inventions.

(4) Participation in intra-EEC transnational co-operation in technology transfer and the management of innovations.

(5) Setting up of innovation centres in various regions of Greece.

(6) Utilisation of capital funds for the promotion of new forms of finance, such as venture capital, and so on.

(7) Establishment of a data bank network across the country for the benefit of SMEs.

(8) Provision of technical assistance to SMEs and information of technological, economic and legal matters.

(9) Provision of training for entrepreneurs in SMEs in the fields of management, new technologies, and so on.

OVERVIEW

SME policies in Greece are largely marked by an absence of regional specificity. This has resulted in many cases in an inefficient utilisation of public resources on the part of the entrepreneurs through investing in declining sectors, mainly because of limited information about sector competitiveness and local conditions (for example, selection environment, industrial structure, inter-industry linkages, export prospects, and so on).

Lack of regional orientation also leads to an over-concentration of firms in sectors reliant upon a local market. This excludes them from policies which promote competitiveness through organisational improvements, managerial training, export promotion and marketing. Non-locally orientated policies also retard the spread of new technologies in specific firms or specific sectors which would benefit because of either their current weaknesses or their exceptional potential.

There remain some key uncertainties: for example the contribution of individual entrepreneurs to their difficulties is no easy task to assess. It is also difficult to assess the role which small/large firm relationships play in this context. Nevertheless, policies focusing on these points would enhance the potential of the SME sector in Greece and thus contribute more effectively towards the goal of equity, which is the main issue of concern in the policy-making framework of recent years.

REFERENCES

Camagni, R. and R. Cappellin (1983) Sectoral productivity and regional policy. Research report, Milan.

Davelaar, E. I. and P. Nijkamp (1986) The urban incubator hypothesis: old wine in new bottles. *Research Memorandum, Free University, Amsterdam.*

Giaoutzi, M. (1984) Innovation patterns in Greek industry. *School of Engineering, University of Thessaloniki, Research Report* (mimeographed).

—— (1985a) Factors affecting the capacity of technological change: the case of the less developed countries. *Papers of the Regional Science Association, 58,* 73–82.

—— (1985b) Problems and prospects of technological change: the case of less developed countries. 25th Regional Science Congress, Budapest.

—— (1986a) Technological change and regional dynamics. Paper presented at the GREMI meeting on Technological Change and Regional Development, Paris (mimeographed).

—— (1986b) Technological change and urban systems. Paper presented at the 25th anniversary of A.S.R.D.L.F. on Technologies Nouvelles at Developpement Regionales, Paris.

Iliopoulou, P. (1987) An evaluation of the Greek regional incentives policy (1972–87). Paper presented at the RSA Congress, Athens.

Rothwell, R. and W. Zegveld (1982) *Innovation and the small and medium size firm.* Frances Pinter, London.

Storey, D. J. (1982) *Entrepreneurship and the new firm.* Croom Helm, London.

281

15

Trends in Migration and Characteristics of Entrepreneurs in the National Periphery of Israel

Gabriel Lipshitz

INTRODUCTION

During the 1970s and 1980s, with the rise in importance of the manufacture of sophisticated products for the national and regional economy, and with the transition to 'intellectualisation of all phases of production' (Nijkamp *et al.*, 1988), the demand for educated manpower of a high technological level also increased. The spatial distribution of knowledge became a central factor in considerations of location among entrepreneurs, and emphasised for them the geographical distribution in labour force quality. Since migration is one of the main factors leading to changes in the spatial distribution and quality of the labour force, it has become one of the most important spatial flows influencing the development potential of each region. For a fuller understanding of this influence, an integrative geographic study should be made of: the characteristics of migrants, the variables which clarify regional emigration (characteristics of region of origin), the variables which clarify regional emigration (characteristics of region of destination), the volume of interregional migration, and so forth.

The present chapter does not conduct such an integrative study, but deals only with the relationship between the characteristics of the entrepreneurs in the 'National Periphery' region and migration to and from such regions. It is important to note that variables which characterise entrepreneurs — such as location, size, type, extent of demand for their product, extent of supply of their product, price of their product — comprise one of the most significant variables, possibly even the most significant, influencing spatial patterns of migration. In practice, these variables determine the employment potential as well as the level of wages there, and these two variables have a decisive influence on the spatial variability of net migration (Todaro, 1976).

Of the characteristics of the entrepreneurs, mentioned above, we shall focus here upon the influence of two of them (size and type of entrepreneur) on migration to and from the regions of the National Periphery of Israel. Such a discussion is certainly *partial*, for other variables — some of them relating to entrepreneur characteristics and others to regional characteristics — also have influence on spatial patterns of migration. The present study examines this influence, not by means of statistical methodology, but through conceptual discussion.

THE COMPARATIVE CONTRIBUTION OF THE LARGE AND THE SMALL-TO-MEDIUM ENTREPRENEUR TO THE PATTERNS OF MIGRATION IN THE NATIONAL PERIPHERY

Most investigators hold that the large entrepreneurs, whether multi-locational or multinational companies, do indeed increase the number of job slots in the regions of the National Periphery, but their contribution towards increasing regional economic welfare — comprising one of the central goals of regional development — is actually quite modest (Holland, 1976; Thomas, 1980).

According to this approach, the large firms in the National Periphery, whether controlled by companies outside the region of independent plants, do create jobs, but these plants, in most instances, are unskilled-worker orientated, that is, they can motivate only the migration of non-professional manpower, and cannot break the outward flow of academics and technological workers. Furthermore, even if we regard large plants in the National Periphery as job generators, it should not be ignored that those plants belonging to multi-location or multinational firms are under the constant threat of cut-backs and closures. These plants may well be the first to suffer during times of economic depression, for reasons captured by the phrase 'out of sight, out of mind'.

The closure of a large plant does not only lead to the unemployment of its workers, but can also cause unemployment at other foci of employment in the same region, thus becoming a factor encouraging emigration. Thus, for instance, the Timna

Works in the Eilat region (Eilat is the southern-most of Israel's cities), which employed, 1,000 workers in 1976, presently employs only 22, due to the drastic fall in the world price of copper. On the other hand, it is argued that large, multi-locational companies can, in difficult times, maintain unprofitable plants in peripheral regions for a longer time, if it is considered that there is a chance of future recovery (O'Farrell, 1980). The resources of such companies provide them with a longer 'breathing space' to tide them over difficult times, for unprofitable plants can be subsidised by the successful plants under its ownership. Furthermore, government involvement in economic activities hinders large companies from closing plants in backwards regions. In Israel, some of the attempts to close large plants of multi-locational companies in development regions have encountered governmental and public opposition of considerable strength, the claim of 'security factors' having much weight in the argument.

What characterises the drive of the large entrepreneur of the last two decades to expand also characterises the change of the 'small' and 'medium' entrepreneur into an important factor in national and regional economic growth (Storey, 1988). Does indeed small and medium entrepreneurship which is stirring to life on this national level — which, studies have shown, is a positive factor in job creation (ibid.) — also contribute to the economic development in peripheral regions? Thus, for instance, can this entrepreneurship prevent the emigration of younger and skilled workers from the regions of the National Periphery, and encourage immigration to them? A positive answer to these questions can be made only when the new entrepreneur in the National Periphery is, in Maillat's words, 'highly productive and not barely surviving' (Maillat, 1988). Only thus can the entrepreneur increase not only the number of jobs available, but also the wages involved. The increasing importance of these two variables will not only prevent emigration from the region, but will also attract 'strong' elements from other regions. In order for such a type of entrepreneur to develop his or her business in the National Periphery, there are requisite conditions, such as: the existence of a reliable labour force in general, a 'regional production environment/structure', in Nijkamp et al.'s terms (Nijkamp et al., 1988). Unfortunately, in most instances the National Periphery does not possess the aforementioned requisites, and the regional infrastructure is very backward in comparison with the core regions. A spatial policy encouraging the migration of 'modern entrepreneurs' to the National Periphery must necessarily be accompanied by a paralleled cultivation of the relevant human capital — and this presents a formidable challenge.

One of the spatial results of what has been described above is negative net migration in the national periphery in most of the countries. What are the migration trends in the National Periphery of Israel and how are they influenced by the size and the type of entrepreneurs there? In the next section, this question will be addressed.

VARIABILITY OF REGIONAL NET MIGRATION IN THE NATIONAL PERIPHERY OF ISRAEL

During the 1950s and 1960s government activities focused on development of *large* industrial enterprises in 'Galilee', the northern National Periphery, and in the 'Negev', the southern National Periphery (see Figure 15.1). Those plants are large employers of manpower and call for little highly skilled labour — thus, they were considered as a most suitable form for the population of the National Periphery, much of which had immigrated within the first decade of the state (Lipshitz, 1986b).

Only in the last decade have the first buddings of modern SMEs begun to appear in the National Periphery of Israel, particularly in Western Galilee. These plants are based on skilled manpower (engineers, computer technicians, etc.), an abundant element in the Haifa region, and on a population which migrated to new 'community settlement' established in the last decade in Western Galilee. A similar development in the establishment of SMEs is taking place in the new Jewish settlements in Judea and Samaria (the 'West Bank'). These regions can also be treated as part of the National Periphery (despite all of the problems thereby involved).

This short background should be of assistance in understanding the empirical results, as is shown below.

Figure 15.2 shows us that the levels of net migration in two peripheral regions (Negev and Galilee) was negative through most of the period under study. However, whereas the net migration in the Negev changed from positive to negative with time, that of Galilee became less negative and, in the early 1980s, even became positive. The positive trends indicated in Galilee characterise each of the sub-regions comprising it. Figure 15.3

Figure 15.1a: Natural regions in Israel and the study regions

Figure 15.1b: Division of Israel into a core–periphery structure

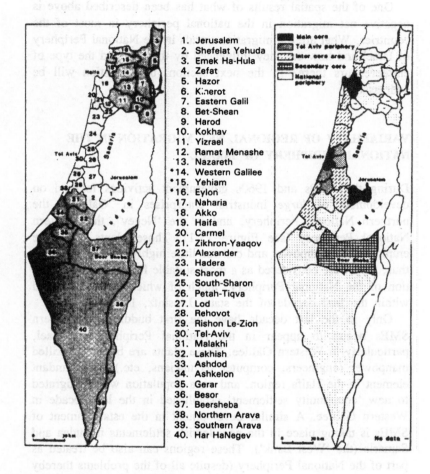

1. Jerusalem
2. Shefelat Yehuda
3. Emek Ha-Hula
4. Zefat
5. Hazor
6. Kinerot
7. Eastern Galil
8. Bet-Shean
9. Harod
10. Kokhav
11. Yizrael
12. Ramat Menashe
13. Nazareth
*14. Western Galilee
*15. Yehiam
*16. Eylon
17. Naharia
18. Akko
19. Haifa
20. Carmel
21. Zikhron-Yaaqov
22. Alexander
23. Hadera
24. Sharon
25. South-Sharon
26. Petah-Tiqva
27. Lod
28. Rehovot
29. Rishon Le-Zion
30. Tel-Aviv
31. Malakhi
32. Lakhish
33. Ashdod
34. Ashkelon
35. Gerar
36. Besor
37. Beersheba
38. Northern Arava
39. Southern Arava
40. Har HaNegev

*Western Galilee = Western Lower Galilee
Yehiam + Eylon = Western Upper Galilee

indicates that the net migration in each of the regions of Galilee became less negative in time and in some of them it turned positive. The trends in the Negev are more complex. Figure 15.4 indicates that combinations of four trends led the net migration balance for the Negev to turn from positive to negative. The first and most important trend is the dramatic decline in the net

286

Figure 15.2: Net migration in the National Peripheries of Israel, 1961–83

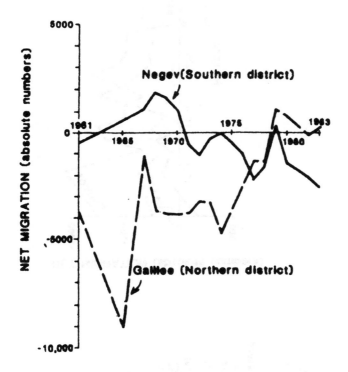

migration of the Beersheba region and its change to a negative balance in the early 1980s. The second trend is the lack of improvement in the net migration of such regions as Gerar and Besor; their net migration is negative, at an almost identical level, throughout the period under study. The third trend is the decline of the net migration of the Har Hanagev region and its change to a negative balance in 1970. The fourth trend is the decline in the positive net migration of the Southern Arava (Eilat) region beginning in 1971).

Of all the regions of the National Periphery in Israel, the Beersheba region in the south and the lower Western Galilee region in the north have undergone the most obvious changes in their net migration patterns (Figures 15.3 and 15.4). Calculations reveal that the changes in net migration of these two regions have influenced above all the net migration of Galilee and the Negev respectively. These changes are the clear result of the spatial

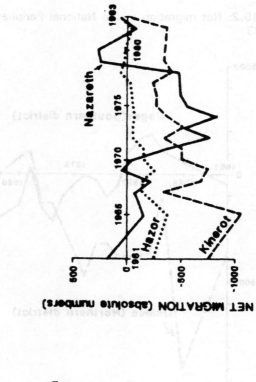

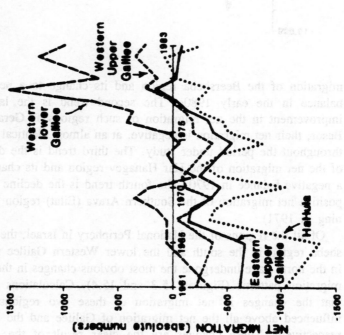

Figure 15.3: Net migration of regions in the northern National Periphery of Israel, 1961–83

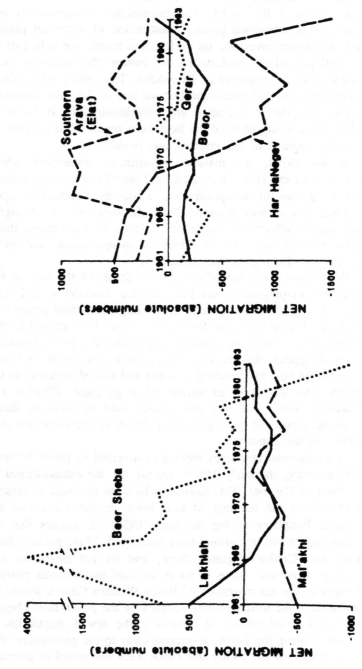

Figure 15.4: Net migration of regions in the southern National Periphery of Israel, 1961–83

policy of the Government of Israel. At the beginning of the 1960s, considerable national resources were diverted to the development of Beersheba. The construction of apartments and their sale at subsidised prices, construction of industrial plants, loans to private investors, on preferential terms, are only part of the official efforts undertaken to ensure the economic and demographic development of Beersheba. This policy indeed bore positive results, and Beersheba became one of the most attractive regions for internal migration and new immigrants. In the mid-1960s, the net migration of the Beersheba region *vis-à-vis* each of the other regions of the country was positive.

In the 1970s, the massive government investment which characterised the 1960s decreased, and Beersheba actually entered into a 'period of independence', while its dependence upon government assistance declined. From the viewpoint of net migration, which reflects the extent of attraction of the region, Beersheba did not meet the challenge of independence, and more persons left the region than entered it.

No serious study has taken place in Israel of the role of the industrial employment structure in the Beersheba and Har Hanagev regions in the change in net migration from positive to negative. According to the few studies which have related to this subject, albeit indirectly (Gradus and Krakover, 1976; Lipshitz, 1987), it appears that the large plants in the Negev did not play a significant role in attracting younger and skilled migrants to the region. The low level of variety of large plants (Gradus and Krakover, 1976) and the low wages paid to workers there, encouraged many of the region's population to migrate to the core regions to the country.

Many national resources were also diverted to lower Western Galilee during the early 1960s, mainly for the establishment of the town of Carmiel. This town was built on the basis of lessons learned from the building of new towns in the regions of the National Periphery during the early 1950s. It appears that the lessons as applied in Carmiel have succeeded. Many persons from Haifa and Galilee migrated there, and its net migration was positive. However, there is no doubt that the obvious positive changes in the net migration of lower Western Galilee should be attributed to the official policy adopted by the government, beginning in the mid 1970s, of increasing the Jewish population in Galilee. During the 1970s, it became clear to the government that the strategies of the 1950s and 1960s were not suited to planning in the 1980s. In other words, the construction of popular housing and its sale, even cheaply, no longer comprised an attractive feature, and certainly not to families in high socio-economic groupings. Thus, the government decided to establish 'community settlements' of various types, the size of each settlement varying between several tens of families to several hundreds.

In these settlements, each family had its own house with attached garden, and in almost all the settlements, the basic services were built, such as kindergartens and shopping centres. High levels of threshold services were also built in the regional centres. From 1975 up to the present, some 40 such community settlements have been established, with their method of establishment varying from one settlement to another.

The existence of a young and highly educated work-force served as the human basis for the establishment of science-based and technological plants in the region. These plants were and are being established by the government and by private investors. A large proportion of these plants employ between five and several tens of workers. Some are based on the convenient climate and beautiful scenery of the region. SME entrepreneurs have exploited these advantages and have established popular touristic enterprises there, such as guest houses. Alongside these, plants and business concerned with 'tourist products' have risen, such as jewellery plants. Other plants are based on the characteristics and skills of the investors themselves. Thus, there are such cases as that of a computer scientist who left a large company to set up a small, independent computer-orientated firm. In most cases, relations amongst plant workers and between them and the management are very good and informal. Such relations spur higher motivation and go far in increasing productivity.

Since the establishment of community settlements in Western Galilee is still an ongoing process, and the majority of the present population there has migrated to the region only in recent years, it would be difficult *at this stage* to evaluate the direct contribution of the SMEs towards the establishment of the region's positive net migration balance. Indeed, there is evidence that the region's positive net migration balance will remain stable, and will even increase (Lipshitz, 1986a), but it would be difficult to evaluate the contributory role of the plants in the region in this trend. Even so, it is already clear that one of the important pull factors is related to livelihood, for in the community settlements and regional centres, the small investor can realise his or her aspirations and make a modest dream come true. In these regions there is a high degree of openness to small investors interested in opening a plant based, *inter alia*, on personal skills. In this age of industrial giants (multi-locational or multinational), which often create social and professional attrition, these opportunities present a great challenge to young investors.

Just as there is no region resembling lower Western Galilee (lying in the shade of a metropolis) in the Negev, in Galilee there is no region resembling the Southern Arava. The specific characteristics, three of which are noted below, are what made this southern region attractive, and it is in fact the only region of all those in the National Periphery — whether in the north or in the south — in which its net migration balance has remained positive throughout the period under study (Figure 15.4). Its main characteristics can be summed up as follows:

(a) it lies at the greatest distance from the centre of the country;
(b) the socio-economic level of the population is among the highest in the country, whether urban or rural;
(c) the southern part of the region (the town of Eilat) lies on the Gulf of Eilat, known for its beauty, and throughout the region fascinating desert landscape is to be found.

Today in Eilat there is no single enterprise employing a major portion of the work-force there. In the past, there were the Timna mines, which employed some 35 per cent of the city's labour force, and the collapse of that enterprise — due to a drop in world prices of copper — seriously harmed the economy of the city, and the positive net migration balance began to decline at that time. Today, a decided majority of the population is employed in SMEs, including hotels and other tourist-related industries. Here, too, it is difficult to evaluated the relative contribution of the SMEs towards the positive net migration balance throughout the period under study. It is clear that the existence of numerous SMEs has assisted the inhabitants of Eilat in locally overcoming widespread national crises, but the relative weight of such smaller businesses in this process is unclear.

Judea and Samaria make up a further geographical region, besides Galilee and the Negev, which can be defined as part of the National Periphery. We shall not delve here into the suitability of this definition, but it should be noted that the term 'periphery' in this case does seem to be suitable geographically speaking, but not from the socio-economic aspect.

In the present stage of Jewish settlement in Judea and Samaria, it would be difficult to speak of 'net migration' as a parameter, for most of the population involved has migrated to the region only in the last decade, and a process of migration from the region has not made itself particularly evident. In 1983, some 15,000 Jews lived in Judea and Samaria (70,000 in 1986). For our purposes, we may note that the population living in these settlements is employed in two main locations: in the metropolitan area of Tel Aviv or of Jerusalem, and within the settlements themselves. Those who are employed in settlements work mainly in SMEs. As in Western Galilee, here too the plants are based on two advantages: the advantage of geographical location, related to the physical and human landscape of the region; and the advantage of personnel, related to the skills of the migrants themselves. Thus, a geologist with an MA degree has established a centre for cave research (caves are found in abundance in the region of this domicile), or an ex-kibbutznik (member of a collective farm) possessing considerable knowledge in modern farming techniques has set up an agricultural laboratory; or a computer person has established a programming consultation office. However, will such small enterprises in these settlements succeed economically, and lead to demographic growth by increasing the number of incoming migrants over the number leaving? The answer will be available only in a decade or so.

CONCLUSIONS

The present study examines the directions of influence of firm size and type on net migration in the National Periphery of Israel. Since there is insufficient data in Israel for *statistical* investigation of the subject, and since many of the smaller firms — particularly those in Western Galilee and Judea and Samaria — were only established in recent years, it is as yet impossible to evaluate their contribution towards migration: thus, the directions of influence have been defined hypothetically. The discussion in this chapter thus comprises a basis for a precise statistical examination of the problem. From the Israeli case, it is clear that the large plants in the National Periphery of the country provided a large additional number of job slots, but because of their characterisation (large work-force, lack of variety, low wages), they did not provide a challenge for the younger and more skilled elements, who migrated to the central regions of the country. It appears that, on the one hand, these large plants tended to be closed down and often because of political and public pressures — but on the other hand, when a large plant was closed down, it led to a serious economic crisis in the region of the National Periphery, and to massive migration from the region.

The small-to-medium investors in the National Periphery of Israel can be classified into two types: the 'traditional' type, based on unsophisticated business; and the 'modern' type, based on a sophisticated plant. It appears that the former type is less stable and tends to close down or to change the nature of his or her business, and does not comprise a challenge to attract persons from within the National Periphery. The second type of investor comprises an attractive force for the skilled and educated. As noted, enterprises of the second type within the National Periphery are in its infancy, and the extent of its contribution to the positive net migration can be evaluated only in another decade or two.

REFERENCES

Gradus, Y. and S. Krakover (1976) The level and nature of industrialization in central and development regions. *The Economic Quarterly*, *23*, 66–78 (in Hebrew).

Holland, S. (1976) *Capital versus the region*. Macmillan, London.

Lipshitz, G. (1986a) Migration to, from and within Galilee, 1961–1983. *The Economic Quarterly* (in Hebrew).

———— (1986b) The stability of spatial patterns of welfare — the Israeli case. *Geoforum*, *17*(3–4), 353–66.

———— (1987) Migration within metropolitan areas in Israel — a periodic comparative analysis. *Papers of Regional Science Association, 61*, 200–21.

Maillat, D. (1988) The role of innovative small and medium-sized enterprises and the revival of traditionally industrial regions. Chapter 4 in this volume.

Nijkamp, P., T. Alsters and R. van der Mark (1988) The regional development potential of small and medium-sized enterprises. Chapter 7 in this volume.

O'Farrell, P. N. (1980) Multinational enterprises and regional development: Irish evidence. *Regional studies*, *14*, 141–50.

Razin, E. (1986) Plant closures in Israel's development towns, 1975–

1983. *Studies in the Geography of Israel*, *12*, 167–84 (in Hebrew).
Storey, P. J. (1988) The role of small and medium-sized enterprises in European job creation: key issues for policy research. Chapter 8 in this volume.
Thomas, M. D. (1980) Explanatory framework for growth and change in multiregional firms. *Economic Geography*, *56*, 11–17.
Todaro, M. P. (1976) Urban job expansion, induced migration and rising unemployment — formulation and simplified empirical tests for LDCs. *Journal of Development Economics*, *3*(3), 211–25.

16

Rural Small-scale Industry in Developing Countries: Indonesian Experiences

Piet Rietveld

INTRODUCTION

Rural small-scale industry has long been considered as a topic of marginal importance for industrialisation in developing countries. Recently, analysts and policy-makers are becoming increasingly aware of the importance of this sector, not only as a medium to survive for poor villagers, but also as a starting-point for industrial growth. In this chapter we will discuss the role of rural small-scale industry for regional development in developing countries. Empirical illustrations will focus on Indonesian experiences with rural small-scale industry.

In a paper based on empirical evidence from a large number of developing and developed countries, Anderson (1982) concludes that changes over time in the size structure of industry tend to take place according to a definite pattern (see also Figure 2.1 in Chapter 2 of this volume). Prior to industrialisation, household and artisanal activities are predominant, but as industrialisation proceeds their share continuously decreases, whilst that of small workshops and factories as well as large factories (with more than 100 workers) increase. Initially, the increase of the share of the first group tends to be much faster than of the second group. Only as the process of industrialisation proceeds further does the increase of the share of small firms come to a halt and large firms start to obtain considerable shares of manufacturing employment. (For some basic reasons as to why it is *small*-scale industry which is the main driving force during the first phase of industrialisation, see Staley and Morse, 1965). This chapter discusses the developments in relation to Indonesia.

Indonesian data on the size distribution of firms are relatively

Table 16.1: Size distribution of industrial firms in Indonesia, 1979

Size of industry	Number of workers	Share in value added (%)	Share in employment (%)
Large and medium	≥ 20	77·6	19·4
Small	5–19	8·8	18·4
Household	1–4	13·6	62·2

Source: BPS (1983) (processed).

scarce, since national data on household and small-scale firms are not collected very regularly. For 1979 some key figures are represented in Table 16.1. The table shows tremendous differences in labour productivity among the size groups. The share of large and medium-sized firms in value added is four times as large as the share in employment. A main reason why the productivity in household and small industry is so low is that work is mainly done by unpaid family workers on a part-time basis, many workers having multiple jobs. Besides, seasonal variations may be large in these firms. Consequently, if labour productivity were computed in terms of value added per worker day, the differences between large- and small-scale industry would be smaller, although quite pronounced differences remain (cf. Poot, 1981).

The conclusion is that the main part of Indonesian industrial employment is in small-scale and household industry where productivity is low. On the basis of these figures one might wonder whether these firms can really contribute in a positive way to economic development. This will be the main topic of this chapter.

In the following sections an investigation will be made of the role of household and small-scale firms in the industrialisation process of developing countries, especially in Indonesia. It will focus on rural industry since it is here that the large bulk of small-scale and household industry is found (see Poot, 1981). In the next section the place of industry in the rural economy will be analysed, while in the penultimate section, the equity aspects of rural industry will be considered. Policy conclusions will be drawn in the final section.

INDUSTRY AND THE RURAL ECONOMY

In most developing countries rural industry is predominantly household or small-scale. Large-scale industry has a strong urban bias (Lipton, 1977; see, however, Wolf, 1986).

Hymer and Resnick (1969) have addressed the role of non-agricultural activities in general and industry in particular in rural areas. Two sectors are distinguished in the rural economy: agricultural and non-agricultural activities. Agricultural goods are exported to rural areas; non-agricultural goods are assumed to be nontradeable. Manufactured goods are imported from urban areas. An implication of the model of Hymer and Resnick is that as productivity in agriculture increases or the transport system improves, the rural economy can gain by increasing specialisation: towards agricultural and at the expense of non-agricultural activities, industry being one of them. Thus, industry would become predominantly an urban activity, most probably large-scale.

The Hymer–Resnick model can be criticised for various reasons. Firstly, no attention is paid to activities directly linked to agriculture such as processing agricultural products, production and repair of agricultural tools, and so on. It is probable that an important part of these activities will be located in rural areas, given the high transport costs involved. In the context of broadly based agricultural growth, this sector has a favourable perspective (see Johnston and Kilby, 1975).

Secondly, the assumption that rural industrial goods cannot be traded to cities because urban products are superior is not always true. The quality of low-wage industrial products in rural areas is not necessarily worse than those produced in urban areas. Besides, the urban poor may, for a long time, remain users of cheap, low quality goods. Furthermore, one must take into account the possibility of subcontracting.

Thirdly, agricultural development would create demand for consumer goods, part of which can be provided most efficiently by rural industry, such as industrial services (repair) and various kinds of construction materials.

Fourthly, Hymer and Resnick assume that in rural areas there is a considerable trade-off between the production of agricultural and non-agricultural goods because of limited labour supply. Thus, they do not regard as probable that in the off-crop season the opportunity costs would be near to zero. However, in countries with high agricultural density such as Indonesia, there is not much to do in agriculture during the dry season, so that work in rural industry during this period does not affect agricultural production. Those workers may be willing to accept non-agricultural work in the off-crop season even if its return would be extremely low, giving rise to multiple jobs.

In this section, some Indonesian results will be presented, based on village data. Two qualifications must be made, however. Firstly, time series data are not available for longer periods at the village level so that use must be made of cross-sectional data. Secondly, the data only allow one to study non-agricultural activities as a whole, rural industry being one of them.

As a theoretical background for the analysis, the economic base approach is used: agriculture is treated as a basic sector, and the incomes generated in this sector lead to effective demand for non-agricultural goods and services. In addition to demand, supply conditions play a role. The supply side will be represented by agricultural density since a high density means that many workers are pushed out of agriculture, implying an extensive labour supply for non-agricultural activities. Furthermore, a land distribution index is added to investigate the influence of distributional aspects in the village on non-agricultural activities. Finally, non-local conditions are taken into account by an accessibility variable: distance to the nearest large city.

The data (observed in 1981–2) relate to a set of 14 villages, mainly located on the densely populated island of Java. The precise definitions of the variables read as follows (for more details, see Rietveld, 1986):

Y: non-agricultural income per household (in Rp. 1,000 per year per household).

X_1: agricultural income per household (in Rp. 1,000 per year per household). The distribution between agricultural and non-agricultural incomes was on average about 50:50, which means that non-agricultural activities are much more important for rural regions than is sometimes thought.

X_2: agricultural density (persons per hectare (ha)). A correction has been made for the intensity of labour use for various types of land. The average agricultural density in the sample is 12.6 persons per ha which reflects the extremely high population density in Java.

X_3: Gini index of land ownership. The average value is 0·52,

Table 16.2: Results of multiple regression on non-agricultural income per household in 14 Indonesian villages, 1981–2 (t-values between parentheses)

Linear	Agricultural income per household	Agricultural density	Gini index landowner-ship	Distance to city	Constant	R^2
	X_1	X_2	X_3	X_4		
Linear	0·811	15·8	−327	−0·691	75·1	0·891
	(4·54)	(5·76)	(2·41)	(−0·99)		

which is considerably lower than in countries characterised by landlordism.

X_4: distance to nearest large city (in km). The average distance is 43 km, which reflects the fact that Java has a rather well developed system of cities.

To come to know about the contribution of each of the independent variables with respect to Y, a multiple regression has been carried out (see Table 16.2). The t-values obtained indicate that the estimated coefficients for X_1 to X_3 are significant at the 5 per cent level. The coefficient for X_4 is only significant at the 20 per cent level. It is agricultural income and agricultural density which are the most important independent variables (as can be seen from the t-values).

The regression coefficient obtained for X_1 indicates that agricultural incomes has very substantial effects on non-agricultural incomes. One would expect a lower value than 0·811, however, since leakages in the village economy must be large, due to its small scale, so that a considerable part of incomes generated in agriculture will be spent outside the village. One must be aware, however, that agricultural incomes do not only play a role via the demand side: indirectly, there will also be effects via the supply side. Thus, for example, agricultural products may be used as inputs for processing activities. In addition, incomes obtained in agriculture are not seldomly used for investments in non-agricultural activities.

The estimation result for X_2 (agricultural density) indicates that there are opportunities for those being pushed out of agriculture (given the high density) to switch to non-agricultural activities. One must not draw overly optimistic conclusions on the absorption capacity of non-agricultural sectors, however. The

300

general impression is, namely, that market satiation is an important problem for many non-agricultural activities.

For land distribution the conclusion reads that the more equal the distribution, the higher the non-agricultural income per household. This is in agreement with conjectures in the literature. Spending patterns of big farmers are unfavourable for local activities since their consumption is usually more orientated towards urban products compared with small farmers.

The last explanatory variable is distance to the nearest large city. Non-agricultural incomes in villages do experience a number of influences from cities, the strength of which depends on distance. Some of the influences are negative (for example, competition by urban products), others are positive (for example, possibility of commuting). As explained in Rietveld (1984), the balance of the two influences may be expected to be positive. Thus, non-agricultural income near cities will be higher than further away from cities. Indeed, a negative sign is obtained for X_4, although its level of significance is lower than for the other variables. In a dynamic context the result would mean that non-agricultural incomes in villages benefit from improvements in accessibility, as took place in Indonesia during the 1970s.

We draw the conclusion that non-agricultural incomes depend strongly on the agricultural conditions in a village. Demand generated by agricultural income plays a main role; and agricultural density and land distribution are also important. Finally, accessibility to a main city also appears to play a role. The important function of demand deserves attention; it is often overlooked in analyses and policies with respect to non-agricultural activities. Thus, for example, most government policies stimulating non-agricultural activities are directed to the supply side (credit, skill improvement).

EQUITY AND RURAL SMALL INDUSTRY

In Figure 16.1 some important features of rural non-agricultural activities are shown in relationship with equity. The figure is based on Indonesian village data (for more details see Rietveld, 1986). Figure 16.1a shows that as the land owned by households increases, the *share* of non-agricultural incomes in total household income decreases. This can easily be understood given the clear positive relationship between agricultural income and land owned.

Figure 16.1: The relationship between landownership and involvement in non-agricultural activities

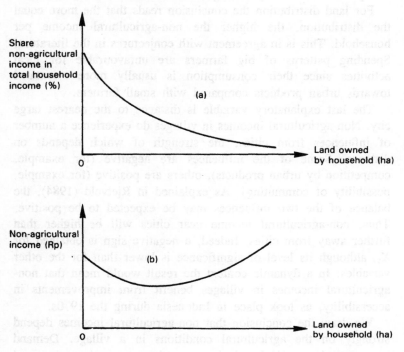

Figure 16.1b may be more surprising at first sight: a *U*-shaped relationship is found between land owned and non-agricultural income. For the group of small farmers a negative relationship exists between land owned and non-agricultural income. Such a negative relationship can be explained by a micro-economic analysis in which labour supply for both agricultural and non-agricultural work is taken into account (see Rietveld, 1986). The more the time spent in agriculture on the own land, the less the urgency to do non-agricultural work. Several reasons can be mentioned why this negative relationship only holds true for small farmers. Big farmers usually have larger households than average, which means that the potential number of workers outside agriculture is larger. Furthermore, big farmers may decide to invest their agricultural profits in non-agricultural activities. In addition, educational attainment will on average be higher in the households of big farmers, so that well-paid non-agricultural jobs can be obtained more easily. This implies, *inter alia*, that it may

become more profitable for big farmers to reduce the involvement in agricultural work as much as possible by using agricultural labourers and tenants, so that the time available for non-agricultural work is increased.

Do non-agricultural activities contribute to equity in the rural economy? The main source of rural inequality in developing countries is usually the inequality in the ownership of land $I(\ell)$. Several mechanisms exist which ensure that inequality in agricultural income $I(Y_a)$ is smaller than $I(\ell)$: for example, by share cropping and agricultural labour the value added created on land owned by landlords partly flows to low income households. In addition, the value added per ha in small firms is often higher than in large firms. Thus we may conclude: $I(Y_a) < I(\ell)$. The second step is from agricultural income to total income. Given the U-shaped relationship between non-agricultural income and land owned, a considerable mitigation of income inequality occurs when total income inequality $I(Y_t)$ is compared with agricultural income inequality $I(Y_t) < I(Y_a)$. Thus, in rural regions, total income inequality $I(Y_t)$ will usually be much lower than inequality in the distribution of land $I(\ell)$, with a major role in this inequality reduction being played by non-agricultural incomes.

POLICY CONCLUSIONS

Although most developing countries have formulated policies to stimulate small-scale enterprise, it is remarkable that in general the weight given to small-scale industry in national development plans has been very limited. One of the backgrounds seems to be the high priority given to the objective of economic growth. Given the low amount of value added per worker in small-scale industry, large-scale industry becomes the natural focus if priority is given to production growth. Of course, if priority would be given to employment creation, small-scale industry would become more central (cf. McCawley, 1981).

Before discussing various policy measures specifically addressed to rural small-scale industry, it is important to note that indirect policies may have a favourable effect on this industry which is much more decisive than the direct policies. Firstly, broadly based agricultural development will be of high importance for rural small-scale industry. As shown in the second section, such a development will especially stimulate agriculture-related

303

industries, but the rise of agricultural incomes in general will also stimulate rural industry via the demand side. At the supply side, profit made in agriculture may be invested in industry. Even though a considerable part of this stimulus may leak towards urban areas (see, for example, Bell and Hazell, 1980), the ultimate effect on rural industry will usually still be strong.

Secondly, a close inspection of general industrialisation policies reveals that these often have both an *urban bias and a scale bias* (cf. Lipton, 1977; Anderson, 1982). In many countries, general industrialisation policies have been in favour of large capital-intensive industry. Import substitution policies, for example, have the effect that large-scale industry is protected against foreign competition, but often also against domestic small-scale industry. Conditions to obtain credit are much more favourable for large firms than they are for small firms. Over-investment in capital-intensive industry means under-investment in agriculture, thus reducing the speed of agricultural development — precisely the area in which small-scale industry has the strongest interests.

The conclusion is that agricultural development and a scale-neutral industrialisation policy would favour rural small-scale industry. Then the question arises what else can governments do for rural small-scale industry? There are essentially three approaches: non-policy, protection, and stimulation.

Non-policy is obviously a modest approach, yet it may be appropriate for several sub-sectors in rural industry, especially in the lower spectrum. The problem with stimulation programmes in many countries is that — despite good intentions — they may give rise to an additional burden for small-scale and household industry. Registration, bureaucratic procedures, corruption, licensing, and so on may become a heavy burden for rural entrepreneurs doing marginal activities. It is not without reason that many of these entrepreneurs try to keep away from government as much as possible.

Protection of rural small-scale industry is another alternative. This will usually occur in the form of constraints on urban large-scale industry or on imports. An example is a constraint on large beer factories so that rural household industry can remain on the market. Other examples relate to the production of bottled drinks, cigarettes, textiles and cement.

How must protection policies be evaluated? Obviously, they are favourable for rural producers, but not for the consumers since price could be lower. The money which could be saved by consumers would partly be used for other expenditures, including rurally produced industrial goods. Thus, a negative side-effect of protection for rural industry can be expected, although the positive primary effect is most probably much larger.

Protection measures come near to the concept of selective spatial closure (Stöhr and Tödtling, 1977). The integration of the rural economy in the national economy is not taken as a self-evident goal or trend. Diffusion of new technology is controlled in such a way that it does not hurt rural industry. Indeed, it must be admitted that (especially in the short run) technological change may have strongly differentiated effects on rural and urban areas, urban areas usually experiencing net benefits and rural areas experiencing net disadvantages (cf. Nijkamp and Rietveld, 1987). However, protection of rural industry will negatively affect the skills of the labour force in rural areas so that its prospects for future industrialisation may become worse. In addition, the various arguments of Little *et al.* (1970) against import substitution policies must be taken into account.

Less rigid forms of protection may be more easily defended, however, for example in the form of a negotiated stepwise introduction of a new technology to prevent all-too-sudden disturbances of the rural economy. Even if government accepts the introduction of large-scale plants there are still ways to mitigate the pains for the rural economy. An effort could be made to locate such plants in suitable rural areas so that rural areas also experience some of the employment benefits of the new plants.

A survey of *stimulation* programmes for rural small-scale industry in various developing countries is given by Chuta and Sethuraman (1984). It is not easy to develop effective stimulation programmes. The number of small-scale firms is so large that it is not easy to approach a sufficient number of them. In addition they tend to be widely dispersed and their accessibility is usually bad.

From a spatial viewpoint, the marketing opportunities for rural industry can be improved by the emergence of small and medium-sized cities in rural areas (cf. Johnson (1970) and Rondinelli (1983)).

Stimulation programmes usually focus on the supply side in the form of training, provision of credit and inputs. An important problem is that many branches in rural industry are so crowded that stimulation of certain firms may endanger the existence of other firms not served by the programme. This problem indicates how difficult it is to evaluate the effectiveness of stimulation programmes: evaluations must not be confined to the firms covered by the programme, but other firms must also be taken into account. Their disappearance may be a consequence of the 'success' of the firms involved in the programme.

Clearly, supply-oriented stimulation policies are most effective in branches not characterised by chronic excess supply. The supply of a scarce input may be ensured, for example, via the creation of co-operatives. Training programmes are another example. Technical training may lead to the introduction of new products so that broader markets can be served and to higher quality so that the competitiveness of small industry is improved. Furthermore, training in the sphere of accounting and organisational design may help entrepreneurs of rapidly expanding firms to prevent the occurrence of large inefficiencies (Anderson, 1982). Given the often very high interest rates people have to pay to money-lenders in rural areas, credit programmes may also be useful tools for stimulating rural industry (Poot, 1981; Anderson 1982).

Demand-oriented policies are not easy to implement (Poot, 1981): for example, the creation of co-operatives to strengthen the marketing of industrial goods produced by rural industry often appears ineffective. This is a pity since such co-operatives could also play an important role in the export of certain products of rural small-scale industry. Other marketing possibilities for small-scale rural industry exist in the direction of large firms, for example, in the form of subcontracting. The most direct way of demand stimulation by the government consists of purchases by the government itself of products from small-scale industry.

The conclusion is that one must not be overly optimistic about the effectiveness of specific stimulation policies addressed to rural small-scale industry. General policies aiming at agricultural development and scale-neutral industrialisation will most probably be more effective.

REFERENCES

Anderson, D. (1982) Small industry in developing countries: some issues. *World Bank Staff Working Paper, Washington, D.C., 518*.
Bell, C. and P. Hazell (1980) Measuring the indirect effects of an agricultural investment project on its surrounding region. *American*

Journal of Agricultural Economics, 62, 75–86.

BPS (Biro Pusat Statistik) (1983) *Statistik Indonesia*. Jakarta.

Chuta, E. and S. V. Sethuraman (eds) (1984) *Rural small-scale industries and employment in Africa and Asia*. ILO, Geneva.

Hymer, S. and S. Resnick (1969) A model of an agrarian economy with nonagricultural activities. *American Economic Review*, 59, 493–506.

Johnson, E. A. J. (1970) *The organization of space in developing countries*. Harvard University Press, Cambridge.

Johnston, B. F. and P. Kilby (1975) *Agricultural and structural transformation: economic strategies in late developing countries*. Oxford University Press, London.

Lipton, M. (1977) *Why poor people stay poor. Urban bias in world development*. Temple Smith, London.

Little, I. M. D., T. Scitovsky and M. F. Scott (1970) *Industry and trade in some developing countries*. Oxford University Press, London.

McCawley, P. (1981) Pertumbuhan Sektor Industria. In A. Booth and P. McCawley (eds), *Ekonomi Orde Baru*, LP3ES, Jakarta, pp. 79–131.

Nijkamp P. and P. Rietveld (1987) Technological development and regional labour markets. In M. M. Fischer and P. Nijkamp (eds), *Regional labour market analysis*. North Holland, Amsterdam.

Poot, H. (1981) The development of labour intensive industries in Indonesia. In Rashid Amjad (ed.), *The development of labour intensive industry in ASEAN countries*. ILO, Geneva, pp. 77–139.

Rietveld, P. (1984) Non-agricultural activities in rural areas. *Ekonomi dan Keuangan Indonesia*, 32, 428–45.

——— (1986) Non-agricultural activities and income distribution in rural Java. *Bulletin of Indonesia Economic Studies*, 22(3), 106–17.

Rondinelli, D. A. (1983) *Secondary cities in developing countries*. Sage, London.

Staley, E. and P. Morse (1965) Modern small-scale industry for developing countries. McGraw-Hill, New York.

Stöhr, W. and F. Tödtling (1977) Spatial equity - some anti-theses to current regional development doctrine. *Papers of the Regional Science Association*, 38, 33–53.

Wolf, D. L. (1986) The rural development of modern manufacturing. In C. MacAndrews (ed.), *Central government and local development in Indonesia*. Oxford University Press, Oxford, pp. 132–56.

307

Index

Note: SME is used for small and medium-sized enterprise, throughout.

308

For Product Safety Concerns and Information please contact our
EU representative GPSR@taylorandfrancis.com Taylor & Francis
Verlag GmbH, Kaufingerstraße 24, 80331 München, Germany